STUDIES IN HONOR OF *JOHN WILCOX*

JOHN WILCOX

· GOLDSMITH · HANAWALT · HOLLINGSWORTH ·

Studies IN HONOR OF

JOHN WILCOX

by

MEMBERS OF
THE ENGLISH DEPARTMENT
WAYNE STATE UNIVERSITY

Edited by

A. DAYLE WALLACE

WOODBURN O. ROSS

Essay Index Reprint Series

· WERRY · WALLACE · WAGNER · SCHUELLER ·

JORGENSON · KIRSCHBAUM · MADSEN · NASH · PRESCOTT · ROSS ·

BABCOCK · BLAYNEY · CABLE · DIAMOND · GAY · GOLDEN

BOOKS FOR LIBRARIES PRESS
FREEPORT, NEW YORK

*PR
14
W44
1972*

Library of Congress Cataloging in Publication Data

Wayne State University, Detroit. Dept. of English.
    Studies in honor of John Wilcox.

    (Essay index reprint series)
    Bibliography: p.
    CONTENTS: Foreword, by L. L. Hanawalt.--Heroic
diction in The dream of the rood, by R. E. Diamond.
--Jonson, Seneca, and Mortimer, by L. Kirschbaum.
[etc.]
    1. English literature--Addresses, essays, lectures.
2. American literature--Addresses, essays, lectures.
I. Wallace, Alva Dayle, 1908-   ed. II. Ross,
Woodburn O., ed. III. Wilcox, John, 1887-
PR14.W44   1972   820.9   76-167433
ISBN 0-8369-2727-3

1-24-74- L11029

PRINTED IN THE UNITED STATES OF AMERICA
BY
NEW WORLD BOOK MANUFACTURING CO., INC.
HALLANDALE, FLORIDA 33009

J OHN WILCOX was born June 5, 1887
into the large family of a teacher-farmer in Warsaw, Indiana, and
attended the public schools there. Upon graduation from high
school, he became first a class-room teacher and then the head of
a small consolidated school. He took a bachelor's degree at Indiana
University in 1911, and thereafter taught school and did newspaper work in three states of the far West. During World War I,
he served as lieutenant in the artillery and the air force, going to
France as an aerial observer. At the close of the war he attended
the University of Dijon for a time, and on his return to the
United States came immediately to Detroit as a teacher in Northern High School.

Mr. Wilcox first made a connection with the institution now
known as Wayne State University in 1921, when David Mackenzie, dean of Detroit Junior College, requested his transfer from
Northern High School to the burgeoning two-year college that
was housed in the old Central High School building on the present campus. In that period certain promising teachers in the high
schools were invited to join Dean Mackenzie's staff. Mr. Wilcox
was to teach English and journalism.

For the Junior College the 1920's were the maturation years,
in which the institution was transformed into a four-year arts
school, the College of the City of Detroit, and in which it grew
rapidly in faculty, student body, and curricula. Rising standards
of professional training led the Board of Education to create or

foster professional schools in close conjunction with the Liberal Arts college. As time passed, the several schools and colleges were incorporated into a university structure, to which in 1934 the name Wayne University was given.

In this lively period, Mr. Wilcox made a distinct impression on the college both by his incisive teaching and by his clear-headed work on faculty committees. He was for a time adviser to some student publications. He was prominent in the faculty group that waged a quiet campaign for more extensive participation by the faculty in decisions on academic policy. He shared in the creation of the local chapter of the American Association of University Professors and remained one of its influential members. As the increasing complexity of university problems more and more required mature and informed faculty consideration, the breadth of his interests caused him to be chosen for service on many faculty bodies, including the Liberal Arts Council, the University Council, and numerous important special committees.

But Mr. Wilcox is perhaps best known among his colleagues for his ardent interest in graduate work and the Graduate School. He began his own graduate studies at the University of Wisconsin, and received the degree of Master of Arts from that institution in 1924. The University of Michigan granted him the degree of Doctor of Philosophy in 1932; he began there the studies which led subsequently to a volume on the Restoration period. His later scholarly writings have dealt chiefly with Elizabethan literature, which he has taught to undergraduate and graduate classes for many years, and with the area of his later special interest, literary criticism. In 1951-52 he spent a sabbatical year at the Sorbonne, in research in the field of criticism.

From the early 1930's, when graduate work began at Wayne, Mr. Wilcox worked continuously in the departmental committees that defined standards and requirements. He was active in the Graduate Council. Over a long period he was the departmental adviser to graduate students and chairman of the department's Graduate Committee. His wife, Nettie Krantz Wilcox, formerly a college teacher of English, shared his intellectual interests and shared too his deep personal concern for the graduate students as individuals. Successive generations of graduate students have enjoyed the friendly welcome and gracious hospitality of the Wilcox home.

In the early 1940's, Mr. Wilcox urged the development of a program for doctoral studies in English at the University, and he kept this objective constantly before the departmental and college committees during the post-war years, when a deluge of veteran students and the accompanying rapid increase in the undergraduate faculty prevented expansion of graduate work. Finally plans for the English doctorate were completed, and advanced students entered classes in September, 1954.

This year, at the age of seventy, Mr. Wilcox is retiring from his professorship. The present Doctor of Philosophy program of the Department of English Language and Literature is in a sense a monument to his thirty-six-year career as a faculty member of the University. He has done more than any other single person to advance that program and to formulate its working details.

This volume of studies, the product of the professional thinking of a number of his colleagues, is therefore a peculiarly appropriate parting-gift from the department in which he labored long and well for the cause of research and scholarship.

LESLIE L. HANAWALT

June, 1957.

vii

BIBLIOGRAPHY

"Defining Courtly Love," *Papers of the Michigan Academy of Science, Arts, and Letters*, XII (1929), 313-325.

"French Courtly Love in English Composite Romances," *Papers of the Michigan Academy of Science, Arts, and Letters*, XVIII (1932), 575-590.

"Love in *Antony and Cleopatra*," *Papers of the Michigan Academy of Science, Arts, and Letters*, XXI (1935), 531-544.

The Relation of Molière to Restoration Comedy (New York: Columbia University Press, 1938), ix + 240 pp.

Review of John W. Draper, *The Hamlet of Shakespeare's Audience* (Durham, N. C.: Duke University Press, 1939), *The Shakespeare Association Bulletin*, XIV (1939), 122-126.

Review of Howard Baker, *Induction to Tragedy* (Baton Rouge, La.: Louisiana State University Press, 1939), *The Saturday Review of Literature*, XX, No. 11 (July 8, 1939), 18.

Review of R. B. McKerrow, *Prolegomena for the Oxford Shakespeare* (New York: Oxford University Press, 1939), *The Shakespeare Association Bulletin*, XV (1940), 59-60.

"Putting Jaques into *As You Like It*," *Modern Language Review*, XXXVI (1941), 388-394.

Review of John C. Adams, *The Globe Play House* (Cambridge: Harvard University Press, 1942), *Philological Quarterly*, XXII (1943), 95-96.

Review of G. S. Alleman, *Matrimonial Law and the Materials of Restoration Comedy* (Wallingford, Pa., 1942), *Modern Philology*, XL (1943), 290-291.

viii

"The Place of Excellence," *School and Society*, LXII (October 6, 1945), 209-212.

'On Reading John Ford," *The Shakespeare Association Bulletin*, XXI (1946), 66-75.

"Imitation Silk Purses," *AAUP Bulletin*, XXXII (1946), 31-39.

"Excellence and Democracy," *School and Society*, LXIII (March 30, 1946), 217-220.

"Othello's Crucial Moment," *The Shakespeare Association Bulletin*, XXIV (1949), 181-192.

"La Genèse de la Théorie de l'Art pour l'Art en France," *Revue d'Esthétique*, VI (published in 1953), 1-26.

"The Beginnings of l'Art pour l'Art," *Journal of Aesthetics and Art Criticism*, XI (1953), 360-377.

Review of William Elton, ed., *Aesthetics and Language* (New York: Philosophical Library, 1954), *Modern Language Quarterly*, XVI (1955), 170.

with R. W. Babcock, *Writing Scholarly Papers: A Manual of Procedure and Form for Essays and Theses and Dissertations* (Detroit: Wayne University Press, 1955), iv + 38 pp.

ALTHOUGH some *Festschriften* are centrally concerned with one subject or one period, it was clear from the beginning that this volume in honor of Professor John Wilcox, if it were so limited, would not truly reflect the variety of his interests and accomplishments. Although a specialist in Shakespeare and the drama of the seventeenth century, he has long been a student of the whole range of literary criticism and has made a special study of the beginnings of the *art for art's sake* movement. In his advising of graduate students and building a graduate program at Wayne he has never forgotten the importance of courses for freshmen and sophomores and has worked untiringly for a sound and stimulating, even exciting, program for undergraduate majors in English and for the general student as well. He has taught, and taught well, a wide variety of courses, graduate and undergraduate. It is fitting, therefore, that this volume, the work of colleagues in the Department of English at Wayne, should range from the Old English period to the present, from English to American figures and subjects.

From the moment that this book was suggested, the Wayne State University Press Editorial Board and the staff of the Department of English have given it enthusiastic and continuing support. The editors are grateful to the members of the Board and the staff of the Press and to each member of the Department who submitted an essay for the volume. Their enthusiasm and cooperation in honoring Professor Wilcox for past accomplishments also manifest their wish for him of many happy years of scholarhip after his retirement.

W.O.R.
A.D.W.

CONTENTS

xiii

xiv

STUDIES IN HONOR OF JOHN WILCOX

1.

Heroic Diction in
The Dream of the Rood

ROBERT E. DIAMOND

Many people who have read *The Dream of the Rood* have been struck by the poet's use of certain heroic phrases in describing the crucifixion. The tree from which the cross was made is said to have been cut down by bold enemies (*strange féondas*, 30b). The Lord is referred to as a young hero (*geong hæleþ*, 39a). He is said to be bold and brave (*strang and stíþmód*, 40a). The cross is said to be wounded with arrows (*strǽlum forwundod*, 62b). The Lord is said to rest for a while after the mighty conflict (*æfter þám micelan gewinne*, 65a). When the poet says that the Lord hastens with great courage (*efstan elne micele*, 34a), he uses a phrase strongly reminiscent of the one used to state that Beowulf hastened to do battle with Grendel's mother (*efste mid elne*, 1493). The executioners of the Lord are twice called warriors (*hilderincas*, 61, 72), the very compound used in *Beowulf* to refer to Beowulf twice (1495, 1576) and to Grendel once (986). The Lord is referred to as a famous ruler (*mǽran þéodne*, 69a). This same phrase is used six times in *Beowulf* to refer to Hrothgar, four times to Beowulf, and once each to Heremod and Onela. The Lord is referred to as a prince (*æðelinge*, 58a). In *Beowulf*, this word is used three times to refer to Beowulf (1596, 2374, 2424), once to Scyld (33), once to Wæls (888), and once to one of the warriors at Heorot (1244). After the descent from the cross, the followers of the Lord sing a dirge for Him (*sorhléoð galan*, 67b). This is the same phrase that appears in *Beowulf* where Hrethel sings a dirge (*sorhléoð gæleþ*, 2460) for his son Herebeald.

It must be apparent at the outset that this heroic language is strangely out of place in a poem about the crucifixion of the Lord. When the poet describes Christ as a bold hero hastening

3

courageously to the mighty struggle, he directly contradicts the story of the crucifixion as related in the gospels; but, more important, he does a kind of violence to the spirit and doctrines of Christianity. The central paradox of Christianity is the everlasting victory through the apparent momentary worldly defeat and humiliation. Our poet seems to have reversed the softening tendency which so often creeps into heroic poetry: for example, in the Serbian heroic song of the Battle of Kossovo, the hero rejects an earthly kingdom in favor of the heavenly kingdom; and one of the heroic figures of the *Mahabarata*—Arjuna—appears in the heroic narrative frame of the didactic poem, the *Bhagavad Gita*, bewailing the senseless slaughter of the approaching battle. There seems to be a point in the heroic poetry of many peoples where the softening tendencies of a more ethical society begin to supersede the old heroic standards of vengeance and glory in battle. In *The Dream of the Rood*, however, the situation is just the reverse: supposedly a Christian poem, presumably informed by the spirit and doctrines of Christianity, it displays in some passages a seemingly atavistic reversion to the heroic spirit.

How can we account for this apparent inconsistency of tone in *The Dream of the Rood*? Scholars and critics have generally assumed that the poet was trying to make his Christian subject matter attractive to an audience that was accustomed to hear heroic poetry. But England had been solidly Christian probably for quite a long time when the poem was composed. It seems likely that the poet lapsed into heroic language not so much in order to please his audience as because he was accustomed to compose in such language. This brings us, of course, to the subject of traditional diction in Old English poetry. Whether or not *The Dream of the Rood* and other such poems were composed orally or with pen in hand can probably never be settled to anyone's satisfaction, but they reflect a kind of oral-formulaic diction, handed down from generation to generation, added to a little here and a little there, comprising a common stock of formulaic phrases which enabled the poets to express almost any idea in correct verses, without casting about for a felicitous turn of expression. A poet who was accustomed to compose songs on heroic subjects would quite naturally apply all the old heroic epithets and formulas to his matter. If he set himself to compose a song on a Christian subject, it was natural that diction reflecting an earlier society should creep in. And, as time went by, a stock of Christian formulas was developed. Many were, of course, formed on older models, using, for example, epithets for kings to refer to the first two persons of the Trinity.

Such a poet, then, is in some sense a captive of his traditional diction. There are not an infinite number of ways to express an idea in correct verses; there are only the traditional ways. While the poet can rely on the traditional diction to help him out of tight places in composing, he is also caught in the net of tradition, so to speak—he cannot compose in any other way. This applies not only to his actual choice of words, but to the themes and narrative technique of his work. The tradition in which the poet was composing was a narrative tradition. Dogmatic or introspective subject matter would most likely be passed over in favor of something that gave the poet a story to tell. To call the thing by its right name: the poets tended to choose subjects from Christian story that were rather sensational. A good example is the Cynewulf poem on the acts of Saint Juliana, which relates a succession of lurid events. Whereas hagiography does not lend itself particularly well to the kind of narrative treatment the Anglo-Saxon poets customarily gave their work, the Apocryphal book of Judith is admirably suited to this kind of narrative treatment and makes an excellent heroic poem. The setting and the proper names are all that distinguishes Judith of Bethulia from a Germanic heroic figure. In *The Dream of the Rood*, the central section of the poem, describing the actual crucifixion, the section where most of the heroic diction occurs, is handled in this narrative manner. The story of the events of the crucifixion is told in a series of swift-moving actions, with little delay.

A strong indication that the poem was composed in the traditional oral-formulaic style is the number of repeated verses. Checking every verse against the entire corpus of Old English poetry reveals that 67 of the 311 verses are repeated elsewhere at least once. This is 21.5 percent, more than one in five. Of course, this poem has a great number of hypermetric verses, 64 to be exact. As one can rarely find a hypermetric verse repeated in its entirety, it is interesting to examine the figures for the normal verses only: 27 percent of the normal verses are repeated elsewhere. This is more than one in four. Such a high percentage of repeated verses would be unthinkable in a poem composed in the modern way. This is not to deny originality to the poet of *The Dream of the Rood:* the dazzling conceit of the cross which tells its own story is not dimmed by the fact that the poet used traditional diction. Within the framework of the tradition in which he was composing, he displayed great inventiveness.

What kind of society can give rise to poems which represent such a strange blend of heroic and Christian elements? It would be no more accurate to say that *Beowulf* is a heathen poem with Christian coloring than that *The Dream of the Rood* is a Christian poem with heathen coloring. Both poems are clearly the work of believing Christians, composed in the traditional style for Christian audiences who were accustomed to certain standards and conventions of composition. They both represent a blend of traditional and Christian elements.

Perhaps we can account for the persistence of the traditional style of poetic composition by assuming that Anglo-Saxon England, while firmly Christian, still preserved many of the conditions of the heroic age. That epoch, from which the traditional style of composing and many of the themes of the poetry can be traced, is usually assumed to be over by the time most of the extant Anglo-Saxon poetry was composed. It is interesting to note, however, that the Cynewulf-Cyneheard episode, related in the Chronicle as having taken place in the year 786, occurred fifty years *after* the death of Bede. Here we have a typically heroic situation, with the loyalty to the comitatus taking precedence over kinship loyalty — half a century *after* the death of the man whose career surely represents the pinnacle of Christian civilization in Anglo-Saxon England. If the comitatus and the meadhall were still functioning so vitally, we can assume that there were two kinds of societies simultaneously in pre-Conquest England: one centering around the great monasteries; and the other a military society depending on the comitatus relationship. We know that oral composition was practiced in the monastic society — from Bede's account of Cædmon and his vision; and we know that heroic themes were sometimes of interest to the poets of this society — from Alcuin's letter mentioning Ingeld. As clerical communities constantly recruit members from lay society, young men who were in contact with the military society and its style and taste in poetry must have been drawn into the monastic centers — and they must have brought the traditional style of poetry with them. If they had not done so, none of the poems would have been preserved, for meadhall composing was for entertainment and not to be written down. It is natural that when the traditional style came to the monastic centers, it should be used for the most part to compose poems on Christian subjects.

It seems likely, then, that the contact between these two societies, the military and the religious, or, if you prefer, these two important and dominant segments of Anglo-Saxon society, gave rise to poetry which preserves the old clichés and formulas of heroic poetry but applies them to Christian subjects.

2. *Jonson, Seneca, and* Mortimer

LEO KIRSCHBAUM

In the 1640 Jonson Folio there is a fragment entitled *Mortimer His Fall*.[1] It consists of "The Persons Names"; a synopsis of the five acts and choruses, called "Arguments"; and sixty-nine lines of text, comprising a forty-five line soliloquy by Mortimer and a twenty-four line dialogue between Mortimer and Isabella. At the end appears an editorial note by Sir Kenelm Digby: "Hee dy'd, and left it unfinished." In an authoritative volume published in 1950, Percy Simpson wrote, "This fragment, with its curious experiment of a chorus that changes its composition in the scheme of the three acts, has the air of being early work."[2] But in 1953 Marchette Chute asserted a completely opposite opinion: "*Mortimer, his Fall* exists only in a fragment — the opening soliloquy and a brief exchange of dialogue — but there is enough to show that Jonson had been planning to write the most rigidly classical play of his life."[3] Which statement is correct?[4] The early or late dating of the piece itself is, I think, relatively unimportant, of academic interest. But what *is* very important is seeing where the piece fits into Jonson's slowly evolving theory and practice of tragedy. That will be the task of this tentative paper.

I say *tentative* deliberately, for I don't think the time has yet come to discuss or judge Jonson's tremendous performances in this genre adequately. We don't want to see what they are, we can't see what they are, we are prone to accept their contemporary failure as more or less final, irrevocable placing. This inability to perceive what Jonson was attempting or to judge it fairly stems, I feel sure, from the conscious or unconscious premise that the Elizabethan dramatist's exemplar, the Roman writer of tragedies, Seneca, was, it must be admitted, vulgar. That is why Ellis-

Fermor can write what to me is an inexplicable remark concerning *Catiline*: "Jonson is not, of course, directly indebted to Seneca for anything in this play except the Thyestean prologue and the choruses, but it is evident that the poetry of Seneca was in his mind throughout, at least, the early parts of the play."[5] I submit that in relation to the Senecan elements of the play as a whole, the words "directly indebted" are almost meaningless. Or take similar words of an otherwise excellent appreciator of what Jonson was attempting: "In fact, most criticism, favorable as well as unfavorable, has centered on such interesting but essentially peripheral matters as Jonson's use of the Senecan ghost and chorus (in *Catiline*), his portrayal of character, his reconstruction of the Roman scene, and, of course, his rhetoric."[6] Such a critical use of *peripheral* tends to omit everything enclosed in the complex artifact except what a particular critic chooses to call the center of interest. It is aesthetic monism with a vengeance!

If T. S. Eliot could recently call *Titus Andronicus*, which is today slowly winning recognition as an excellent and stageworthy example of its type, "one of the stupidest and most uninspired plays ever written," in which "there is nothing really Senecan at all,"[7] I submit that we had better look carefully at the Roman dramatist again, at the same time abjuring our over-delicate fastidiousness and trying to discover wherein and to what degree the Elizabethan dramatists, unabashedly and constantly, from Kyd through Jonson, imitated him. Actually, much of what we today consider highly melodramatic in Elizabethan drama was countenanced by Seneca.[8] We simply must forget all about Greek drama when we are discussing the imitation of the ancients in English Renaissance tragedy. Critics fresh from Attic tragedy or from Horace's *Ars Poetica* remark at the bloody on-stage scenes of Elizabethan drama, pointing out that even in Seneca the horrible is reported. But this is not true. Phaedra commits suicide *coram populo* in *Hippolytus* (1199-1200), and so does Jocasta in *Oedipus* (1034-39). Medea slays her two sons, each at a different time, directly in front of the audience (*Medea*, 967-75, 1018-9).

The poisoned, writhing Hercules appears on-stage in *Hercules Oetaeus*. Theseus puts together the torn parts of his son's body before the spectators' eyes in *Hippolytus* (1247-72). Atreus brings in the heads of Thyestes' three children on a covered platter, which he then uncovers before their father (*Thyestes*, 1004-5). Thus, it all depends on what one means by "non-classical" when he discusses Lavinia's holding Titus' severed hand in her teeth or Macduff's bringing in Macbeth's head. The poisoning of Drusus in *Sejanus* can be thought of as an Italianate motif first appearing in the widely imitated *Jew of Malta*, but poisoning plays a large role in the action of *Medea* and *Hercules Oetaeus*. Kyd's Hieronimo and Isabella are usually thought of as the progenitors of those scenes of tragic madness in which the groundlings so delighted. But Kyd was copying Seneca. Witness the frenzy of Hercules in *Hercules Furens*, of Deianira and Hercules in *Hercules Oetaeus* (1003-24, 1432-40), of Cassandra in *Agamemnon*. We think of Elizabethan divination or necromantic scenes as going back to *Doctor Faustus*. But when Jonson wrote the spectacular scene in *Sejanus* in which the flamen performs a ritual before Fortune's altar and the goddess' statue turns its head, he was imitating the Roman: Medea's sacrifice to Hecate (*Medea*, 740-844), the on-stage divination of Tiresias and his off-stage magic reported by Creon (*Oedipus*, 296-392), Atreus' bloody sacrifice (*Thyestes*, 641-788). We can see that the ghost of Sylla which introduces *Catiline* goes back to Tantalus' ghost which introduces *Thyestes* and Thyestes' revengeful spirit which introduces *Agamemnon*. But we do not so clearly see that the ghost in *Hamlet* goes back not alone to the ghost of Andreas in *The Spanish Tragedy* but also to the ghost of Hercules which suddenly forms in mid-air on-stage, speaks, and then vanishes at the end of *Hercules Oetaeus* and the vengeance-seeking ghost of Agrippina which appears on-stage and then disappears in *Octavia* (593-645).[9] Conversely, we can view Sejanus, Catiline, and Mortimer as descendants of the Machiavellian Barabas-Tamburlaine line,[10] or we can view them as Renaissance re-creations of the powerful, egoistic, and ruthless Senecan tyrants, Lycus in *Hercules Furens* and Nero in *Octavia*.[11] We think of the revenger as typical of English Renaissance drama, but we must not forget the doubt-ridden but forceful Medea and the sadistic, hypocritical Atreus. The first recalls Hamlet; the second, Sejanus and Catiline. Even non-observance of unity of place was countenanced by *Hercules Oetaeus*, where the scene is first Euboea and later Trachin; and non-observance of unity of time, by *Octavia*, whose dramatic action covers two days (see 592, 646-53). Herford and Simpson write: "[Jonson] intended in *Mortimer* to provide a chorus . . . a chorus loosely enough adapted, it is true, to classical precedent, for it consists of at least three several bodies — 'ladies,' 'courtiers,' 'country justices and their wives,' who intervene respectively after the first, second, and third acts."[12] But Jonson did have "classical precedent" in Seneca's *Agamemnon*, where there is a chorus of Argive women and a chorus of captive Trojan women; and in *Octavia*, where there is a chorus sympathetic to Octavia and a chorus sympathetic to Poppaea. Even the satiric scenes of Jonson's completed tragedies (which Lisideius, in Dryden's *An Essay of Dramatic Poesy*, deplored[13]) had classical justification in the ever-present mordant scorn and irony of Seneca's plays.

Seneca, perhaps the Italian and French Seneca, the Seneca of the English academic and popular stage, Senecan closet drama, the medieval tradition of tragedy as a sudden fall from high place (although this also is stressed in the Roman plays), Machiavellism, and pseudo-Machiavellism, Renaissance critical theory — all these went to make up the Jonsonian type of tragedy. *Mortimer His Fall* had it been completed would have been the most purely Senecan of the three. Yet it would also have been remarkably like the last act of Marlowe's *Edward II*, in which, likewise, a boasting, double-dealing, ruthless Mortimer, at the very pinnacle of his fortune, falls to ruin and death. Aside from dignity of utterance, it is not in inner spirit or characterization or shocktechnique or even action that Jonson's tragedies differ from

Hoffman or *Titus Andronicus*: they differ mainly in outward form.[14] Let us review, therefore, the evolution of Jonson's work in this category.

By 1598 Jonson had already achieved some reputation as a writer of tragedies for the popular stage, for in *Palladis Tamia* Francis Meres included him among those who "are our best for Tragedie." We get information concerning these lost plays from Henslowe's *Diary*. On December 3, 1597, Jonson was lent a pound for a play which he promised to finish by Christmas and the plot of which he showed to the Admiral's company (43 *v*). On October 23, 1598, Chapman was paid for "ij ectes of a tragedie of bengemens plotte" (51 *v*); perhaps this was the plot of the previous December. In August and September, 1599, Jonson and Dekker were paid eight pounds for "the lamentable tragedie of pagge of plemoth" (63 *v*, 64). This must have been a domestic tragedy like *Arden of Feversham* or Wilkins' *The Miseries of Enforced Marriage*.[15] Between September 3 and September 27, 1599, Jonson, Chettle, Dekker, "and other Jentellman" received four pounds, ten shillings in earnest for "Robart the seconde kinge of scottes tragedie" (64 *r - v*). On September 25, 1601, Jonson was paid two pounds for additions to *The Spanish Tragedy* (94); and on June 22, 1602, ten pounds for the same or further additions and "in earneste of a Boocke called Richard crockbacke" (106 *v*). This completes the references to Jonson's lost tragedies mentioned by the *Diary*. Apparently, then, Jonson, like a typical playwright of the Henslowe group, was ready to turn his hand to Kydian imitation, chronicle tragedy, domestic tragedy, *etc.* If the extant additions to *The Spanish Tragedy* are his, we can see how very well he could do the lush melodramatic sensationalism which the groundlings loved. But what Jonson himself thought of his co-workers and the popular stuff he had to write is not hard to guess.

How Jonson broke away from bondage to the current dramatic mode in comedy need not be repeated here. But in 1601, disgusted with the reception his recent comedies had received, in the "apologeticall Dialogue" to *Poetaster* he told his audience,

> And, since the *Comick* MVSE
> Hath prou'd so ominous to me I will trie
> If *Tragoedie* have a more kind aspect.

If he please but one,

> So he iudicious be; He shall b'alone
> A Theatre vnto me:

What he will create, the product of long hours in his cell to win the bays, will cause wonder, spite, and despair. It will be poetic drama, "That must, and shall be sung, high, and aloofe." Knowing Jonson's reverence for the past, his respectful but non-pedantic and vitalized following of the ancients, his desire to please the more cultured minds of his audience, we can almost guess what *Sejanus* will be like in a good many respects. But before we continue our short survey of Jonson's tragedies, let us remember one thing: the tendency sometimes on Jonson's part, when what he had done was not appreciated, to exaggerate rather than to eliminate those very attributes which had bored or irritated his auditors.

In the writing of the original *Sejanus* (1601-3) Jonson had a collaborator. But since the extant version is by Jonson alone, it may be regarded as representing his own idea of what the ancient model adapted to the exigencies of the contemporary stage should be. The epistle "To the Readers" in the 1605 Quarto tells us much about what this idea in the abstract was:

> First, if it be obiected, that what I publish is no true Pöeme; in the strict Lawes of *Time*. I confesse it: as also in the want of a proper *Chorus*, whose Habite, and Moodes are such, and so difficult, as not any, whome I haue seene since the *Auntients,* (no, not they who have most presently affected Lawes) haue yet come in the way off. Nor is it needful, or almost possible, in these our Times, and to such Auditors, as commonly Things are presented, to observe the ould state, and splendour of *Drammatick*

Poemes, with preseruation of any popular delight. But of this I shall take more seasonable cause to speake; in my Obseruations vpon *Horace* his *Art* of *Poetry,* which (with the text translated) I intend, shortly to publish. In the meane time, if in truth of Argument, dignity of Persons, grauity and height of Elocution, fulnesse and frequencie of Sentence, I haue discharg'd the other offices of a *Tragick* writer, let not the absence of those *Formes* be imputed to me, wherein I shall giue you occasion hereafter (and without my boast) to thinke I could better prescribe, then omit the due use, for want of a conuenient knowledge.

A true tragedy, therefore, should observe the unity of time. It should have a proper chorus, *i.e.,* like that of a Seneca play. These requirements Jonson has omitted. But truth of argument he has carefully adhered to; witness the plenitude of bibliographical references to sources scattered through the margins of the 1605 Quarto. As to "the other offices of a *Tragick* writer," we need only turn to the text to see them fulfilled. And following Horace's dictum and the usual practice of Seneca, the horrible destruction of Sejanus' body is reported by Terentius, and the horrible deaths of Sejanus' children and the agony of their mother are reported by a Nuntius. It is amusing to note the intransigent Jonson designating the normal Elizabethan custom of music between the acts, "CHORVS — *Of Musicians.*" One aspect of the play which might be noticed is that Jonson gets an effect similar to the Senecan small cast by having his characters fall into groups as much as possible, so that actually there is no more difference between a group's individual members than there is between Guildenstern and Rosencrantz. For example, in the first act Sabinus, Silius, Cordus, and Arruntius are alike as peas in a pod; so are the informers, Natta and Latiaris; so are Natta, Latiaris, Satrius, and Sejanus when they are sycophantic to Tiberius. (There is grouping *and* also very careful differentiation between characters in *Catiline,* but not in *Sejanus.*)

But despite its Machiavellian superman; its Tiberius cast along the lines of the English conception of the lecherous and hypocritical Italianate nobleman;[16] its off-stage poisoning of Drusus; its Clytemnestra-Aegisthus relationship between the debased Livia and Sejanus; its lurid Macro, who has an admirable comic scene in Act V with a consul who constantly wanders off-stage; its reported omens; its spectacle of the priest of Fortune and the statue's turning its face; its bustling and exciting last act, replete with suspense; its satirical comedy of Eudemus and Livia — despite such theatricality, *Sejanus* was a bad failure. In his Folio dedication to Lord Aubigny, Jonson writes that it "suffer'd no less violence from our people here, than the subiect of it did from the rage of the people of Rome." But *Sejanus*, he continues, has won to itself "a greater fauour," "the loue of good men." Some of them prefixed poems to the Quarto: Chapman, Hugh Holland, Marston, William Strachey, etc.

Catiline His Conspiracy was first presented in 1611. It was written by a man who was fresh from great triumphs in comedy, who must have felt quite sure of himself. It is much more Senecan in mood and execution than its predecessor. In his dedication to Lord Pembroke in the 1611 Quarto, Jonson was not afraid to call it "a legitimate Pöeme":

> I must call it so, against all noise of opinion: from whose crude, and ayrie reports, I appeale, to that great and singular faculty of iudgement in your Lordship, able to vindicate truth from error. It is the first (of this race) that ever I dedicated to any person, and had I not thought it the best, it should have beene taught a lesse ambition. Now, it approcheth your censure cheerefully, and with the same assurance, that innocency would appear before a magistrate.

My insistence that it was in outward form mainly that Jonson reformed the popular neo-Senecan tragedy is borne out by an examination of *Catiline*. According to him, *Sejanus* was "no true Pöeme" because it did not observe the neoclassic unity of time and because it did not have "a proper *Chorus*." Yet neither does *Catiline* observe the unity of time. But Jonson does call the latter tragedy "a legitimate Pöeme," for *Catiline* does have a proper background chorus of Roman citizens (which in classic fashion speaks philosophically or generally on state matters between the acts and which engages a few times, as in Seneca, in dialogue); and *Catiline* does have in Sylla's ghost, which acts as prologue, a direct imitation of the vindictive ghost of Thyestes which prefaces Seneca's *Agamemnon*.

As to Jonson's conception of neoclassic tragedy, the epistle "To the Reader in Ordinarie," in the Quarto of *Catiline*, can perhaps yield more information than critics have extracted from it. Let us look at a much quoted sentence:

> *Though you commend the two first Actes, with the people, because they are the worst; and dislike the Oration of Cicero in regard you read some pieces of it, at Schoole, and vnderstand them not yet; I shall find the way to forgive you.*

This scornful statement does not mean that Jonson was ashamed of the first two acts. It does mean that at the time Jonson in writing a neo-Senecan drama was perfectly willing to include material that would satisfy the popular audience. That Jonson thought highly of the "grauity and height of Elocution" of Cicero's oration does not mean that he was not satisfied with the satiric comedy of Act II, which is as forceful as any part of the play in depicting the corruptness of the Catiline faction, and with the Senecan imitations of Act I: Sylla's ghost; the ambitious and ruthless Catiline; the unnatural relationship between Catiline and Aurelia (cf. *Thyestes, Oedipus,* and *Hippolytus,* where this thrill is exploited); the bloodthirsty Cethegus; the ominous portents of darkness, underground groans, and fiery light; the drinking of the slave's blood by the conspirators. That Jonson knew that such material would please the Jacobean audience inasmuch as it had already pleased them in other plays does not mean that he was still not copying his Roman exemplar. For example, Sylla's list of Catiline's crimes reminds us of similar catalogs by Barabas and Aaron, but it also reminds us of the prototype, Atreus' words at the beginning of *Thyestes*. And there is no difference in kind

between the first act and the last two acts. In them an unchanged
Cethegus shocks with his blood-greediness. "It thunders, and
lightens on the sodaine" at the end of Act III, and the portents
continue in Act IV. There is also the neo-Senecan report of
Catiline's death by Petreius. Another classical touch, in imitation
of Plutarch, is furnished by the set addresses to the armies made
by Petreius and Catiline. And in *Catiline*, too, there is the truth
of argument so important to the imitator of *Octavia*; the main
sources are Sallust and Cicero.

But *Catiline*, like *Sejanus*, was also a failure. And Jonson is
bitter in his denunciation of the theatre-goers in Quarto's dedica-
tions, "To the Reader in Ordinarie," and "To the Reader extraordinary." And once more he appeals to the better judgment of the
cultivated few. Beaumont, Fletcher, and Nathan Field prefix
encomia.[17]

Sejanus had failed. And Jonson had become more formally
Senecan in *Catiline*. *Catiline* had failed. Even without the authority of Sir Kenelm Digby, we could, on the basis of internal
evidence alone, determine that the fragment, *Mortimer His Fall*,
was a late production:

> The later *Mortimer* shows an even wider divergence still from
> popular practice through the increasing stress of scorn for popu-
> lar opinion; it must have embodied almost all the limitations
> imposed by the outward form of Roman tragedy.[18]

In the abstract, its plot (as shown by "Arguments") is not essentially different from the plots of the preceding Jonson tragedies.
It is again the sudden fall of a titanic and hypocritical state-
villain. Mortimer's extant soliloquy is boastful Machiavellism neat
— or Seneca neat, as one chooses. And the adulterous relationship
between the hero-villain and the Queen Mother, Isabella (*cf.*
Sejanus and Livia) can remind us of Edmund and Goneril — or
of Aegisthus and Clytemnestra.[19] But *Mortimer* in the matter of
form was to be far different from the current tragedies. Gone is
the kind of comic appeal which Jonson had previously admitted.

Gone is the crowded stage. Like a Seneca play, *Mortimer* has a small cast of eight plus a Nuntius and Chorus. Gone are the crowded action and bustling incident. Like a Seneca play, the action deals only with the climax. And like a Seneca play, relatively little is to happen on the stage. There are to be only dialogue before action, dialogue after action, and reported action. The first two acts and choruses set the situation. The first act shows Mortimer's pride and security, the Queen's favor, the Machiavellian counsels of Worcester against Lancaster, who suspects the favorite. The first chorus of Courtiers celebrates the worthiness of Isabella, Mortimer, and Worcester. Act II shows Edward III's refusal to suspect Mortimer and the Queen, and his imputing the scandal to Lancaster's malice. The second chorus, of Ladies, praises the King for this stand, lauds his piety, and describes their own happiness under him. So far there has been that charged kind of stasis so characteristic of Roman tragedy, preparation for action but not action itself. But the plot begins to operate in Act III. However, there is still no action on-stage. Apparently, the Nuntius was to report to the Earl of Cornwall a vision in which his blind brother had seen "the horrors of their Father's death" and the murder of their uncle, the Earl of Kent, "by Mortimer's hired practise." (Cf. Cassandra in *Agamemnon* and Tiresias in *Oedipus.*) The third chorus, of Country Justices and their wives, relate how they had been tricked to believe the late king had been alive in Corfe Castle. In Act IV, Edward and Cornwall decide "to explore the truth of those reports." The fourth chorus relates how Mortimer, at the height of his boastful career, has been discovered in Isabella's bedchamber and sent to execution. The fifth act presents Lancaster's reception of what has happened. And apparently the final chorus was to be responsible for "the Celebration of the Kings Justice." So much for the Seneca-like action. Furthermore, as Charlton surmises, "it looks also as if the unities were to have been ostentatiously adopted."[20]

Mortimer His Fall, then, shows how far Jonson's imitation of

Roman tragedy went. It is not Jonson's first attempt in tragedy but undoubtedly his last.

NOTES

1. All quotations from Jonson's plays are from *Ben Jonson, The Man and His Work*, ed. C. H. Herford, Percy Simpson, and Evelyn Simpson (11 vols., Oxford, 1925-52), hereafter cited as *Herford-Simpson*. *Sejanus* is in Vol. IV; *Catiline*, Vol. V; and *Mortimer*, Vol. VII.
2. *Herford-Simpson*, X, 383.
3. *Ben Jonson of Westminster* (New York, 1953), pp. 345-46.
4. The irresponsible Fleay, in contradiction to Gifford, called *Mortimer* "the very first production of his without coadjutor, that has come down to us." (*A Biographical Chronicle of the English Drama 1559-1642* [London, 1891], I, 356-57). But Greg (*Henslowe's Diary* [London, 1908], II, 188-89), Charlton (*The Poetical Works of Sir William Alexander* [Edinburgh and London, 1921], I, clxxiii-vi), and Chambers (*The Elizabethan Stage* [Oxford, 1923], III, 374) all regard it as late work. Cf. A. C. Howell, "A Note on Ben Jonson's Literary Methods," *Studies in Philology*, XXVIII (1931), 187: "If, as I believe, the *Discoveries* is the raw material out of which he created his poetry, it should contain hints as to projected work of the poet. It seems fairly certain that in the numerous quotations from Machiavelli's *Il Principe*, Lipsius' *Politicorum, sive Civilis Doctrinae*, Seneca's *De Clementia*, Erasmus' *Institutio Principis Christiani* and others, found in Pars. 77-101, Jonson was making preparations for his projected tragedy, *Mortimer His Fall*. A perusal of the Argument prefixed to the play will almost indicate the points at which his various notes would be used."
5. *The Jacobean Drama*, (2nd ed., London, 1947), pp. 111-12, n. 3.
6. J. A. Bryant, Jr., "*Catiline* and the Nature of Jonson's Tragic Fable," *Publications of the Modern Language Association*, LXIX (1954), 265-77. There is similar limited and limiting understanding of what Seneca meant to Jonson in the same author's "The Significance of Ben Jonson's First Requirement for Tragedy: 'Truth of Argument,'" *Studies in Philology*, XLIX (1952), 195-213.
7. "Seneca in Elizabethan Translation," *Selected Essays 1917-32* (London, 1932), p. 82. This essay, which first appeared in 1927 as an introduction to *Seneca His Tenne Tragedies* (see next note), has recently been reprinted without change in T. S. Eliot, *Essays on Elizabethan Drama*, Harvest Books (New York, 1956).
8. I have utilized the text and numbering of *Seneca's Tragedies*, Loeb Classical Library, ed. F. J. Miller (2 vols, London and New York, 1927). When necessary I have checked with the reprint of the 1581 *Seneca His Tenne Tragedies*, Tudor Translations XI (2 vols., London and New York, 1927).
9. See also the revengeful ghost of Achilles which motivates the action but whose fearsome appearance is merely reported by Talthybius in *Troades* (168-202).
10. See Mario Praz, *Machiavelli and the Elizabethans*, Annual Italian Lecture of the British Academy (1928), pp. 17-19; see also pp. 25-26 on Seneca's Hercules as the prototype of Marlowe's Tamburlaine. I am much indebted to Praz's insistence on the Senecan origin of much that has been termed Machiavellian. But Praz in turn doesn't appear to see altogether clearly that an either-or viewpoint has to be given up, that Machiavellism and Senecanism were so intertwined in the Renaissance that apportioning shares is impossible in most cases.

11. Praz points out that whereas Shakespeare's 3 *Henry VI*, III, ii, 193 has "And set the murderous Machiavel to school," *The True Tragedy* has, "And set the aspiring Catalin to Schoole" (*ibid.*, p. 32). Shakespeare did not make the change, as Praz thinks; the reporter did; and it is interesting to see that for the reporter the two terms were synonymous. The subject of Catiline was not new to the English stage. Gosson wrote the now lost *Catiline's Conspiracies* (Chambers, *Elizabethan Stage*, III, 323), and Chettle and Wilson were given money by the Admiral's men in 1598 to write "cattelanes consperesey," which may never have been finished (Greg, *Henslowe's Diary*, II, 196).

12. II, 6. Varying the constituency of the chorus was no new thing in neo-Senecan tragedy. In *Mustapha*, Fulke Greville has "Chorus Primus of Basha's or Caddies," "Chorus Secundus Of Mahometan Priests," "Chorus Tertius of Time: Eternitie," "Chorus Quartus of Conuerts to Mahometisme," and "Chorus Quintus Tartarorum." *Alaham* has "Chorus Primus Of Good Spirits," "Chorus Secundus, Of Furies...," "Chorus Tertius A Dialogue; Of Good, and Evill Spirits," and "Chorus Quartus Of People." See Vol. II of *Poems and Dramas of Fulke Greville*, ed. Geoffrey Bullough (Edinburgh and London, n.d.). Sir William Alexander's *Croesus* has a "Chorus of some countrymen" and a "Chorus of all Lydians."

13. *Essays of John Dryden*, ed. W. P. Ker (Oxford, 1926), I, 60-61. Jonson's defense of the satiric scenes in *Sejanus* and *Catiline* would undoubtedly be similar to what he says at the conclusion of *Discoveries*, in which he discusses unity of action (Gifford ed., 1816, IX, 249-51): a scene is to be judged not separately but functionally — in relation to the rest of the play. As I say below, nothing contributes more to our sense of the depravity of the Catiline group than Act II. Cf. Harry Levin in his introduction to *Ben Jonson, Selected Works* (New York, 1938), p. 15: "It would be rash to conclude that the satiric spirit is hostile to tragedy. On the contrary, Jonson's tragedies come most to life when his courtiers are fawning or when his women, whose psychology is never more than cosmetic-deep, are gossiping. The very satire which called the story of Sejanus to Jonson's attention, Juvenal's tenth, is almost mediaeval in its stress upon tragic reversal of fortune. The tragedian of an age of satire, Seneca, was the unavoidable model for every Elizabethan dramatist who aspired to the buskin."

14. One might add *tempo*. The violence of a Seneca play is rather of speech and thought than of act and gesture. (Though the second, as I have tried to indicate, are by no means absent.) That is why, according to one's viewpoint, the Roman playwright can be termed active or static, spectacular or rhetorical, melodramatic or lyric.
    For verbal parallels between Seneca and Jonson, see J. W. Cunliffe, *The Influence of Seneca on Elizabethan Tragedy* (London and New York, 1893); F. L. Lucas, *Seneca and Elizabethan Tragedy* (Cambridge, 1922), pp. 130-31.

15. The title of a contemporary broadside reads: "The Lamentation of Master Pages wife of Plimmouth, who being enforced by her Parents to wed him against her will, did most wickedly consent to his murder, for the love of George Strangwidge, for which fact she suffered death at Bar[n]staple in Devonshire." (Greg, *Henslowe's Diary*, II, 205).

16. What I am trying to indicate by these descriptions of Tiberius and Sejanus is that they would be recognizable types already popular on the stage. But, of course, they are truly Senecan, too. So are most of the other elements I mention in this paragraph. Note how well Seneca employs suspense — as in *Hippolytus*.

22

STUDIES IN HONOR OF JOHN WILCOX

17. *Catiline,* to the present writer, is a much finer play than *Sejanus.* It is not difficult to see why it was popular in the late seventeenth century. The manner in which the dramatist has Cicero deal in a surprisingly laudatory way with Fulvia and Curius and then suddenly has him reveal in soliloquy that he knows what they truly are (III, 438 ff.) is a most masterly dramatic treatment. It humanizes Cicero beautifully.
18. Charlton, *op. cit.,* I, clxxvi.
19. That the Elizabethans were quite conscious of the Senecan prototype is indicated by Malevole's speech to the Machiavellian Mendoza, the queen's paramour, in I, v of *The Malcontent: Mal.* . . . a, you whore-sonne hot rayned hee *Marmoset, Egistus,* didst ever here of one *Egistus? / Mend. Gistus? / Mal.* I *Egistus,* he was a filthy incontinent Fleshmonger, such a one as thou art. / *Mend.* Out grumbling roage. / *Mal. Orestes,* beware *Orestes.*
20. *Op. cit.,* I, clxxvi.

3.

Chivalric Themes in
Samson Agonistes

RALPH NASH

1. The Analogy with *Gerusalemme Liberata*

THE ACTION of Tasso's *Gerusalemme Liberata* turns upon the dispersal and reassembling of Godfrey's best soldiers, who are led astray by their passions, especially love, and who must subordinate themselves to Godfrey's will and reason before God's people in Jerusalem can be liberated. Chief among those soldiers are Rinaldo and Tancred, who are explicitly called champions of the Christian faith. Both these champions are made prisoners of love.

Tancred is pursued throughout the poem by Erminia, who is herself a prisoner of her love for Tancred (6.58; 19.83, 95, 100) and who wishes to make Tancred "mio prigioniero" under love's "giogo di servitù dolce e leggiero" (6.84).[1] Tancred seems relatively safe from her pursuit because he is completely enthralled by his love for the pagan Clorinda. At one point his search for Clorinda leads him to a magic castle, to whose defenders he announces proudly: "That Tancred am I who always buckle on the sword for Christ, and am his champion" (7.34). Yet immediately thereafter he becomes a prisoner through magic, and thus unable to fight a single-combat for which Godfrey had chosen him from among his "champions" (6.19, 25).

Rinaldo, of course, is carried to Armida's garden, bound in the most clinging chains of privet blossoms, lilies and roses (14.68). The old hermit tells Rinaldo's rescuers that he is in a far-away prison (14.47) and must be brought back from this distant and hidden prison (14.71), which is described as having doors ornamented with the tales of Achilles in Skyros and Anthony at Actium (16.2-7). In such a prison of love lies the champion of the Christian faith: "Quivi fra cibi ed ozio e scherzi e fole / Torpe il campion de la cristiana fede" (15.44). He has become, as Fairfax[2] puts it, "a carpet champion for a wanton dame" ("egregio campion d'una fanciulla"; 16.32).

If John Milton preferred at times to read Fairfax's translation of this poem of Christian champions caught in the toils of love, he would find the prisoner of love imagery increased and "champions" in every few stanzas, for Fairfax is very fond of the word. And in Spenser the Bower of Bliss and Castle Joyous — as also Duessa's House of Pride, with its women "forgetfull of their yoke" (I.5.50) — emphasized and amplified the morality implicit in Tasso's poem, although Spenser's enormous plan makes the freeing of Verdant (II.12.72-82) a very minor incident, quite unlike the crucial event in the *Gerusalemme*. The Tasso-Fairfax-Spenser complex has been generally thought of as contributing to Milton's epic poems.[3] But certainly it seems probable that the poet's imagination was enriched with reminiscences of Renaissance chivalric poetry when he meditated and elaborated on the meaning of the story of Samson, God's champion against the Philistines and Dalila's prisoner of love.

That Milton should conceive of Samson as the champion of his God was inevitable, since the idea is thoroughly imbedded in the tradition that had grown up around the Samson story.[4] It is natural, then, that details from chivalric romance should find a place in the poem. The chivalric tradition very evidently lies behind Samson's three formal challenges to Harapha (1150-53, 1174-77, 1220-23) as his rising spirits move him to offer himself as God's champion once more. Less evident, perhaps, is the diction of chivalric romance in Samson's earlier speech, when he is still feeling the shame of the once-glorious, defeated champion, the knight unhorsed:

> *Dagon* hath presum'd,
> Me overthrown, to enter lists with God. . . .
> Dagon must stoop, and shall e're long receive
> Such a discomfit, as shall quite despoil him
> Of all these boasted Trophies won on me (462-70).[5]

Such echoes of the manners and language of chivalry must have seemed to Milton appropriate to the story of a champion who betrayed his role because foul effeminacy held him yoked the bond-slave of a woman who wished to hold him as her prisoner and Love's (410-11; 808). But there is more than surface detail to suggest that Milton may have been mindful of Renaissance chivalric poetry as he worked out his tragedy. As the poet meditated upon the prophecy that Samson would "begin to deliver Israel out of the hand of the Philistines" (*Judges* 13:5), he could readily see how his material had affinity with Tasso's poem, for Samson's political career was centered upon the champion's effort to deliver God's people from the pagan yoke. The entire action was, in a sense, *Israel Delivered*.

2. Prison within Prison

In the long speech in which Dalila makes the most of her alibi of "love," she says that she knew Samson "mutable of fancy" (793-4) and feared she would be abandoned like the Timnian bride. Therefore, she explains, she wished to make Samson a prisoner of love:

> I was assur'd by those
> Who tempted me, that nothing was design'd
> Against thee but safe custody, and hold:
> That made for me, I knew that liberty
> Would draw thee forth to perilous enterprises,
> While I at home sate full of cares and fears
> Wailing thy absence in my widow'd bed;
> Here I should still enjoy thee day and night
> Mine and Loves prisoner, not the *Philistines*,
> Whole to my self, unhazarded abroad,
> Fearless at home of partners in my love.
> These reasons in Loves law have past for good,
> Though fond and reasonless to some perhaps (800-812).

This is admittedly an explanation after the fact, but Dalila brings forth again much the same proposal when she proffers Samson recompense for her past misdeeds:

> Though sight be lost,
> Life yet hath many solaces, enjoy'd
> Where other senses want not their delights
> At home in leisure and domestic ease,
> Exempt from many a care and chance to which
> Eye-sight exposes daily men abroad (914-19).

The sensual suggestion of "solaces" and the delights of "other senses" makes it easy to believe that the cares and chances to which eye-sight exposes men include not only the "perilous enterprises" of line 804, but also the danger that her husband's mutable fancy might be attracted to partners in her love. That is, Dalila once more is speaking in terms of making Samson the prisoner of her "love." She will bring him "from forth this loathsom prison-house" (922) only to plunge him into another, more loathsome prison.

Precisely on this level Samson answers her. He has been liberated, delivered from her Circean charms:

> I know thy trains
> Though dearly to my cost, thy ginns, and toyls;
> Thy fair enchanted cup, and warbling charms
> No more on me have power (932-5).

If she slighted and sold him in the flower of his youth and strength, he asks:

> How wouldst thou use me now, blind, and thereby
> Deceiveable, in most things as a child
> Helpless, thence easily contemn'd, and scorn'd,
> And last neglected? How wouldst thou insult
> When I must live uxorious to thy will
> In perfet thraldom, how again betray me,
> Bearing my words and doings to the Lords
> To gloss upon, and censuring, frown or smile?
> This Gaol I count the house of Liberty
> To thine whose doors my feet shall never enter (941-50).

The play upon the idea of prison here is one of the recurrent themes of the tragedy. Eyeless in Gaza, Samson is already doubly imprisoned. "My self my Sepulcher, a moving Grave," says Samson (102), and the Chorus echoes him:

> Which shall I first bewail,
> Thy Bondage or lost Sight,
> Prison with Prison
> Inseparably dark?
> Thou art become (O worst imprisonment!)
> The Dungeon of thy self (151-6).

Yet the levels of imprisonment are at least triple. The Chorus is not quite accurate when it announces "To lowest pitch of abject fortune thou art fall'n" (169). The "worst imprisonment" is not blindness in captivity, as Samson himself recognizes: for if at one moment he exclaims, "O loss of sight, of thee I most complain" (67), he soon is willing to say, "Yet that which was the worst now least afflicts me, / Blindness" (195-6). There may be surface contradictions here, perhaps enough to make us feel that the *Agonistes* did not receive a final polishing, but there is no real confusion. Samson very clearly spells out his understanding of his plight:

> Foul effeminacy held me yok't
> Her Bond-slave; O indignity, O blot
> To Honour and Religion! servil mind
> Rewarded well with servil punishment!
> The base degree to which I now am fall'n,
> These rags, this grinding, is not yet so base
> As was my former servitude, ignoble,
> Unmanly, ignominious, infamous,
> True slavery, and that blindness worse than this (410-18).

It is no wonder that Samson counts his prison the house of liberty as compared to Dalila's. He is aware that he has escaped from a prison worse than any the Philistines can devise. Of course he is harsh and unsympathetic with the woman who ensnared and betrayed him, costing him his eyes and his status as God's chosen man: he does not care to experience prison within prison within prison.

The motif of the prisoner of love has more bearing on our views of Dalila, the imprisoner, than of Samson, the imprisoned. Because Samson is already free of that bondage when the play opens, and never tempted to return to it, its effect on his role lies largely in affording opportunity for verbal ingenuities. As he developed this conventional motif inherent in his subject, Milton naturally had a poet's awareness of its relation to other aspects of the story of a man in bondage to blindness, to sin, and to pagan enemies. However, the subtleties in his variations on Samson's triple imprisonment should not cause us to overlook the plain effects that follow from giving Dalila a literary ancestry that includes Circe, Dido, Alcina, Armida, and Acrasia. With such antecedents for Dalila, her champions among readers may begin to sound like *advocati diaboli* in *Paradise Lost*. It is not really probable that Dalila is a "fine woman"[6] who wants the same happiness for Samson that Manoa wants and "presents it just as lovingly,"[7] nor that she comes without conscious designs[8] to make "a selfless proposal,"[9] or even "a reasonable offer"[10] — for we cannot believe that her reasons "are all good reasons."[11]

The phrases just quoted from various critics would scarcely fit even if Milton were depicting merely the story of a broken marriage. But it is by no means true that the poet "has departed from the design of the tragedy in depicting the personal relations of Samson and Dalila and in ignoring the conflict between the representative of Philistia and the champion of Israel."[12] On the contrary, Milton is bent upon reminding the reader that Dalila and Samson are figures in the struggle to free God's people from domination by Dagon's worshippers. The entire situation is political by its very nature, and the last half of the scene with Dalila is heavily laced with the language of politics: "Traytor" (832; cf. 959), "Magistrates / And Princes" (850-51), "civil Duty" (853), "A common enemy" (856), "the public good" (867), "thy countries foe" (884), "law of nations" (890), "men conspiring to uphold thir state" (892), "suing / For peace" (965-66). In addition are allusions to patriotism (893-4), civil obedience (895) and censorship (947-8), plus of course Dalila's parting speech on her "public marks of honour and reward" (975-95). No doubt Dalila's hope of public renown is a sorry consolation, but the idea fits her character. From her own view of her combat with her husband she can claim, as Professor Scott-Craig observes, "to have out-Samsoned Samson . . . as the saviour of her country from the 'fierce destroyer.' "[13] From the reader's view, she can appear as a partially comic venturer in politics, whose feminine wiles have failed but whose feminine vanity remains.[14]

Failure to see in Dalila either comedy or alliance with godless political forces may damage our view of the poem by making it difficult to understand Samson's reaction to her visit. But in addition to encouraging such false leads as misogyny and settled ferocity, sympathetic views of Dalila as reasonable and right will also miss the irony of the whole situation. Dalila has her reasons for coming,[15] but she is a fool to think that she can still exercise power over Samson. Samson may know that he is sung and proverbed for a fool, but he is not such a fool as all that. Perhaps his vehemence in this scene suggests indignation that Dalila should assume that his folly is unlimited. In Dalila's brazenness there is, in turn, something of the folly of Satan in *Paradise Lost*. She is blind to reality, unable at first to fathom the consequences of what she has done, and finally forced to tell herself that she is content with the lot which she has been trying to avoid through reconciliation with Samson. Yet Milton has let her present her case so skillfully that she actually wins adherents among readers persuaded to believe that blinding and imprisoning a husband is after all a venial affair. As with Satan's wonderful rhetoric, Milton's very success obscures the grandeur of his enterprise.

The poet's emphasis upon the political aspect of the relationship is thoroughly appropriate. Like Armida in the *Gerusalemme*, Dalila is the tool of God's enemies and our judgment of her is to be affected accordingly. Likewise, Samson's mission as God's champion is to deliver Israel from bondage to the Philistines, and he has failed in it through Dalila. How does this affect Samson? It is true that the failure of that mission is not altogether upon his head, for Israel is guilty of much the same "servil mind" that Samson showed in succumbing to Dalila:

> What more oft in Nations grown corrupt,
> And by thir vices brought to servitude,
> Then to love Bondage more then Liberty,
> Bondage with ease then strenuous liberty (268-71).

But although it is weak and sinful in the Israelites to neglect "Gods propos'd deliverance" (292), Israel's weakness is no excuse for Samson's. "All wickedness is weakness," says Samson. Now that he has repented of his wickedness with Dalila, where shall the strong man find strength?

Characteristically, Milton refuses to remain content with the surface of his story. The simplicity of Rinaldo's awakening will not suffice. Awareness of the temptress's true nature, shame at having been caught in her toils, repentance for having neglected God's commission — these are almost the whole story for Rinaldo, but for Samson the merest beginning. Nevertheless, after much inward struggle, Samson must come to much the same conclusion as does Rinaldo: he must offer himself as God's champion once more, ready to return to his abandoned mission if God will accept him. From God must come his strength for that return.

The necessity of the champion's return to action makes it proper that he reject not only the specious Dalila, but also Manoa's earnest offer of a quiet life — "to sit idle on the houshold hearth" forgetful of "My Nation, and the work from Heav'n impos'd" (566, 565). In one respect, however, Manoa is right. If God's

champion has fallen into prison because Dalila ensnared him in
her prison of love, he must be ransomed. The deliverer must be
delivered.

3. The Deliverer Delivered

Milton's major elaboration on his Scriptural material is his
emphasis on Samson's political role.[16] Such procedure can be
thought reminiscent of Tasso's collocation of champion, prisoner
of love, and deliverer, although also thoroughly in accord, for instance, with the manner of Elizabethan tragedy. Samson's mission
as deliverer of Israel has not been made much of by critics.[17] Yet
no word in the poem is more plangent than *deliverer,* and no idea
is more recurrent or subject to more ironic variations.

Samson as deliverer of Israel appears in *Judges* 13:1,5 and
15:18, a meager showing by comparison with eight specific references to deliverance in the poem (39-40, 225-6, 245-6, 273-4,
278-9, 292, 1214, 1270), plus distinct allusions to this function
of the Israelite champion (317, 680-81, 1661-3, and cf. 1714-16).
Indeed the word *deliver* appears as frequently in the Biblical account with reference to Samson's being handed over to his enemies (*Judges* 15:12,13; 16:23,24), in which sense it also occurs
in Milton's verse.[18]

Because of this second sense, the dominant usage of the word
in Milton's poem, to mean Samson as liberator of Israel, carries
ironic significance for the fallen champion, as appears in his first
bitter reference to his mission:

> Promise was that I
> Should *Israel* from *Philistian* yoke deliver;
> Ask for this great Deliverer now, and find him
> Eyeless in *Gaza* at the Mill with slaves (38-41).

The great deliverer has been delivered to his enemies and Philistia
now celebrates her "deliverance from the hands of *Samson*"
(*Argument,* 12-13; cf. 434-9, 984-6, 989-90). Blinded and imprisoned by the foe, neglected by the nation he hoped to liberate

(245-6, 273-4, 278-9, 292), apparently abandoned by the God he served (632), Samson takes on something of the character of the unsuccessful statesman: he is sensitive to criticism and quick to give a rationale for his political activity. To Dalila he expounds the law of nature and of nations (876-900), to Harapha he justifies himself against the charge of "league-breaker" (1182-1216), to the Philistian Officer and the Chorus he discourses on the claims of the civil power (1354-79, 1404-9). Clearly Milton felt that Samson as political figure deserved a goodly proportion of his tragedy's sharply limited space.[19]

The invention of the visits of Manoa and Dalila, both of whom offer deliverance to the imprisoned deliverer, gave obvious opportunity for dramatic irony, as noted above for Dalila and long since observed by critics remarking on Manoa's "sub-plot," which needs no further comment here. In the course of his futile efforts Manoa speaks, without apparent discrimination, of *ransom* (483, 604, 1460, 1471, 1476, 1573; cf. *Argument*, 10), *deliverance* or *delivery* (603, 1505, 1575; cf. *Argument*, 24) and *redemption* (1482; cf. *Argument*, 15). The inevitable Christian overtones of *ransom* and *redemption* may carry the willing reader even further. For although traditional views of Samson as prototype of Christ do not seem to enter the poem markedly, it is certain that Milton's tragedy is somehow concerned with the martyrdom of saints.[20] The manner in which that concern is developed calls for yet further discussion of the deliverance of God's proposed deliverer.

4. The Better Fortitude of Patience

When Harapha departs somewhat crestfallen, the Chorus breaks out in a jubilation that is rapidly tempered by second thoughts:

Oh how comely it is and how reviving
To the Spirits of just men long opprest!
When God into the hands of thir deliverer
Puts invincible might
To quell the mighty of the Earth. . . .

But patience is more oft the exercise
Of Saints, the trial of thir fortitude,
Making them each his own Deliverer,
And Victor over all
That tyrannie or fortune can inflict,
Either of these is in thy lot,
Samson, with might endu'd
Above the Sons of men; but sight bereav'd
May chance to number thee with those
Whom Patience finally must crown (1268-96).

In the light of the preceding discussion of *deliverance*, we cannot miss the ringing significance of "Making them each his own Deliverer," contrasted with the idea of political deliverance through invincible might (1268-72 ff.). These are real alternatives: "Either of these is in thy lot." The Chorus does not merely "go on to sing of patience as the final crown of saints"[21] or state feebly "that he may simply have to bear his lot with patience."[22] Samson is at this crucial point said to be even more likely to be numbered with the saints than with the victorious deliverers of God's people. The announcement of this possibility is perhaps the furthest point Milton could attain in transforming the old legend into something nearer his conception of the better fortitude of patience and heroic martyrdom. Bound by the Scriptural story, Milton had to be willing to "fall short of an exposition of true martyrdom,"[23] if "true martyrdom" means a patient suffering that renounces violence. Readers who accept a late date for the tragedy may very probably feel that he "had regained some of his old desire for heroic action," rather than heroic martyrdom.[24] At least, being committed to the Biblical story with its violent catastrophe, Milton could not alter it further than pointing out an alternative to the road that Samson actually followed.

That Samson chooses the path of action, rather than saintly suffering, seems clear. The Biblical story could hardly be made into a legend of passive martyrdom, the trial of Samson's fortitude; he chooses of his own accord to make other trial of his strength (1643-44). He becomes, indeed, his own deliverer, but not in the manner implied in the Chorus's speech. In response to Manoa's proposals to arrange ransom, Samson four times states that he hopes for oft-invocated death as his only cure and the close of all his miseries (575-6, 590-98, 629-30, 648-51), and he even returns to the subject after Harapha's departure:

> But come what will, my deadliest foe will prove
> My speediest friend, by death to rid me hence (1262-3).

The idea of death as Samson's ransomer and deliverer, implicit in these passages, is made explicit in Manoa's lament:

>   O all my hope's defeated
> To free him hence! but death who sets all free
> Hath paid his ransom now and full discharge.
> What windy joy this day had I conceiv'd
> Hopeful of his Delivery (1571-5).

Here then is the close of Milton's elaboration on the central idea of *deliverance*. The deliverer delivered to his enemies has delivered himself in a manner acceptable to God, but yet not through the exercise of saints.[25] Samson has quit himself like Samson and heroically finished a life heroic — not saintly. He dies redeemed, the acknowledged and victorious champion of God, and in the terms of the poem a successful liberator of his people:

> O dearly-bought revenge, yet glorious!
> Living or dying thou hast fulfill'd
> The work for which thou wast foretold
> To *Israel*, and now ly'st victorious
> Among thy slain self-kill'd
> Not willingly, but tangl'd in the fold
> Of dire necessity (1660-66).[26]

Yet with this congratulation by the chorus Milton does not necessarily avoid the debated question of Samson's martyrdom, of whether in this heroic fulfillment of his political mission,

"Samson was not really a martyr at all because he fought and destroyed himself, while martyrs suffer rather than fight and are destroyed in consequence of their patience."[27] If the choric speech at lines 1268-96 is really presenting two alternatives that are "in Samson's lot" — the one active, the other passive — it seems persuasive that the glorious dearly-bought revenge, through which Samson is ransomed by death who sets all free, is in the spirit of the first alternative, befitting the strenuously active, quasi-military career of Israel's champion and deliverer, but not attaining to the saintly patience whose exercise makes each his own deliverer. Thus the latter portion of the speech (1287-96) may be seen as a means by which Milton has been able to introduce into his drama his evaluation of the better fortitude of patience and heroic martyrdom, even though those qualities are scarcely central to the Biblical action he had chosen for his subject.

This discussion of Milton's tale of the deliverance of an imprisoned champion has concerned itself with three recurrent motifs, inherent in the Scriptural account and the exegetical tradition, but also familiar to the poet from literary sources. There is an assumption here that Milton would find it natural and efficient to draw upon familiar traditions in exploring the ironies of champions lodged in physical or spiritual prisons, or of deliverers delivered over to their enemies until they have learned to deliver themselves from their prisons. If chivalric poems provided Milton a frame within which to weave his poem, or if they merely offered him some threads for his design, the reader can improve his ability to enjoy the poem by recognizing these inventions. There is no necessity to expect this play to be built upon only one source, related to only one literary form. Diversity — even ambiguity — is characteristic of *Samson Agonistes*, whose very title carries simultaneously at least three meanings, possibly more. How should we expect to find Milton's richly stored memory drawing only upon the text of Scripture, or only upon Christian exegetics, or only upon "the Ancients or Italians," or least of all upon his personal experience alone? The poem is consonant with all these sources, limited to none of them.

As with the poem, so with the poet. Both are complex and of independent nature. Milton was trained to be content to work within the limits of his subject, to carry his assertions only to the height permitted by his Argument. Yet he might desire a deeper inward purgation than appeared in the text of *Judges* or in such an analogous story as Rinaldo's delivery from Armida. His method for attaining greater depth is neither to alter radically the main outlines of his source, nor to reject literary themes suitable to the subject because earlier literature may have left those themes rather superficial. Accepting the limits of his source and accepting pertinent literary tradition, he works upon his material by repeating his themes with significant variations until the deliverance of a champion from prison becomes so freighted with meaning that the reader can see how this story from the Old Testament, in its own right a strong assertion of God's justice, becomes also a precursor of the victorious agonies of the saints and martyrs of Christianity.

Clearly this discussion is suggesting that Milton was helped to a discovery of the possibilities in his subject by his awareness of chivalric literature, especially Tasso's poem. But even if one should wish to insist that Milton discovered these possibilities in the bare Scriptural text, or in Christian exegetics, the difference is not great. Whatever their origin, the themes discussed here are so widely spread through the poem, so interwoven in it, and so important to its development, that without taking account of them we cannot recognize all that the poet's invention and technical abilities have achieved.

NOTES

1. Torquato Tasso, *Gerusalemme Liberata,* a cura di Luigi Bonfigli (Bari, 1930).
2. Edward Fairfax, *Godfrey of Boulogne* (2nd ed., London, 1624).
3. For extensive suggestions based on Spenser alone, see Edwin Greenlaw, "A Better Teacher than Aquinas," *Studies in Philology,* XIV (1917), 196-217.
4. See F. M. Krouse's discussion of the word ἀγωνιστής, in *Milton's Samson and the Christian Tradition* (Princeton, 1949), pp. 108-118. In English litera-

ture at least as early as Chaucer Samson is "this noble almyghty champioun" (*Monk's Tale*, line 2023), and the persistence of the concept scarcely needs documenting (e.g., Fletcher and Quarles as cited in *Paradise Regained, etc.*, ed. Merritt Hughes, New York, 1937, pp. 430, 433).

5. Lists, despoil and Trophies seem obvious. Stoop (It. *chinarsi, abbassarsi*) and *discomfit* (It. *sconfitta*) are also from chivalric combat. For other suggestions on chivalric diction, see Allan H. Gilbert, "Samson Agonistes, 1096," *Modern Language Notes*, XXIX (1914), 161; cf. D. C. Boughner, "Milton's Harapha and Renaissance Comedy," *Journal of English Literary History*, XI (1944), 297 ff.

6. E. M. W. Tillyard, *Milton* (London, 1949), p. 341.

7. James W. Tupper, "The Dramatic Structure of *Samson Agonistes*," *Publications of the Modern Language Association*, XXXV (1920), 383.

8. James Holly Hanford, ed., *Poems of John Milton* (New York, 1936), p. lxxxv.

9. Don Cameron Allen, *The Harmonious Vision: Studies in Milton's Poetry* (Baltimore, 1954), p. 90.

10. Paull F. Baum, "Samson Agonistes Again," *Publications of the Modern Language Association*, XXXVI (1921), 360.

11. M. E. Grenander, "*Samson's* Middle: Aristotle and Dr. Johnson," *University of Toronto Quarterly*, XXIV (1954-55), 383.

12. Tupper, *op.cit.*, p. 382.

13. T. S. K. Scott-Craig, "Concerning Milton's Samson," *Renaissance News*, V (autumn, 1952), p. 48.

14. Is it helpful to recall here Ben Jonson's women politicians, especially the promises of renown made (very cynically) by Cicero to the whorish Fulvia?

> What an honor
> Hath shee atchieued to her selfe! What voices,
> Titles, and loud applauses will pursue her,
> Through euery street! What windores will be fill'd,
> To shoot eyes at her! What enuy, and griefe in matrons,
> They are not shee! . . .
>   All this is, while shee liues.
> But dead, her very name will be a statue. (*Catiline*, 3.344-52;

in *Ben Jonson*, ed. Herford-Simpson, Oxford, 1925-52).

15. Readers who take seriously Dalila's alliance with the company of Circean mistresses can agree with Samson that Dalila's professed motive of "conjugal affection" (739) is rather "furious rage/To satisfie thy lust" (836-7). She comes to lure Samson back to "solaces" and "domestic ease" because she regrets her "hast'n'd widowhood" (958; cf. 806).

16. F. M. Krouse's survey of the Samson tradition cites a number of Church fathers and exegetes who emphasized Samson's political mission (*Milton's Samson*, pp. 92-3). None of these would serve as literary models — hence the suggestion here of analogs in Renaissance literature.

17. Sir Richard Jebb's insistence on the political content has obvious relation to what is said here, but Jebb is largely content with finding a Hebraic nationalism in the tragedy ("Samson Agonistes and the Hellenic Drama," *Proceedings of the British Academy*, III, 1907-1908, 341-8). Professor Baum, agreeing with Jebb, refers to "the main theme, Samson's double failure as a Nazarite and as a leader of his people" (358). But generally critics are almost silent or inclined to minimize, as does Professor Parker: "We care little about the 'national cause' of Israel, and less about Dagon and the Philistines" (*Milton's Debt*

to Greek Tragedy in Samson Agonistes, Baltimore, 1937, p. 231). Allegorists confine their remarks to passages that suggest Restoration London.

18. The Philistines celebrate Dagon's delivery of Samson into their hands (437-8) and Harapha reminds Samson that his own God has delivered him over to his enemies (1158-9). Cf. the generalized reference in 692-6 and the image of Samson "turned out" like a shorn sheep among his enemies (537-40).

19. More than a hundred lines are devoted to exposition of political theory and observation, if we add to the passages just cited Manoa's classification of the Philistine aristocracy (1457-71).

20. For *Christus Agonistes,* see Krouse, *op. cit.,* pp. 40-44, 119-24, *et al.,* and T. S. K. Scott-Craig, *op. cit.,* p. 46.

   For Samson as saint and martyr, see Krouse, *op. cit.,* pp. 15-16, 97-8, 107-8, *et al.* Professor Krouse's views are at variance with the main line of the remarks being introduced here.

21. James Holly Hanford, "*Samson Agonistes* and Milton in Old Age," in *Studies in Shakespeare, Milton and Donne,* University of Michigan Publications in Language and Literature, Vol. I (New York, 1925), p. 176.

22. Grenander, *op. cit.,* p. 387. And surely the structure of this speech does not convey the idea that Samson has already won saintly patience and become his own deliverer (W. R. Parker, *op. cit.,* p. 48).

23. Kenneth Fell, "From Myth to Martyrdom: Towards a View of Milton's Samson Agonistes," *English Studies,* XXXIV (1953), 148.

24. Tillyard, *op. cit.,* p. 301.

25. Samson in the Philistian theatre is "patient but undaunted" (1623), but it is difficult to see this description of his demeanor while performing for the Philistines as a significant repetition. On unintentional repetition in the poem, see Allan H. Gilbert, "Is *Samson Agonistes* Unfinished?" *Philological Quarterly,* XXVIII (1949), 103-5.

26. So also Manoa says that Samson "To *Israel*/Honour hath left, and freedom, let but them/Find courage to lay hold on this occasion" (1714-16). These passages certainly imply that Samson has been successful, at least within the limited scope of the prophecy that he would "begin to deliver Israel" (*Judges* 13:5).

   For exegetical views on Samson's political success, see Krouse, *op. cit.,* especially pp. 42, 65-66, 84-85, 91-93.

27. Krouse, *op. cit.,* p. 75, summarizing Cornelius a Lapide, *Commentarius in Ioshue, Iudicum, Ruth* (Antwerp, 1664), p. 178.

4.   *A Reading of "Musicks Duell"*

WILLIAM G. MADSEN

Aᴅᴍɪʀᴇʀs ᴏғ Crashaw's "Musicks Duell" have praised it largely as a virtuoso piece, a *tour de force* of the baroque sensibility. It is a "wonderful piece of word-craft," "infinitely rich in artifice," "the secular triumph of the Crashavian style."[1] Attention is rightly called to its tricks of style, its blending of the senses, and its approximation to music, or rather its "endeavour to produce an emotional effect equal" to that which Crashaw gained from music. But just and even penetrating as many of these judgments are, none of them suggests that "Musicks Duell" has any structure other than the narrative one supplied by Strada's original, or that its imagery operates in any other way than to "suggest the ecstasy of musical experience" and incidentally exemplify the workings of a baroque sensibility. It is my contention, rather, that "Musicks Duell" is built up on a basic intellectual contrast between the music of the man and the music of the nightingale that is not found either in Strada's poem or in any of the other translations and paraphrases of it,[2] and that this basic contrast is supported by the imagery.

I

Strada's *Prolusion* has almost nothing of what may be called intellectual structure: the nearest thing to an idea is the moral of the last line, "Vsque adeo & tenues animas ferit æmula Virtus," which in Robert Vilvain's translation reads, "Even so smal Souls such emulous Virtu hav." It is, in fact, the contrast between the smallness of the bird and the grander resources of the lutenist that is mainly emphasized by Strada, a contrast that is made quite pointed by the juxtaposition of *grandia* and *paruis* in these lines:

> Nam dum discrimina tanta
> Reddere tot fidium natiua & simplice tentat
> Voce, canaliculisque imitari grandia paruis.

Strada's failure to endow his singing-duel with any real symbolic significance is hard to understand in view of the fact that there already existed two well-defined traditions regarding the music of the nightingale and its relation to the instrumental music of man. In the first of these the natural music of the nightingale is contrasted to the artificial music of man:

> Sed quid tibi videtur? qui vel tibiis canunt vel cithara, atque hujusmodi instrumentis, numquidnam possunt lusciniae comparari? D. Non. M. Quid igitur distant? D. Quod in istis artem quamdam esse video, in illa vero solam naturam.[3]

Strada seems to be making this contrast in the passage quoted above (natiua & simplice . . . Voce), but in another passage he blunts the contrast by endowing the bird with art: "& artem Arte refert."

It is not surprising in an age that was so concerned to define the relationship between nature and art, that it is St. Augustine's contrast that informs most of the English adaptations of Strada's poem. In the best and most famous of these (next to "Musicks Duell"), the opening scene of John Ford's *The Lover's Melancholy*, the musical battle is described as

> The sweetest and most ravishing contention
> That art and nature ever were at strife in.

The nightingale is "nature's best skilled musician," "whom art had never taught cliffs, moods, or notes," while the man "had busied many hours to perfect practice." Again, in Robert Vilvain's *Enchiridium Epigrammatum Latino-Anglicum* there appears a fairly literal translation of Strada into English verse with the following heading: "Epigram III. AEmulatio musica. Famianus Strada. The 2 Musicians (a Natural Vocal, and Artificial Instrumental) which contended for Mastery." Tied down as he is to the original, Vilvain cannot do much with this contrast, but we see it fully developed in the anonymous burlesque, *Strada's Musical Duel*, published in 1671, in which the nightingale becomes a kind of musical Shakespeare:

> first to fill
> With sweetest *Breath*; then send it up to that
> So sweetly Chirping *Natu'ral* — *Flagellat*:
> To be carv'd out in as sweet *Tones* of *Voice*:
> And so't straight was; in thousand *Wild notes choice*
> Far above those of *Art*; as, if the same
> For *kind*, *Wild Fowl* much sweeter is than *Tame*.

And as early as 1586 John Case, in *The Praise of Musicke*, had spoken of the nightingale in terms of the nature-art contrast.

In the other tradition with which we are concerned, the nature-art antithesis is replaced by the more integrated and perhaps more Christian view that music, whether natural or instrumental, is a symbol of world harmony and of man's union with God. Music is that art, says William Austin in his commendatory verses to Thomas Ravenscroft's *A Briefe Discourse of . . . Musicke* (1614), *"Whose* Concord *should expresse that* Peace in Heaven," and this same idea appears in the more complicated structures of Milton, Donne, Herbert, and Herrick, too familiar to require rehearsal. In medieval versions of this tradition, as Spitzer has shown, the nightingale takes its place as a member of the great "world-consort." The anonymous *De Luscina*

> after leading us from the Grace-endowed bird to the song of man affirming God's gifts . . . ends with the praise of Christian dogmas (trinity — resurrection). There is no rift between dogma and the natural, spring-time elation of bird and man: sincerely they partake of Grace: . . . the most insignificant member of the world-concert, the little bird, can stir up thoughts on the greatest mysteries revealed to Christianity. . . .[4]

Now while it is obvious that the narrative structure of Strada's poem makes it an apparently unsuitable vehicle for the expression of Christian ideas of world harmony, it is nevertheless remarkable that of all the adaptations I have read, only in Crashaw's does the musical duel appear to have religious significance.

II

A close examination of "Musicks Duell" reveals first that while Crashaw employs few technical terms from music (in contrast, for example, to the anonymous *Strada's Musical Duel*), the terms he does use are chosen with the greatest care. Thus in describing the bird's song he uses "divisions," "melody," "Aires," and "ground-worke," while in describing the music of the lute he uses "turne," "harmonious" and "Harmony," "Rapsodyes," "aires," and finally *"Diapason."* The point is that the bird's music, however various and complicated, is purely melodic or horizontal, while the music of the lute is both melodious and harmonic or vertical. It is significant, I think, that this distinction, which (as we shall see) is part of a larger pattern of meaning in "Musicks Duell," is ignored altogether in the other adaptations. Translating Strada's

> Miratur Fidicen parvis e faucibus ire
> Tam varium tam dulce melos,

William Strode, for example, writes that the lutenist wondered

> how so choise,
> So various harmony should issue out
> From such a little throate.

Here perhaps, as in Ford's and Mr. Wilson's use of "harmony," what is meant is not harmony in the modern sense, but the older meaning of pleasing intervals in the melodic line. The anonymous lampooner, however, is more explicit:

> all these she so *blends,* as her smal Breast
> Had been of all siz'd *Viols* a full *Chest.*
> And all *together* sounding in the Hands
> Of (for all *Parts*) best skill'd musicians.

And Ayres (in a poem not based on Strada's) addresses the nightingale thus:

> Then feather'd Atom, where in thee
> Can be compriz'd such Harmony?
> In whose small Fabrick does remain
> What composition can contain.[5]

This fundamental contrast between the nightingale's melody
and the lute's harmony is emphasized by a thread of imagery that
runs through the rich fabric of Crashaw's baroque tapestry. The
song of the bird is again and again imaged as a river:

> Hee amazed
> That from so small a channell should be rais'd
> The torrent of a voyce, whose melody
> Could melt into such sweet variety   (43-6)

> Bathing in streames of liquid Melodie;   (68)

> Still keeping in the forward streame,   (86)

> Shee opes the floodgate, and lets loose a Tide,
> Of streaming sweetnesse, . . .   (93-4)

In contrast, the music of the lute is imaged, though not so frequently, as the sea:

> Following those little rills, hee sinkes into
> A Sea of *Helicon;*   (123-4)

> The Lutes light *Genius* now does proudly rise,
> Heav'd on the surges of swolne Rapsodyes.   (135-6)

Melody is like a flowing river; harmony like the eternal sea. The
full significance of this contrast is revealed in the last lines of
the poem:

>   thus doe they vary
> Each string his Note, as if they meant to carry
> Their Masters blest soule (snatcht out at his Eares
> By a strong Extasy) through all the sphæares

Of Musicks heaven; and seat it there on high
In th' *Empyræum* of pure Harmony.   150
At length (after so long, so loud a strife
Of all the strings, still breathing the best life
Of blest variety attending on
His fingers fairest revolution
In many a sweet rise, many as sweet a fall)
A full-mouth *Diapason* swallowes all.
          This done, hee lists what shee would say to this,
And shee although her Breath's late exercise
Had dealt too roughly with her tender throate,
Yet summons all her sweet powers for a Noate   160
Alas! in vaine! for while (sweet soule) shee tryes
To measure all those wild diversities
Of chatt'ring stringes, by the small size of one
Poore simple voyce, rais'd in a Naturall Tone;
Shee failes; and failing grieves, and grieving dyes.
She dyes; and leaves her life the Victors prise,
Falling upon his Lute; o fit to have
(That liv'd so sweetly) dead, so sweet a Grave!

This passage, together with the forty lines immediately preceding
it, is an expansion of the last eighteen lines of Strada's poem:

> Scilicet erubuit Fidicen, iraque calente,
> Aut non hoc, inquit, referes Citharistria siluæ,
> Aut fracta cedam cithara. Nec plura loquutus
> Non imitabilibus plectrum concentibus vrget
> Namque manu per fila volat, simul hos, simul illos
> Explorat numeros, chordaque laborat in omni,
> Et strepit, et tinnit, crescitque superbius, & se
> Multiplicat relegens, plenoque choreumate plaudit.
> Tum stetit expectans, si quid paret æmula contra.
> Illa autem, quanquam vox dudum exercita fauces
> Asperat, impatiens vinci simul aduocat omnes
> Ne quidquam vires. Nam dum discrimina tanta
> Reddere tot fidium natiua & simplice tentat
> Voce, canaliculisque imitari grandia paruis;

Impar magnanimis ausis, imparque dolori
Deficit & vitam summo in certamine linquens
Victoris cadit in plectrum, par nacta sepulcrum.
Vsque adeo & tenues animas ferit æmula Virtus.

"Poore simple voyce, rais'd in a Naturall Tone" translates Strada's "natiua & simplice tentat Voce," but it is a question here not of nature and art, but rather of nature and grace. The distinction that is implicit in these lines is the same one that Henry More was later to make explicitly:

> A Nightingale may vary with her voice into a multitude of interchangeable Notes, and various Musical falls and risings, and yet be but a Nightingal, no Chorister: But should she but sing one Hymn or *Hallelujah*, I should deem her no bird but an Angel. So the highest improvement of Natural Knowledge, or mere Morality, will argue no more than the Sons of Men: But to be of one will completely with God, will make us, or doth argue us to be the sons of God.[6]

The superiority of the lute, regarded in the Renaissance as the noblest of instruments,[7] lies in the fact that its "full-mouth *Diapason*" can express that sea of eternity into which flow the rivers of time, the *"Empyræum* of pure Harmony" that lies beyond the spheres, the abode of those who, with Donne, have joined God's "Quire of Saints for evermore."

III

Perhaps it will be objected that this interpretation impoverishes the poem, that it reduces the secular triumph of the Crashavian style with its wonderful word-craft and rich baroque sensibility to a thin allegory of time and eternity, earth and heaven, nature and grace. But it is not as abstract allegory that I would interpret the poem. To use the language of biblical exegesis with which Crashaw was familiar, the significance of "Musicks Duell" is not allegorical (Ford's nature versus art), nor tropological (Strada's "æmula Virtus"), but anagogical. The poem invites us to lift our minds from the narrative to a contemplation of the eternal verity of which it is a concrete embodiment: earthly realities, while not losing their rich particularity, become symbols — or types, to continue the biblical terminology — of spiritual realities. Again and again in seventeenth century religious books, Protestant and Catholic alike, the reader is instructed to derive spiritual profit from earthly things. "Let us make use then," says John White of Dorchester,

> of those things which are of ordinary use, to raise up our hearts to heaven by meditations, and by them teach and instruct our Brethren, as a way most easy, both to the Speaker and Hearer, and most profitable, and lastly ordained by God Himself, who hath not onely imprinted some resemblances of Spirituall things, upon those which are Naturall, but hath set us this taske, to study Spiritual things in the Book of Nature; and to ascend up to Heaven by these things on Earth.

"It is a point of holy wisdome," says Henry Mason, "to take occasion for heavenly meditations, by the mention or sight of earthly things." "There is no page in the book of nature unwritten on," says Thomas Adams, the prose Shakespeare of Puritanism:

> The very bread we eat, should put us in mind of that bread of life; our apparel, of that garment of righteousness which doth justify us, and of glory that shall crown us; our houses below, of those eternal mansions above; the light of the sun invites us to that everlasting light in heaven; the winds in their airy regions, of that sacred Spirit which blows and sanctifies where he pleaseth; the running streams summon us to that crystal river, and fountain of living waters; the earth, when it trembles, remembers us of the world's final dissolution.[8]

Anagoge is not allegory: in the passage from Adams earthly houses do not "stand for" heavenly mansions, they "put us in mind of" them. Similarly in "Musicks Duell" the nightingale is a nightingale, the lute, a lute, and the man, a man. At the same time, however, the reader trained in the anagogical mode of

thought would have been quick to see melody and harmony as
types or symbols of time and eternity, and if he had looked at
the poem's profusion of imagery more closely, he would have
found that it too contributed to the total meaning. Without looking for such point to point correspondences as an allegorical
interpretation would demand, let us examine a few images more
closely to see how they may enrich our understanding.

Take lines 57-104, a passage based on only five lines of the
original:

                her supple Brest thrills out
Sharpe Aires, and staggers in a warbling doubt
Of dallying sweetnesse, hovers ore her skill,
And folds in wav'd notes with a trembling bill,   60
The plyant Series of her slippery song.
Then starts shee suddenly into a Throng
Of short thicke sobs, whose thundring volleyes float,
And roule themselves over her lubricke throat
In panting murmurs, still'd out of her Breast
That ever-bubling spring; the sugred Nest
Of her delicious soule, that there does lye
Bathing in streames of liquid Melodie;
Musicks best seed-plot, whence in ripened Aires
A Golden-headed Harvest fairely reares   70
His Honey-dropping tops, plow'd by her breath
Which there reciprocally laboureth
In that sweet soyle. It seems a holy quire
Founded to th' Name of great *Apollo's* lyre.
Whose sylver-roofe rings with the sprightly notes
Of sweet-lipp'd Angell-Imps, that swill their throats
In creame of Morning *Helicon,* and then
Preferre soft Anthems to the Eares of men,
To woo them from their Beds, still murmuring
That men can sleepe while they their Mattens sing: 80
(Most divine service) whose so early lay,
Prevents the Eye-lidds of the blushing day.
There might you heare her kindle her soft voyce,
In the close murmur of a sparkling noyse.

And lay the ground-worke of her hopefull song,
Still keeping in the forward streame, so long
Till a sweet whirle-wind (striving to gett out)
Heaves her soft Bosome, wanders round about,
And makes a pretty Earthquake in her Breast,
Till the fledg'd Notes at length forsake their Nest;   90
Fluttering in wanton shoales, and to the Sky
Wing'd with their owne wild Eccho's pratling fly.
Shee opes the floodgate, and lets loose a Tide
Of streaming sweetnesse, which in state doth ride
On the wav'd backe of every swelling straine,
Rising and falling in a pompous traine.
And while shee thus discharges a shrill peale
Of flashing Aires; shee qualifies their zeale
With the coole Epode of a graver Noat,
Thus high, thus low, as if her silver throat   100
Would reach the brasen voyce of warr's hoarce Bird;
Her little soule is ravisht: and so pour'd
Into loose extasies, that shee is plac't
Above her selfe, Musicks *Enthusiast*.

The original is pretty thin by comparison:

Hoc etiam Philomela canit dumque ore liquenti
Vibrat acuta sonum, modulisque interplicat æquis;
Ex inopinato grauis intonat, & leue murmur
Turbinat introrsus, alternantique sonore
Clarat, & infuscat ceu martia classica pulset.

Whether or not the primary purpose of Crashaw's amazing display is to provide emotional equivalents of the effect of music, the passage contributes to the anagogical meaning in several ways. For one thing, it is the perfect example in English poetry of what Spitzer, speaking of St. Ambrose, calls the "Christian poetics of kaleidoscopic transformation of symbols." "In Christian art," Spitzer continues (p. 426),

earthly images may easily appear, to melt away and vanish, since to the Christian no single phenomenon has the importance that it did to the pagan. Here we have not the dualistic device of the Ciceronian simile, but metaphoric fusion. . . . Synaesthetic apperception always bears witness to the idea of World Harmony as . . . all the senses converge into one harmonious feeling.

But earthly things are not therefore unreal. The sheer variety of the imagery reveals a natural world of rich particularity; if the melody of the bird represents nature, or earth, or time, it is certainly not by way of abstract allegory. In addition, the images tell us something of the relation between nature and grace. Thus the way the imagery is distributed between the nightingale and the lutenist suggests a complex interaction between nature and grace rather than the irreconcilable conflict that the bare narrative might suggest. For example, the suggestions of growth, progress, and aspiration in the description of the bird's song, culminating in lines 102-104, together with the references to "holy quire," "Angell-Imps," "Anthems," and "Mattens," imply that nature seeks to rise above itself toward its fulfillment in grace, that man, as Hooker said, has a natural desire for the supernatural. Conversely the fact that the music of the lute contains all the elements of the nightingale's song, that it is described as "still breathing the best life/Of blest variety," suggests that grace presupposes nature, that the order of grace is simply the natural order raised to a supernatural level. The difference between them is that nature is inadequate without grace. Momentarily the bird's "little soule is ravisht" and "she is plac't/Above her selfe," but in the end she fails and falls. It is only in the final diapason, "the Generalitie, or whole state of consent and concord, which is perfect musicke,"[9] that the "Hoarce, shrill strife," the rise and fall, the discords of earthly existence are resolved. Nature may "lay the ground-worke of [our] hopefull song," but only grace can raise us to "th' *Empyræum* of pure Harmony."

NOTES

1. The following secondary sources are referred to in this article: Leo Spitzer, "Classical and Christian Ideas of World Harmony," *Traditio*, II (1944), 409-64; Ruth Wallerstein, *Richard Crashaw: A Study in Style and Poetic Development* (Madison, Wisconsin, 1935); and Austin Warren, *Richard Crashaw: A Study in Baroque Sensibility* (Baton Rouge, Louisiana, 1939). The paragraph quotes from Wallerstein, p. 127, and from Warren, pp. 108-9, 110.

2. The following translations and adaptations of Strada's *Prolusion* are referred to: John Ford, *The Lover's Melancholy*, I, i; William Strode, "A Translation of the Nightingale Out of Strada," *Poetical Works*, ed. Bertram Dobell (London, 1907), pp. 16-18; Robert Vilvain, *Enchiridium Epigrammatum Latino-Anglicum* (London, 1654), pp. 177a-177b; Mr. Wilson, in *Poems by Several Hands and on Several Occasions*, Collected by N. Tate (London, 1685), pp. 405-8; Anon., *Strada's Musical Duel* (London, 1671). My attention was called to these poems by the references in Warren and in L. C. Martin, *The Poems of Richard Crashaw* (Oxford, 1927). All quotations from Crashaw and Strada are taken from Martin's edition.

3. St. Augustine, *De Musica*, I. iv. 6, in Migne, XXXII, 1086, cited by Spitzer, p. 458.

4. Spitzer, pp. 455-6.

5. P. Ayres, "To the Nightingale," *Poems by Several Hands* (London, 1685), p. 71.

6. Henry More, *Discourses on Several Texts of Scripture* (London, 1692), p. 408, quoted by W. Fraser Mitchell, *English Pulpit Oratory* (London, 1932), p. 294.

7. Agostino Agazzari, *Del sonare sopra il basso*, in Oliver Strunk, *Source Readings in Music History* (London, 1952), p. 428.

8. John White of Dorchester, *A Commentary Upon the Three First Chapters of . . . Genesis* (London, 1656), Book II, p. 45; Henry Mason, *Hearing and Doing. The Ready Way to Blessednesse . . .* (London, 1635), pp. 14-15; Thomas Adams, *Meditations Upon Some Part of the Creed*, in Nichol's *Standard Divines* (Edinburgh, 1862), III, 175.

9. Quoted in NED from Holland's *Pliny*, I. 14.

Absalom and Achitophel
as Epic Satire

CHESTER H. CABLE

THE DEPENDENCE of the satiric hits in Dryden's *Absalom and Achitophel* upon a theory of the epic and the theoretic relationships between epic and satire is frequently obscured by its more obvious qualities as satire. Dr. Johnson, a perceptive critic and himself something of a satirist, at the same time that he censures the structure of the poem, lists those more obvious qualities as clearly as anyone can: "If it be considered as a poem political and controversial, it will be found to comprise all the excellences of which the subject is susceptible; acrimony of censure, elegance of praise, artful delineation of characters, variety and vigour of sentiment, happy turns of language, and pleasing harmony of numbers; and all these raised to such a height as can scarcely be found in any other English composition."[1] Among students and general readers, the poem is too frequently remembered in an even more limited appreciation, only for the individual "characters." It is my thesis that as satire and as poetry, *Absalom and Achitophel* gains its real and its persuasive force by the arrangement of its narrative and the treatment of its characters according to one recognizable epic theory of the time. The kind of action chosen for narration, the singleness of the action, the probable and necessary quality of it, and the causal relationship between characterization and action are to be distinguished from the casual sequence of events found in such a narrative as Butler's *Hudibras* or the historic events of the series of the various "Instructions" to painters.[2] Dryden himself makes the same distinction when he rejects his "Annus Mirabilis" as epic because of its "broken action, tied too severely to the laws of history. . . ."[3]

History, as particular events, furnishes the subject matter of the satire of the period. I suspect that great satire in English has always tended to be provoked by particular individuals and specific situations and to attack those individuals in those situations. But from time to time, fashions and situations brought about changes in the mode of attack; conditions and the poet came together to form, in *Absalom and Achitophel,* an effectively convincing example of the usefulness of epic devices in satire. The qualities which emerge from Dryden's application here of the period's ideas of "epic" are the ones which point the way to the later great satires in English verse.

Epic qualities were not associated with satire throughout the seventeenth century. Mid-century satire strayed into something of a blind alley in its complete dependence upon the conceit, as in most of John Cleveland's satire in the 1640's,[4] or upon the philosophic, point-by-point answer of such a piece as Martin Lluellyn's "A Satyr, Occasioned by the Author's Survey of a Scandalous Pamphlet, Intituled *The Kings Cabinet Opened.*"[5] Both writers have real power and the devices have their uses. To say, as does Cleveland, of the lords and commoners who made up the Westminster Assembly, that they are behaving like clandestine lovers and that the birth which will result will be a "gaol-delivery"[6] is a witty conceit and a scandalous innuendo; it may be doubted that it is a device likely to persuade anyone to change his opinion about the individuals Cleveland is attacking. Nor is Lluellyn's device of the point-by-point answer to an attack on the king, though the argument is forceful and the language witty, of any great persuasive power to the undecided or the antagonistic. It required a more comprehensive structure for either of these devices to operate persuasively, as their use in Dryden's satire would indicate.

In part, the sharp division in the public for which satire might be written during the middle of the seventeenth century made for less attention to the persuasive qualities in satire. At the time of the Civil War in England, during all of the period of the controversy and the settlement which excluded a whole section of the people from participation in public affairs, each satire was written for a public already convinced of the satirist's point and usually by a man on the losing side who found this his only method of gaining any kind of satisfaction. Under these conditions, rough language and a fairly direct attack are almost inevitable. It is remarkable that bitterness is not the only quality to be found in such satires.

In the various theories advanced about satire early in the century, almost the lone voice for indirection and persuasiveness had been that of Heinsius, in his edition of Horace and the discourse "De Satyra Horatiana."[7] For the rest, the chief advice had been of the kind with which Barten Holyday prefaced his translation of the satires of Persius: "For indeed when a Satyrist, set on fire to see the desperate security of prophaneness; the furie of his passion doth so transport him, that there is no time left for the placing or displacing, choosing or reiecting of some particular word; but as most commonly their passions are vneuen, rough, and furious: so is that also which they write being in this poeticall perturbation."[8] Later in the century, Milton subscribed to this view whole-heartedly.[9] And, in general, satirists remained more perturbed than persuasive.

But with the return of the monarchy in 1660, the problem of the satirist changed. His readers were no longer clearly divided into two opposed camps; instead, men were to be persuaded to take one stand or another, and satire was one method toward such persuasion. This was clearly so in 1681, when Dryden wrote *Absalom and Achitophel,* as his statement "To the Reader" would indicate: "The Commendation of Adversaries, is the greatest Triumph of a Writer; because it never comes unless Extorted. But I can be satisfied on more easy terms: If I happen to please the more Moderate sort, I shall be sure of an honest Party; and, in all probability, of the best Judges; for the least Concern'd are commonly the least Corrupt: And, I confess, I have laid in for those, by rebating the *Satyre* (where Justice would allow it), from carrying too sharp an Edge. . . . The Violent on both sides will condemn the Character of *Absalom,* as either too favourably or too hardly drawn. But they are not the Violent whom I desire to please." In the same statement, Dryden remarked, "I can write Severely, with more ease, than I can Gently." And the problem of appealing by satire to the moderate is indeed a double one. For it means establishing, within the structure of the satire, the norm from which the situation and the individuals depart, since the readers will not belong to a closed society in which such norms may merely be assumed. And in addition, it also means presenting any departures from that norm as at the least ridiculous, possibly vicious, and probably dangerous. Dryden's statement about personal satire is pertinent here:

> There are two reasons for which we may be permitted to write lampoons; and I will not promise that they can always justify us. The first is revenge, when we have been affronted in the same nature, or have been any ways notoriously abused, and can make ourselves no other reparation . . . . and . . . the second reason which may justify a poet when he writes against a particular person . . . is, when he is become a public nuisance. All those, whom Horace in his Satires, and Persius and Juvenal have mentioned in theirs, with a brand of infamy, are wholly such. 'Tis an action of virtue to make examples of vicious men. They may and ought to be upbraided with their crimes and follies; both for their own amendment, if they are not yet incorrigible, and for the terror of others, to hinder them from falling into those enormities which they see are so severely punished in the persons of others. The first reason was only an excuse for revenge; but this second is absolutely of a poet's office to perform: but how few lampooners are there now living, who are capable of this duty![10]

Here is the reason for and the ideal of those character sketches for which *Absalom and Achitophel* is most generally admired. But the means by which their "public nuisance" quality is demonstrated is not to be found in them as isolated characters. They are not, strictly speaking, lampoons at all, but rather agents toward the epic action — the fable — which the poem sets about to narrate.

Dryden gives several hints in his conduct of the poem that *Absalom and Achitophel* is to be compared to epic. His introduction of Absalom, for instance, insists upon the two traits of a hero which were proper to epic — his renown in war and his natural attraction in love. He also makes Absalom the son of a king, a recommended epic procedure. In addition, the action is an important one, in the epic sense. Corneille, in his "Discours du poëme dramatique," had considered several possibilities and decided that such action should involve some great interest of state and center about a passion more noble or more evil than love, such as ambition or vengeance.[11] Absalom is ambitious, Achitophel is vengeful, and David's throne is in doubt. It is almost as though Dryden had checked off the points he intended to make.

Even the phrasing alludes pointedly at times to the contemporary epic, Milton's *Paradise Lost*. The lines in which Dryden first mentions Achitophel describe him as "manifest of Crimes, contriv'd long since," in defiance to his Prince; "manifest" is here a Latinism not usual in Dryden, but familiar enough in Milton. And the couplet introducing his first speech to Absalom is phrased in inverted form and alludes to Satan, the serpent:

> Him he attempts with studied Arts to please
> And sheds his Venome in such words as these.[12]

In addition, there is the roll call of the "legions of Satan," beginning with Zimri — an obvious epic device, even without Milton's "Say, Muse."

In short, no reader in Dryden's time could have missed the ironic overtones of the epic comparison. A norm of heroic struggle with a serious outcome is thus established.

The narrative scheme is also a "fable" in the sense that Dryden, following Le Bossu, discusses it in his "Preface" to *Troilus and Cressida*: it begins in a "precept of morality" and it develops the plot through the probable and necessary, as they were then interpreted. Corneille's struggle with those terms in his "Discours de la tragédie" led to the conclusion that if one treated a historical subject, the audience would have to say it could happen because it had happened; the treatment of individual characters in individual scenes could then be freer than in an invented subject. In his use of a biblical narrative, Dryden places little dependence upon the idea that "because it has happened, it obviously could happen."

The plot is, of course, slight. But it is a plot. Achitophel, finding life dull and the multitude ripe for change, chooses Absalom, the charming but illegitimate son of King David, as a tool to bring about that change. Absalom begins by resisting any criticism of the king. But Achitophel finally persuades him that his father, the king, is weakly good-natured and that the queen and the king's brother may do away with David and put Absalom's very life in doubt. And Absalom thereupon goes about the country, rousing people to the danger of the Jebusite plot, which he says is led by the queen and the brother of David, until the king rouses himself and asserts his kingly power, marvellously supported by the Almighty.

The story of Absalom and Achitophel is thus to some extent an account of character change in one individual, in the impressionable Absalom, and of a contrast between his malleable qualities and the firm limits to the "stretch of grace" in the king. Most obviously, the characters furnish materials for this action. But what is more to the point, the interplay of character displayed in the tale raises, without putting them irrevocably into words, pertinent questions about qualities of character necessary to a king and qualities of character necessary to any man in public life. The action, the plot itself, helps to give the reader some standard, larger than individual prejudice or individual injury, by which to judge the men. A man may be a villain or a fool, but that is of importance only to his friends and enemies unless he has public influence. And here the fable proves the public influence of the individuals. By relating one individual to another, Dryden manages also to bring out the many kinds of influences at work within the opposition. To the extent that people like Buckingham could work upon other men in the party, and through the party, upon the public, they were "public nuisances." And so the character of Zimri is satire on two levels: It strikes off a personal score with Buckingham by showing him as ridiculously ineffective; and by relating his individual qualities to the larger fabric, it displays them as potentially dangerous in a public figure.

Furthermore, not only is it fable, but as epic it implies standards of "manners," of epic characterization, especially of appropriateness to a general type. Dryden, in discussing this problem, says:

> . . . the manners must be suitable, or agreeing to the persons; that is, to the age, sex, dignity, and the other general heads of manners: thus, when a poet has given the dignity of a king to one of his persons, in all his actions and speeches, that person must discover majesty, magnanimity, and jealousy of power, because these are suitable to the general manners of a king.[13]

Le Bossu's commentary on Aristotle discusses at some length what the poet should do if the appropriate behavior of one of his characters differs from what history reports of him;[14] the satirist, of course, finds such discrepancy to his advantage; and in Dryden's case here, the discrepancy is extremely useful for the satiric treatment of Shaftesbury and Oates, to name the most obvious examples; for one, as an elder and wise statesman, should be considerate of the public welfare and is not; and the other, as a priest, should be spiritual and unworldly and is not.

Just in case the reader might have missed the epic implications of the story, it is also biblical. And Dryden has managed to carry a number of implications of censure through the choice of biblical names. For example, Dryden said that he avoided mention of greater crimes in his satire on Buckingham; but he chose a biblical name for him with the proper association with greater crimes, for a Zimri in the Bible was slain as an adulterer. Dryden had no need to say specifically that Buckingham had slain the Earl of Shrewsbury "while his adulterous countess held his horse. . . ."[15]

Dr. Johnson compares the persuasive power of Dryden's "The Medal" with that of *Absalom and Achitophel* to the disadvantage of the former because, as he says, "The superstructure cannot extend beyond the foundation; a single character or incident cannot furnish as many ideas, as a series of events, or multiplicity of agents."[16] It may be noted that when Dryden used this more limited descriptive framework he was not hoping to persuade but simply writing for partisans.

Marvell may also have been writing for partisans when he composed his "Last Instructions to a Painter" (1667).[17] He uses the couplet skilfully and he makes use of the epic comparison and of exalted descriptions of nature to suggest the dignity of epic from which human nature departs. But although he is narrating events, involving many characters and leading to an important matter of state, he does not construct a plot which is based upon a single precept of morality nor lay the groundwork for their part in the action in his characterizations of the persons involved. And the result is a falling away in persuasive power. Marvell must, because of the casual quality of his narrative — its being tied too severely to history — directly denominate the norm from which each character has fallen away; he does so vividly enough, but the weight of the censure tends to fall back on the satirist unless the reader is already of his party.

But even within the framework of a plotted story, few of Dryden's contemporaries managed to get such full satiric value from the epic description of individuals. John Caryll, whose *Naboth's Vinyard*[18] preceded *Absalom and Achitophel,* made the most of the moral fable-contemporary situation relationship; and the characters are truly living ones. But the action is not heroic in the sense Dryden's is, his scene is less crowded, and he manages to center upon fewer full-length portraits than does Dryden. The effect is that he gets less emphasis upon the "public nuisance" quality of his characters. And although the authors of

Absalom Senior[19] and of *Azaria and Hushai*[20] recognize the opportunity to introduce many contemporary characters, they fail to relate them firmly to the action of the story, or, for that matter, to the biblical background. They are considerably less expert than Dryden, too, at making the traits of character which identify individuals true parts of general types of character, and then at making those general types open to censure as they display shortcomings in their part in the general action being narrated. For the most effective satire, the character must be displayed in an action which is open to censure, be shown performing that action because of the type of character he is, and be identifiable, within that type, as a contemporary person. To be satisfied, as the authors of *Absalom Senior* and *Azaria and Hushai* most frequently are, merely with tying a biblical name to a contemporary individual and identifying the individual by reciting several of his idiosyncrasies, cannot rise above the petty spite of the lampoon, nor demonstrate the "public nuisance" quality of true satire, nor, certainly, maintain the appearance of impartiality in the satirist. For satiric narrative, then, as well as the epic, the rule laid down by Le Bossu would seem to be useful: The traits of character should be shown as having some firm relationship to the action if the satirist is to push the pleasure home, to entertain as well as to censure, even adequately to amuse.

It was not until almost the end of his life that Dryden connected epic and satire explicitly, saying of Boileau's *Le Lutrin:* "Here is the majesty of the heroic, finely mixed with the venom of the other; and raising the delight which otherwise would be flat and vulgar, by the sublimity of the expression. . . . Had I time, I could enlarge on the beautiful turns of words and thoughts, which are as requisite in this, as in heroic poetry itself, of which the satire is undoubtedly a species."[21] But in his practice, he had discovered epic devices as a means to persuasive satire at least as early as *Absalom and Achitophel*. And sensitive and expert satirists of succeeding periods followed his lead to the best of their ability.

NOTES

1. *Lives of the English Poets* (London, 1912), I, 320.
2. The most complete list of these painter poems I have seen is to be found in J. Woodfall Ebsworth, ed., *The Roxburghe Ballads: Illustrating the Last Years of the Stuarts* (Hertford, 1883), IV, 546-47. The four volumes of *Poems on Affairs of State* (1697-1707) contain thirteen; Ebsworth cites twenty.
3. Preface to "Annus Mirabilis," *Essays of John Dryden*, ed. W. P. Ker (Oxford, 1926), I, 11.
4. See for example "The Rebel Scot," "A Dialogue between Two Zealots upon the &c in the Oath," "Smectymnuus, or the Club-Divines," "The Mixt Assembly," conveniently found in *The Poems of John Cleveland*, ed. John M. Berdan (New Haven, 1911).
5. *Men-Miracles. With other Poemes* (London, 1646), pp. 101 ff.
6. "The Mixt Assembly," lines 69-86.
7. Daniel Heinsius, *Quintus Horatius Flaccus, De Satyra Horatiana* . . . (Leyden, 1629).
8. *A. Persius Flaccus his Satyres. Translated into English*, 3rd ed. (London, 1635).
9. "An Apology for Smectymnuus," *The Works* (New York, 1931), III, Part I, 228-29.
10. "Original and Progress of Satire," *Essays*, II, 79-81.
11. *Oeuvres* (Paris, 1862), I, 24.
12. *The Poems of John Dryden*, ed. John Sargeaunt (London, 1935), p. 52, lines 228-29.
13. Preface to *Troilus and Cressida*, *Essays*, I, 214.
14. *Monsieur Bossu's Treatise of the Epick Poem* . . . (London, 1695), pp. 180-85. Book IV, chap. 7.
15. The Story of Zimri occurs in Num. xxv. 6-15. See Sir Walter Scott, ed., *The Works of John Dryden* . . ., 2nd ed. (Edinburgh, 1821), IX, 270, n., and J. Q. Wolf, "A Note on Dryden's Zimri," *MLN*, XLVII (1932), 97-99.
16. *Lives of the Poets*, I, 321.
17. *Poems and Letters*, ed. H. M. Margoliouth (Oxford, 1927), I, 142.
18. London, 1679.
19. Elkanah Settle, *Absalom Senior: or, Achitophel Transpros'd* . . . (London, 1682).
20. Samuel Pordage (London, 1682).
21. *Essays*, II, 108.

SAMUEL A. GOLDEN

As soon as farce began to develop, practicing dramatists attempted to halt its growth. It came under direct attack as early as 1668 when Edward Howard, probably disturbed by such stage presentations as *The Cutter of Coleman Street, Sauny the Scott,* and *Albumazar,* reflected that this upstart genre was undermining the dignity of the stage. In the epistle to *The Usurper,* he lamented that farce "has so tickled some late Audiences, with I know not what kind of Jollity, that true *Comedy* is fool'd out of Countenance, and instead of Humor and wit, (the Stage's most Legitimate issue) leaves it to the inheritance of Changlings."

Three years later, in the preface to *An Evening's Love; or, The Mock Astrologer,* John Dryden joined in the attack.

But I have descended, before I was aware, from Comedy to Farce; which consists principally of grimaces. That I admire not any comedy equally with tragedy, is, perhaps, from the sullenness of my humour; but that I detest those farces, which are now the most frequent entertainments of the stage, I am sure I have reason on my side. Comedy consists, though of low persons, yet of natural actions and characters; I mean such humours, adventures, and designs, as are to be found and met with in the world. Farce, on the other side, consists of forced humours, and unnatural events. Comedy presents us with the imperfections of human nature: Farce entertains us with what is monstrous and chimerical. The one causes laughter in those who can judge of men and manners, by the lively representation of their folly or corruption: the other produces the same effect in those who can judge of neither, and that only by its extravagances. The first works on the judgment and fancy; the latter on the fancy only: there is more of satisfaction in the former kind of laughter, and

61

in the latter more of scorn. But, how it happens, that an impossible adventure should cause our mirth, I cannot so easily imagine.[1]

Edward Ravenscroft is generally credited with beginning the vogue of farce in 1672 with *The Citizen turn'd Gentleman*, but Professor Hughes says that it gained a strong foothold somewhat earlier.[2] However, it was not until this play, with James Nokes in the role of Old Jordan, that farce won the acclaim of the public and the favor of Charles II, a good judge of that sort of play. When it was reprinted in 1675, Ravenscroft, with pardonable glee, stated that it was performed thirty times. Downes observed that "This Comedy was look [*sic*] upon the Cricks for a Foolish Play; yet it Continu'd *Acting* 9 Days with a full House."[3] On the sixth day, Ravenscroft added a couplet to the prologue in order to annoy the critics.

The Cricks come to Hiss and Damn this play,
Yet spite of themselves they can't keep away.

Allardyce Nicoll, in *A History of Restoration Drama 1660-1700*, states that "no writer had more of an influence on the usual fare of the theatre than had Ravenscroft."[4] But, in *British Drama*, he writes:

Of little intrinsic importance, but of considerable historical value, two minor dramatists, Nahum Tate and Edward Ravenscroft, must now be considered. Both were varied playwrights, producing tragedies and tragi-comedies as well as purely comic works, but their merit lies almost wholly in the last-mentioned species. To them more than to any others we owe the development and establishment of English farce.[5]

In 1685, Nahum Tate, after his uneven success as an adapter of Shakespeare, brought out *A Duke and No Duke*, based on Sir Aston Cockayn's *Trappolin Suppos'd a Prince*. The preface contains a weak and meagre defense of farce. He felt that its existence had to be justified in the face of the adverse comments and that his purpose was to establish it on a level with tragedy and comedy by finding classical precedents.

Yet, with monotonous regularity, writers continued to carp at the encroachment of farce on the provinces of comedy and tragedy. In 1689, Thomas Shadwell expressed disappointment when the audience failed to distinguish comedy from farce in *A True Widow*. With poor grace, he said:

> In the Action, many doubted which belong'd to the Farce in the Play, and which to the Play it self, . . .For some, I believe, wish'd all the Play like that part of a Farce in it; others knew not my intention in it, which was to expose the Style and Plot of Farce-Writers, to the utter confusion of damnable Farce, and all its wicked and foolish Adherents. But I had rather suffer, by venturing to bring new things upon the Stage, than go on like a Mill-Horse in the same Round.

In 1691, William Mountford raised his small voice in protest in the prologue to his comedy, *Greenwich-Park*.

> When we can see the Town throng to a Farce
> And Hamlet not bring charges.

In 1692, in the preface to *Cleomenes*, Dryden threatened to write a satire on the subject.

> . . . at a time when the World is running mad after Farce, the Extremity of Bad Poetry, or rather the judgment that is fallen upon Dramatique Writing . . . Were I in the humour, I have sufficient cause to expose it (Farce) in its true colors; but . . . I will forbear my Satyr . . .

In 1693, Tate brought out the second edition of *A Duke and No Duke*. *The Gentleman's Journal* of January, 1692/3, printed a pithy and informative notice which indicated the play's popularity.

> A Duke and No Duke, being often acted now, and scarce, is reprinted, with the addition of a curious preface by our Laureat, concerning farce.

The "curious preface" may well be the most important contribution in the Restoration period to the subject of farce. Nicoll recognized its importance when he stated that Tate "saw fit to increase what had been but a page and a half of preface to his *A Duke and No Duke* into a full-blown discourse 'concerning Farce'."[6] Tate himself considered the preface so important that he mentioned it on the title page: "now added a Preface concerning Farce: With an Account of the *Personae* and *Larvae,* etc. of the Ancient Theatre." He said that he had intended ransacking the classics to prove the existence of farce in them, but that his task had been simplified when he had found an obscure Latin work entitled *De Personis, et Larvis earumque apud Veteres Usus, & Origine Syntagmation* written by Agesilao Mariscotti, and first printed in 1610.

Mariscotti was an Italian scholar and apostolic prothonotary under Pope Paul V. His survey of the use of masked actors and dancers in the classical period had served as background for discussion of the Carnival of Venice. His work was not concerned with dramatic problems; it merely called attention to the abuse of masks and vizards in the great pre-Lenten celebration. He disapproved of the "Demonstration of Distraction and Frenzy of all sorts" and "the Impious Practices and Debaucheries" at the Festival.

Tate lifted the first part of the book for the basis of the preface. He followed Mariscotti up to the discussion of the evils at the Carnival of Venice, and, therefore, up to this point, the preface was largely a loose translation.[7] He credited Horace and Ovid with mention of the *personae* and added that the ancients believed in "pompous and splendid dresses" as proper for tragedy. From tragedy he moved to satire, which, he claimed, was "but a species of the former." From satire, he made a swift transition to the subject of masks and vizards for representation of individuals, and by this, showed that satire had developed into a dramatic means of criticising well-known people. At first, disguises had been used to represent famous people; later, to heighten mirth.

Mariscotti had pointed out that by the use of masquerade, people hid their identities and conducted themselves in a wicked fashion in the great Venetian carnival.

After Tate had shown that the ancients had used *personae* on the stage, he launched a direct discussion of farce. He pointed out that it was reasonable to believe that the *personae* and vizards had found a genuine and natural use among ancient "Farce-Players." To strengthen his argument, he referred to Molière's comedies and recalled that they had been denounced as farcical. He then carried the discussion to a consideration of English plays, and, having established that farce was capable of satire and not inconsistent with good sense, applied his conclusion to the comedies of Ben Jonson and John Dryden.

While he sought a definition, he stated that he "dare not be the first that ventures to define it." Just as Dryden could not understand why farce was popular, so Tate could not understand "by what Fate it happens (in common Notion)" that farce was considered "the most contemptible sort of the Drama." Nor could he understand why farce brought "least Reputation to an Author."

Farce, according to Tate, could not be confined by strict rules and regulations. It could have a plot or be without one and did not necessarily have to be within the bounds of nature and probability. He argued that when comedy exceeded the limits of nature and probability it became farce, but that while the dramatist had the right to exceed these limits he had to exercise judgment in order to "heighten . . . Mirth without too grosly [*sic*] shocking [the] Senses."

The essay was designed to establish farce, on the one hand, divorced from comedy, and, on the other, separated from burlesque and buffoonery. He insisted that farce was different from comedy because comedy stayed within the limits of probability; that it was not burlesque and buffoonery because these deviated from "good sense." Farce, therefore, was a dramatic form beyond the limits of probability but within the bounds of "good sense." Upon such a basis, Tate claimed that Jonson's *The Alchymist* was farce until Act V, scene ii, when the intrigues of Subtle, Face and Dol were exposed. He considered this action improbable because in life such rascality was not likely to occur.

Farce was something more than a bundle of nonsense. It could be satiric through the use of "drollery, banter, buffoonry, vagaries, and whimsies." Therefore, according to his understanding, such plays as *The Rehearsal, The Knight of the Burning Pestle* and even *Love and a Bottle* came within its limits. In them were improbability of action, satirical elements, and heightening of mirth. The point that mirth should not be accompanied by a gross shocking of the senses put a limit on farce. Tate would have objected, for example, to *The Royal Flight, or The Conquest of Ireland,* labelled "a new farce," in which King James's disastrous flight was burlesqued in a shameful manner. While the play was beyond the realm of probability, it could not possibly be a farce because it was derisive.

In *A Duke and No Duke,* Tate had carefully followed the principles he had laid down in his essay. He succeeded in turning a poor tragi-comedy of five acts into a sparkling farce of three, by judicious excision and tightening of the action. He worked with a sure hand and never allowed the material to get out of control. The improbability was never strained; it managed to border on reality without ever trespassing into the field of comedy. Nor did the play dwindle into buffoonery. Its immediate success and long, durable history demonstrate the practicality of Tate's critical observations.[8]

The improbability arises from the magic transformation of Trapolin, "a Parasite, Pimp, Fidler and Buffoon," into an exact copy of the Duke. When he suddenly finds himself mistaken for the Duke, he retains his fun-loving nature but takes full advantage of his new situation. Even though he realizes that eventually he must return to his original character, he enjoys his lot without abusing his power and does not become pompous and severe like the real Duke. When the transformation was completed, Trapolin says:

The Dress is just like him, and for ought I know, it is Dress that makes a Duke . . . Trust me for Duking of it: I long to be at it. I know not why every man should not be Duke in his turn.

Tate inserted satirical passages.

Trap: Our Highness means to take exact account of Affairs; I left an honest Fellow here, call'd *Trappolin*. What's become of him?

Barb: Your Highness gave me charge to banish him.

Trap: Why there's the Pillar of our State gone. You took him for a Buffoon, but I found him one of the best Politicians in Christendom. . . .

Trap: . . . I love dispatch in Affairs, tell me therefore quickly what you take to be the duty of a Statesman?

Barb: To study first his Royal Masters profit,
And next to that his pleasure; to pursue
No sinister design of private gain;
Nor pillage from the Crown to raise his Heirs,
His base-born Brood in Pomp above the Race
Of old descended Worth; —

Trap: . . . I have travel'd, and can tell you what a Statesman should be. I will have him ten times prouder than his master; I, and ten times richer, too. To know none of his old Friends, when he is once in Office; to inform himself who has Merit, that he may know whom to do nothing for; to make Sollicitors wait seven years to no purpose, and to bounce thr'o a whole Regiment of 'em. . . .

The intention of the speech in the Justice scene is undisguised.

Well, here sits the Government: In the first place I would have the Court take notice, that in Affairs of State, I think that words are not to be multiply'd. . . . So that in this Assembly, he that speaks little, will speak better than he that talks much; and he that says nothing, better than they both.

Cockayn's Trapolin was at times a buffoon, but not so Tate's. In the original play, the first act ended with Trapolin riding on the back of Barberino. Tate cut out this nonsense.

Trapolin, a good-natured man, wants everybody to be happy. He sympathizes with Prudentia, the Duke's sister, and her lover, Brunetta, who are forbidden to marry by order of the real Duke. Trapolin himself is in love with Flametta, but their love never becomes mawkish. Tate might have changed him into a sentimental character but avoided this pitfall. Flametta, a refreshing character, is neither coy nor maudlin. When her lover is banished, she does not become the traditional woman in distress, ready to die, but fights to bring him back. Throughout his exile, she maintains a nice sense of humor. The scene in which she seeks the aid of Barberino is effective.

> Fla: I gave my heart before I knew his Vices,
> But it will be my triumph to reclaim him,
> I do beseech your Honour to call him home.
> Barb: And what Return may I expect for this?
> Fla: Goodness has always been it's [sic] own reward;
> But to convince you that your Courtesie
> Shall not be wholly thrown away upon me,
> By Day or Night you shall command——
> Barb: What?
> Fla: My Prayers.
> Barb: A very hopeful Recompence;
> What Statesman ever yet took Prayers for pay?

Except for the use of the obscure Mariscotti, the preface is, probably, a collection of what had been thought about farce for a long time. The point is that no one before Tate had seen fit to write an orderly and comprehensive treatise on the subject. For example, as far back as 1688, Aphra Behn, in the dedication of *The Emperor of the Moon*, said she had "endeavour'd as much as the thing wou'd bear, to bring [this farce] within the compass of Possibility and Nature," but she had failed to elaborate.[9] Tate's hopes for a better understanding of the nature of farce through critical discussion were futile. No controversy developed because writers of farce did not bother to present a case; they were content to see their plays prosper.

Nevertheless, the opponents continued short, sporadic attacks. In the preface to his son's comedy, *The Husband His Own Cuckold,* John Dryden said:

> There is scarce a Man or Woman of God's making in all their Farces, yet they raise an unnatural sort of laughter, the common effect of Buffoonery; and the Rabble which takes this for Wit will endure no better, because 'tis above their Understanding.

Nicholas Brady contributed to the general attack in the prologue to *The Rape.*

> Now awkward Farce prevails with dull Grimace.
> Thus little poets cheaply get a name.

Nicholas Rowe expressed his opinion in the prologue to *The Ambitious Step-Mother.*

> O cou'd this Age's Writers hope to find
> An Audience to Compassion thus inclin'd,
> The Stage would need no Farce, nor Song nor Dance,
> Nor Capering Monsieur brought from Active FRANCE.

Similar sniping continued well into the eighteenth century. Writers of tragedy and comedy spoke in unison against farce; writers of farce simply smiled at their more serious contemporaries. Popular success was their goal and they had reached it. There was no common battleground. By 1693, farce was too well established to need any defense. In spite of the fact that the best writers had labeled it a genre incapable of being taken seriously, the audiences were to give it wholehearted support.

Without champions or opponents, Tate's essay was ignored. Had it appeared at a more auspicious time, it might have had an important place in the stage history of the late seventeenth century. Notwithstanding, it still is a valuable document in the study of farce. It brought together, for the first time, in an orderly and cogent manner, the principles then current upon which farce could find some solid footing.

NOTES

1. *The Essays of John Dryden*, ed. W. P. Ker (2 vols.; Oxford, 1900), I, 135-136.
2. Leo Hughes, *A Century of English Farce* (Princeton, 1956), pp. 131-132.
3. John Downes, *Roscius Anglicanus*, ed. M. Summers (London, 1928), p. 32.
4. Allardyce Nicoll, *A History of Restoration Drama 1660-1700* (Cambridge, 1923), p. 244.
5. Allardyce Nicoll, *British Drama* (New York, 1925), pp. 248-249.
6. Nicoll, *A History of Restoration Drama 1660-1700*, p. 240.
7. See A. H. Scouten, "An Italian Source for Nahum Tate's Defense of Farce," *Italica*, XXVII, No. 3 (September, 1950), 238-240. He says that Tate leaned heavily on Mariscotti. Such an exposition is pointless because Tate stated clearly that he was presenting an abstract of Mariscotti's work. Tate often translated entire passages and occasionally added his own remarks. Scouten gives an excellent example of Tate's translation.

   Scouten states that there were editions in 1639, 1699 and 1735. There was, however, another edition in 1691, printed in *Miscellanea Italica Erudita*, Tom. II, Collegii Gaudentius Robertus Carm. Cong. Parmae, Typis Hippolyti, & Francisci Mariae de Rosatis, Anno, 1691. This work, never translated into English, was not mentioned by any important writer and Tate may have been the first to refer to it. It may be that the 1639 edition was not circulated in England and that the work was unknown to English writers until 1691. Had Tate known of Mariscotti's work in 1684, he might have written his lengthy essay for the first edition. Since he did not write it until 1693, it is very possible that the 1691 edition was the one which had influenced him.
8. *Ten English Farces*, ed. Leo Hughes and A. H. Scouten (Austin, Texas, 1948), pp. 5-7.
9. *Ibid.*, p. 46.

7.

Le Texier's Early Years
In England, 1775-1779

A. DAYLE WALLACE

W<small>HEN</small> A. A. <small>LE TEXIER</small> arrived in England in 1775, only a few Englishmen could have known that he was any different from other visiting Frenchmen who normally came to England for a few weeks or a few months. Actually, this particular Frenchman remained for more than a quarter of a century, was accepted in fashionable and literary circles, made a place for himself as a one-man show and as amateur actor and director of amateur theatricals, edited a journal in French for English readers, and for one season superintended the Italian operas at the Opera House in London. In his early years in London he set the pattern he was to follow during his stay: success, even brilliance, in reading plays for fashionable audiences counterbalanced by failure or near-failure in other ventures, in some of which his financial and social difficulties caused embarrassment to his friends and supporters.

In the five years before he came to London,[1] Le Texier had become the talk of a considerable segment of fashionable society on the Continent: first in provincial Lyons; then at Paris; and briefly at Ferney (where he read and played before Voltaire) and at Brussels. Born in Lyons about 1736 or 1737, "bien né," as M. de la Place was to write to Garrick on September 15, 1775, in a family whose status made it impossible for him to become an actor without losing social position, Le Texier became a civil servant. In the office of the *Ferme générale* (farming of the public revenues) at Lyons he rose to the responsible position of cashier. But the theatre was his avocation and consuming interest. Whenever opportunity offered, he and other amateurs played in private theatrical performances. In 1770 the provost of the merchants at Lyons arranged with Rousseau, who was in the city, for his

71

Pygmalion, "scène lyrique" not yet printed, to be acted before some important guests. Le Texier in the title role created a sensation. (Except for half a dozen words at the end, spoken by the statue-come-to-life, the piece is a monologue.) Capitalizing upon his great powers of mimicry and flexibility of voice, he decided to become his own company of actors, that is, to read all the parts of a play, giving the voice, bearing, and suggestion of action suited to each character in turn. At first he even changed some parts of his dress for each character, but he soon gave up this distracting device as unnecessary: voice, facial expression, gesture, and action were sufficient. After more than three years of apprenticeship, studying and reading plays in fashionable gatherings, he decided to leave his post at Lyons.

The next scene is Paris. In 1774 he took the capital by storm, and had his discretion matched his talents he might have remained there indefinitely. Grimm's *Correspondance littéraire* for March, 1774, indicates the enthusiasm with which he was received:

> M. Le Tessier, receveur général des fermes de Lyon, homme d'esprit, ayant la passion du théâtre, et étant comédien de la tête aux pieds, a imaginé de former sa voix, naturellement flexible, à lire tous les rôles d'une pièce, en leur donnant à chacun le ton de leur âge et de leur caractère. Cette mutation subite, sans charge et sans saccade, est d un effet surprenant, et produit une illusion complète. Aucun des personnages n'est négligée; tous font leur effet. Son visage, qui passe subitement à l'expression qu'il faut rendre, est toujours juste. Il joint à la perfection de la lecture tous les petits accessoires du costume de la pièce qu'il lit. Deux séances ont suffi pour établir sa réputation, et bientôt il n'a plus été question que de lui. Il a été retenu, dès huit jours après son arrivée, pour tout le temps de son séjour. Nos princes ont voulu l'entendre, chacun a voulu l'avoir à souper; c'est un délire complet; mais il faut avouer que rien n'est plus extraordinaire ni plus agréable.

But his triumph was short-lived. He was too sure of himself. When he was invited to read a play before Louis XV at Madame du Barry's, the king, tired from a day of hunting, fell asleep. To wake him, Le Texier banged his book on the table. On discovering what had happened, the king let it be known that Le Texier was too noisy. Thus the doors of royalty and nobility and gentry and all of fashionable society at Paris were closed to him. Questions also began to be asked about his government post at Lyons. Who had given him leave to come to Paris? Were his accounts in order? There were rumors that he had appropriated or misused some of the money collected by his office. Since he might well have been sent to the Bastille as a result of these or less weighty rumors, he thought it best to leave Paris. After brief stays at Ferney and Brussels, he arrived in England in 1775.

With him Le Texier brought a letter of introduction from M. de la Place to Garrick which gained him not only the friendship of Garrick but also the protection of the Duc de Guines, French ambassador in London. Frequently Le Texier, who was made free of Drury Lane, went to see Garrick act, and in their notes and letters Garrick became Le Texier's "mon cher maître" and "mon cher père," and Le Texier became Garrick's "mon cher fils." The relationship between Garrick and Le Texier has been traced by Frank A. Hedgcock in his *A Cosmopolitan Actor David Garrick and His French Friends*.

Le Texier's reading of French plays to fashionable audiences in England has also been touched upon by Hedgcock and by W. Roberts in his "M. Le Texier: Reader of Plays," in the *Times Literary Supplement*, September 19, 1936 (p. 752). Although these two accounts could be supplemented, Le Texier's activity as a professional reader of plays at his house in Lisle Street, Leicester Square, belongs to a period later than that covered in this paper and is therefore not of central concern at the moment.

Le Texier, to be sure, had more to do than to watch Garrick's acting or to read plays. During his first four years in England he was making many social contacts and was making himself agreeable by acting in amateur performances at country houses. For a year, from June, 1777, to May, 1778, he edited a periodical, *Journal étranger de littérature, des spectacles et de politique*. In 1778 he found himself involved in a newspaper quarrel as a result of his attempt to become one of the managers of the Opera House, and when this venture came to nothing, the new managers hired him to superintend the Italian operas there for one season, 1778-1779. To enlarge upon these activities in the early years of his stay in England is the purpose of this paper. No attempt will be made to glean all the references to Le Texier in contemporary letters; the emphasis will be upon unpublished or generally inaccessible material.

I

From the beginning of his stay Le Texier went much into society. He was the guest of Garrick, the Duc de Guines, Horace Walpole (who had heard from Madame du Deffand of the readings in Paris in 1774), Topham and Lady Diana Beauclerk, and many others. An unpublished letter from Le Texier to Mrs. Thrale will serve to suggest the kind of social life he led and to show how his circle of friends was enlarged. I am grateful to the owner of the letter, Mr. Wilmarth S. Lewis of Farmington, Conn., for permission to print it.

Londres, samedi 30 auguste 1777.
Madame,
J'ay vu Mr Garrick ce matin qui m'a dit que vous n'aviés pas reçu la lettre que j'ay eu l'honneur de vous écrire lundy, de Twickenham ou j'étais chez Mr Cambridge, pour vous présenter mes excuses de ne pouvoir pas profiter de l'honneur de votre invitation pour le mercredy suivant; j'avais prié Mr D. Garrick le samedy chez Mr Walpoole [*sic*] ou je dinai avec luy de vous témoigner tous mes regretes, et lundy j'ay pris la liberté de vous écrire pour vous prier de

les recevoir; je ne puy pas concevoir par quel hazard cette lettre ne vous est pas parvenue. Je vous prie, Madame, d'etre persuadée que j'étais trop sensible a l'honneur que vous m'avies fait pour ne pas vous en témoigner ma reconnaissance ainsi qu'a Monsieur Trhale [Thrale]. Ce hazard malheureux pour moy a pu me faire passer un moment dans votre esprit pour un homme négligent et même malhonnête, ayant surtout aussy peu l'honneur d'être connu de vous; peut-être depuis ce moment vous avés reçu ma lettre qui, sans doute, sera arrivée trop tard, mais qui vous prouvera au moins le chagrin que j'avais de ne pouvoir pas répondre avec bontée.

    J'ay l'honneur d'être avec respect, Madame,
      Votre très humble et très obeisant serviteur,
                        LE TEXIER
Permettes moi de présenter icy mes complimens et mes excuses a Monsieur Trhale [Thrale].

Le Texier's two hosts mentioned in this letter, Richard Owen Cambridge and Horace Walpole, were neighbors at Twickenham. Cambridge, poet, miscellaneous writer, and tireless gossip, had a house on Twickenham Meadows not far from Walpole's Strawberry Hill. Garrick's villa was in the neighboring village of Hampton. In a verse epistle to Lady Cecilia Johnston, August 19, 1777, inviting her and her husband General Johnston to dinner on August 23, the dinner Le Texier alludes to, Walpole mentions that the other guests would be Garrick, Kitty Clive, her brother George Raftor, and Le Texier, "a whole theatre in one from France."

Le Texier's graceful note of apology to Mrs. Thrale, which perhaps parades proper names overmuch, is the kind of note of acceptance or regret that he must have written in great numbers. For example, he very likely exchanged notes with Lord Villiers and Lady Craven concerning the amateur theatricals mentioned below, and with host and hostess on many similar occasions.

Two amateur theatrical performances at country houses, the first in Oxfordshire and the second in Berkshire, will serve to illustrate another facet of Le Texier's activity. On January 4, 6, and 10, 1777, he again played the title role in Rousseau's *Pygmalion*, used in this particular entertainment as the after-piece to Vanbrugh's *The Provok'd Husband*, in which he had no part. The performances, presented in a theatre fitted up by Lord Villiers at Bolney Court, near Henley-on-Thames, are fully described in *Passages from the Diaries of Mrs. Philip Lybbe Powys* (ed. Emily J. Climenson, 1899, pp. 178-194): "The famous Monsieur Tessier is to perform *Pygmalion*." ". . . Tessier spent some weeks with him [Rousseau], perfectly to comprehend the author, as he declared he wrote it to express by action every passion to the eye." In *Pygmalion*, she wrote after the performance,

> [Le Texier] was, I suppose, twenty minutes in all the attitudes of tragic woe, deliberating whether he should withdraw the veil, so fearing the sight of this too lovely object. His powers are certainly astonishing; 'tis said no one equals him. Some *partial English* flatter themselves *their Garrick* might come up to him. I own myself of that number; but then as not a perfect mistress of the French, I fear one's opinion would go for nothing, tho' he speaks so just and distinct, I understand by far the greater part of the *whole*.

After the plays were over on the third night Le Texier further showed his versatility. First he played the violin while Lord Villiers and Lord Malden performed "an excellent burlesque on fine stage dances." Next he sang a little French song which he had composed after dinner and which neatly complimented Lord Villiers and his family.

It should be noted in passing that these amateur performances of *Pygmalion* at Bolney Court were responsible for its translation into English in 1779: *Pygmalion, A Poem. From the French of J. J. Rousseau.* It was dedicated to "Miss Hodges," the Galathée in the performances at Lord Villiers's:

The charming Dignity, the attractive Loveliness of your Figure, fully justified, in the Opinion of every Spectator present, the Passion of Pygmalion, even for the supposed Statue; while the inimitable Action, the ardent Expression, and the eloquent Enthusiasm of Mr. Texier, seemed to deserve from the Deities a Miracle in his Favor.

In the *Morning Post, and Daily Advertiser,* May 18, 1778, a "correspondent of the *ton*" sent in an account of an entertainment given "the week before last at the seat of Lord Craven, near Newbery in Berkshire." The first piece was *The Sleep-Walker,* translated from *Le Somnambule,* 1739, written by Madame du Deffand's friend, Antoine de Ferriol, Comte de Ponte-de-Veyl. The cast of characters is listed, including "Clipman, a Dutch gardener, Monsieur Le Tessier," and Lady Craven as Countess Belmour. Although Le Texier spoke at this time "broken English," as Mrs. Powys noted in the account cited above, Clipman's English is supposed to be atrocious, and Le Texier's Dutch-French accent in the play could have done no harm; indeed, it probably heightened the comedy of the scenes in which Clipman appears. To this play, with prologue and epilogue written by Lady Craven, was added the after-piece, "a French Musical Entertainment." "The performance was repeated three several evenings, to very crowded houses. Tickets of admission were five shillings each; and the money arising from them was distributed to the neighbouring poor." Later in the year *The Sleep-Walker* was printed at the Strawberry Hill Press. Many years later, after Lady Craven had become the Margravine of Anspach, Le Texier assisted with the amateur theatricals at Bradenburgh House, an indication that Lady Craven found him both agreeable and talented.

II

In June, 1777, appeared the first number of a periodical edited by Le Texier, *Journal étranger de littérature, des spectacles et de politique. Ouvrage periodique.* The list of 144 subscribers, a small but select group, suggests a kind of "social register" for the time, over half the number having titles of knighthood or nobility. Appearing in the list are the names of the Duke and Duchess of Argyll, Topham and Lady Diana Beauclerk, the Duchess of Bedford, the Duke and Duchess of Buccleuch, Richard Owen Cambridge, Lord and Lady Derby, the Duke and Duchess of Devonshire, David Garrick, Edward Gibbon, the Duke and Duchess of Marlborough, Lord and Lady North, the Duchess of Richmond, George Selwyn, Lord and Lady Villiers, and Horace Walpole. After the June issue, a double number of 308 pages, the remaining twenty-two numbers, two each month, ranged from 140 to 188 pages each. A large part of the magazine was devoted to poetry, fiction, reviews of books, accounts of new scientific discoveries, spectacular trials or events, and news from various European capitals, but the part which attracted most attention was the theatrical criticism, dealing with plays and operas in both Paris and London and occasionally in Berlin. A few of the essays were translated into English and printed in the newspapers. Two of these, printed in the *Public Advertiser*, will serve to illustrate the nature of Le Texier's criticism and his close attention to the problems of the actor and theatrical manager.

On September 15, 1777, the editor of the *Public Advertiser* noted: "In compliance with our correspondent's suggestion we here give Mons. Le Texier's opinion of Mr. Henderson's performance of *King Richard III*, translated from No. 6 [the first number for September] of *Journal étranger*." The essay which follows covers two and a half columns of the newspaper, a much greater space than English newspapers gave to an actor or a play. Henderson, "the Bath Roscius," was attracting great attention at the Little Theatre in the Haymarket, where he first played Richard III on August 7, 1777. Many thought of him as the successor to Garrick and fully as versatile as Garrick. Le Texier, without naming "mon cher maître," compares him with Henderson, to Henderson's disadvantage: "When at the sally upon his tent, he says, 'Give me a horse — bind up my wound' — a noble juncture!

which we have seen performed! as we shall never again see it. . . ."
As for the scene "A horse! a horse!" Henderson delivers the speech
very well with his voice, but his short steps take away the air of
probability. In the death scene "the Great Master [Garrick] tri-
umphed." Henderson, however, excels in the role of Shylock,
"which of all the parts he has played is beyond contradiction that
in which he approaches nearest to perfection; so near, indeed,
that without entering into particulars, we think we may say it is
not possible to perform it better." Le Texier thus puts himself on
record in both specific and general criticism.

Another of his critical essays on the performances at the Little
Theatre in the Haymarket appeared in the *Public Advertiser* on
September 20 (with two corrections of the text noted in the issue
of September 22), this time containing comments upon Digges,
The Spanish Barber (better known as *The Barber of Seville*),
and Colman as manager, "from the *Journal étranger* for the
present month." Le Texier did not see Digges in *Cato*, but for
Digges' Wolsey in *Henry VIII*

> . . . we think we may venture to pronounce him to be a very
> valuable acquisition for the British theatre. A noble figure, in
> this part particularly admirable, an excellent deportment, a
> clear conception, and judicious support of his character, a pleas-
> ing voice, and good delivery (though the English accuse him of
> a vicious pronunciation) render him, in my opinion, one of the
> best actors now on the stage.

Next he praises Colman's free translation and his production of
The Spanish Barber, but laments "the very considerable curtail-
ments from the original French." Finally, he praises Colman for
his "uncommon pains" taken with the Little Theatre at the beginning of his managership.

> It is but just that he should have been amply recompensed;
> for we may truly aver, that since the late loss sustained by the
> retirement of Mr. Garrick, we have not seen so many interested
> particulars collected together, as in the course of the present

summer. It is to be hoped, for the entertainment of the public, that this example will create a laudable emulation in the direction of our winter theatres, who rely rather too much perhaps on the national partiality to the stage.

At this time the critic for the *London Magazine* voiced many times Le Texier's implied strictures on the managers of Covent Garden and Drury Lane, but not even he, in his attempt to be a responsible critic, analyzed the problems of *acting* (voice, gesture, delivery, action, etc.) as minutely and precisely as Le Texier did. The comment on Colman also shows a strong interest in the problems and the potentialities of the theatrical manager.

Having praised Garrick at the expense of Henderson, who had many enthusiastic admirers, Le Texier was sure to be challenged. His detailed, critical commentary was sharply attacked by a correspondent who signed himself "Textorius" in the *Public Advertiser*, September 25, 1777. Le Texier, he charges, has "misrepresented Henderson" in criticizing the first soliloquy. "Soliloquy is a species of dramatic language in which the Bath Roscius is unrivalled." Textorius also refers to Le Texier's "critical parade, learned jargon, and sophisticated prancing," "such whip-syllabub, such frothy declamation." In another letter in the same newspaper five days later Textorius grants Le Texier "perfect knowledge of the beauties of his own language. His admirable recital of the most animating passages in the French writers is a sufficient proof of it." But Le Texier does not understand Shakespeare, and the "description of Garrick's dying in Richard is highly laboured," although Textorius grants that Garrick's performance "was a masterpiece of acting."

As a result of these attacks Le Texier was satirized in the *Public Advertiser*, October 14, 1777, in "Sketches for Modern Designs" as "a Critic without knowing his text — Monsieur T——." Among the thirteen others satirized in the same squib were Bute, North, Sandwich, Burke, Colman, and Mrs. Macaulay. The inclusion of Le Texier in such a list is in itself an indication that his name was fairly well known to the public.

At the end of the first year of publication of his *Journal étranger,* Le Texier inserted two long advertisements in the news columns of the *Morning Post,* May 21 and 29, 1778. In the first he announced:

> Mr. Le Texier, perceiving the daily success of the *Journal étranger,* and flattered to see that the pains he has taken as editor of that periodical publication have been acceptable to his subscribers, is come to a determination of reducing the volumes to one half, that he may be able to reduce the price, which in its present state may appear too high to many individuals. His intention being to employ his leisure hours in a manner agreeable to society and to himself whilst he remains in England, where some undertakings, in their nature no way incompatible with the above work, are likely to fix him for some time, he has resolved to publish only twelve volumes annually; . . . excepting the political matters on which he means to remain silent, on account of the present critical situation of affairs. This want will be abundantly supplied by a choice of any new and interesting matter, both in prose and verse, that may appear in the foreign journals. He proposes also to pay particular attention to all theatrical performances, foreign and domestic; this article having hitherto appeared very acceptable. Each volume concluding with an accurate catalogue of all the new books published in any of the living languages.
>
> The first volume upon this improved plan will be published at furthest on the 15th of June, in order to have sufficient time to receive the subscriptions; the others will follow on the first of every succeeding month.
>
> Subscriptions, at three guineas each, are to be paid at the time of subscribing, are taken in at Mr. Le Texier's, Davies Street, Berkeley Square; also at Messrs. La Boissierre, Bookseller, St. James's Street, and Elmsley, Bookseller, Strand.

In the second advertisement he explains that he will be unable to reduce the price because of the expense of subscribing to all the foreign journals, paying his correspondents in the various capitals, etc. For those who find it inconvenient to pay the three-guinea subscription in advance, he offers "a proper method of making easy, to every individual, the subscription" by giving a note of hand payable at the end of the year. After outlining the contents — theatrical news, trials, novels, anecdotes, important events, "interesting discoveries in mechanics, natural history, and even physics," extracts from new books, music (particularly for the harp), and a catalogue of new books — he adds: "In fine, nothing shall be spared to render the *Journal étranger* the most entertaining and useful work of the kind. Its utility will especially be experienced by those who want to become conversant in the French language." After all of this fine prospectus, the journal did not continue. Why? Probably because there were not enough subscriptions to make it pay, three guineas being, as Le Texier was well aware, a high price for a magazine. Even though many of his fashionable subscribers might have been willing to renew their subscriptions, he clearly wished to widen the circle of appeal. Anti-French sentiment may have contributed, for England and France were in fact at war, although no formal declarations had been made on either side. At any rate, Le Texier would not be idle. One of his "undertakings" alluded to above, the superintending of the performances at the Opera House, would keep him occupied.

III

As early as February, 1777, Le Texier appears in the character of would-be theatrical entrepreneur. In the *London Chronicle* for February 1-4 is notice of a design which appears to have been well advanced in its planning stage:

> The French comedians who are to perform here under the management of Mons. Texier, in order to evade the Act of Parliament passed in the 10th of George II will act by subscription, and the tickets of admission are to be half a guinea each; but no money will be taken at the door.

Apropos of this venture, which came to nothing, Horace Walpole wrote to William Mason, February 27, 1777: "Poor Mr. Garrick labours under the infirmity of age: he has complained of Monsieur Le Texier for thinking of bringing over Caillaud [Caillot] the French actor in the Opéra-Comique, as a mortal prejudice to his reputation." Le Texier's venture was similar to that of "Breslaw and His New Italian Performances" in Cockspur Street, Haymarket, as advertised in the *Morning Post,* January 13, 1778. Various devices were used to present dramatic performances without disturbing the privilege of the patent theatres, Covent Garden and Drury Lane.

In February, 1778, the public learned that Le Texier had envisioned a much more ambitious project, the management of the Opera House, or King's Theatre in the Haymarket. Following the announcement that Richard Brinsley Sheridan and Thomas Harris had completed arrangements with the proprietors, Mr. and Mrs. Brooke and Mr. and Mrs. Yates, to become the managers, a paragraph appeared in the *Morning Post,* February 5, suggesting that Le Texier had been "in treaty for the Opera House . . . in order . . . to have amused the English *noblesse* with the antics of some *theatrical French puppets,*" that is, a company of French actors. The next day this statement was modified: Le Texier, "in conjunction with a gentleman of character and considerable property, had absolutely entered into articles for the King's Theatre, though not to convert it into a stage for French *performers,* but to conduct it upon the usual plan of Italian *operas.*" Le Texier's coadjutor in this plan was Giovanni Andrea Battista Gallini, a famous dancer and dancing-master who later became one of the proprietors of the Opera House. At about this time Horace Walpole encouraged Le Texier to take over the Opera House on the "present plan," as is indicated by Walpole's letter to Mason a few weeks later, March 4. On February 13, the *Morning Post* reported that Le Texier had started a Chancery suit against the Brookes and the Yateses for breach of contract, Mrs. Brooke, actual manager for the proprietors, having signed a sale agreement which had not been observed, and the sale had been made to Sheridan and Harris. In the same issue was a letter from Mrs. Brooke to the editor, calling upon the author of the anonymous paragraph "in your paper of this day" "to publish his name" and give the details of the supposed agreement,

> . . . as Mrs. Brooke never, till after the agreement with Messrs. Sheridan and Harris was signed, heard any person hinted at, as concerned with Mons. Le Texier . . . except Mr. Garrick and Mr. Colman. If the author of this paragraph refuses this, he is a vile and infamous assassin of reputation, and deserves a much severer punishment than the mildness of our laws can inflict.

Clearly, the dispute was growing warm, and on February 16 another paragraph and another letter did nothing to reduce the heat of argument. The paragraph chides Mrs. Brooke for bringing Garrick and Colman into the discussion, as neither "ever entertained the most distant idea of being concerned in any manner with the Opera House, Mr. G. having quitted all thoughts of theatres when he left Drury Lane; and Mr. C. thinking one side of the Haymarket fully sufficient for him." The letter is from "The Writer of the Paragraph" to which Mrs. Brooke objected. He refuses to retract his statements, asserts that Mrs. Brooke drew up an agreement in behalf of the proprietors to sell their joint property of the Opera House for "20,000£ or guineas," and says that legal authorities have judged the agreement binding. On February 18 Mrs. Brooke denied that there was ever an agreement with Le Texier; there was merely "a set of different propositions, drawn up by her (as the basis of a treaty), to not one of which Mons. Le Texier ever acceded."

The discussion had gone so far that Le Texier sent a letter to the *Morning Post* to state his view of the situation. The letter appeared February 23:

To the Editor of the *Morning Post*.

Sir,

I am too much affected by, and interested in, the several paragraphs in your paper, relating some transactions concerning the Theatre in the Haymarket, to remain silent, according to my first resolution; but, out of respect to the sex in general, I restrain myself from expressing my thoughts upon that subject; notwithstanding, as it is essential for me that the truth should appear in its proper light, I declare, for the first, and last time, that I have, in my hands, proposals, and conditions of a treaty, made, and written by the hand of Mrs. Brooke herself, in the name of Mr. Brooke, and Mr. and Mrs. Yates. They gave me a week for my decisive answer, till Sunday morning, the 25th of January. On Friday, the 23d, Mrs. Brooke had notice from a respectable quarter, which she cannot deny, and again, on Saturday the 24th, from myself in person, that I was ready to accept the conditions, and that the money was ready. We gave, and received, our respective words of honour, and she told me she expected her brother in town, and that, immediately upon his arrival, she would appoint a time for the execution of the contract.

On Monday, the 26th, they met clandestinely, and signed, at nine o'clock on Tuesday morning, another contract with the purchasers, for 1000 guineas more. This I can and will prove, whenever it shall be found necessary, in another place, being absolutely resolved to take no more notice of any misrepresentations that may appear in the public papers, declaring that nothing shall proceed from me that is not signed with my name.

I am also very sorry to have seen the names of Mr. Garrick and Mr. Colman mentioned so often in this business; and I think myself obliged honestly to declare that they have never been concerned in this treaty in any manner whatever.

I am, Sir,

Your humble servant,

LE TEXIER

Friday, Jan. [Feb.] 20, 1778

The tone of this letter, in comparison with that in some of the preceding paragraphs, is firm, matter-of-fact, and restrained, and there is no sign of the arrogance that is said to have developed in Le Texier's relations with Garrick. It is possible that an English friend suggested a judicious rather than an emotional declaration.

If Le Texier hoped to have the last word in the dispute, he was disappointed. On the following day, February 24, appeared a paragraph concerning his word *clandestinely*, which might be thought to reflect on the new proprietors:

> . . . we have authority to declare that those gentlemen, whose treaty was begun long before Mr. Texier's, had never the least intimation of the proposals offered or received by Mr. Texier, till within a few days of their purchase, and then only by the report of a third person; nor had they the smallest confirmation of such a treaty ever having existed until after they had signed and sealed. In fact, the treaty which ended in the present purchase was so far from *clandestine* that it was never a secret, even to Mr. Texier's friends.

Mrs. Brooke then had her final word, in a long paragraph on February 25.

> Mrs. Brooke having seen . . . a letter signed *Le Texier*, complaining of misrepresentation, . . . thinks it necessary to say there have been no misrepresentations . . . but what appear to have proceeded from himself or his friends. He not only knew of the treaty with Messrs. Sheridan and Harris, but that the first application had been made . . . by those gentlemen; indeed, both applications were sufficiently public, and had been the subject of general conversation many days before the agreement

with Messrs. Sheridan and Harris had been signed. Mrs. Brooke certainly did not give any word of honor to Mons. Le Texier, as he supposes; on the contrary, she told him she believed Mrs. Yates was at that instant, Saturday night, January 24th, treating with Mr. Sheridan, which was really the case. The paper he alludes to . . . was written and sent the *first* of January, so that, from his own account, his decisive answer should have been given the *eighth*. But as he has mentioned honor, Mrs. Brooke begs leave to observe how little his declaration in that letter respecting Mr. Garrick and Mr. Coleman is reconcilable on that principle with his having mentioned one of those gentlemen as the friend on whom he depended to support him in the purchase,* and the other, as having applied to him with the intention of bringing English plays to the Opera House. As Mrs. Brooke has neither time nor inclination for altercations of this kind, which prove little more than that both parties are angry, she must decline taking notice of what may, in future, be inserted in the public prints.

*[Editor's note.] Quaere, — Does not this border a little on the improbable, when it is well known to the Managers that Mons. Gallini was the man who had the money ready to complete the above purchase?

On this note the discussion ended: Sheridan and Harris had purchased the franchise of the Opera House, and Le Texier had started or was planning to start a suit for damages. The settlement of these difficulties was announced in the *Morning Post*, March 13: "The dispute between Messrs. Sheridan and Harris, and Mons. Le Texier . . . is at length finally and amicably adjusted; the later has given up all pretensions to it [the Opera House], and the former, in consequence thereof, have appointed him superintendent of the Italian Opera at that theatre." Two days later the new plan for the Opera House for the season of 1778-1779 was announced in the same newspaper: "The entertainments are to be the operas on the usual nights, plays twice a week, and probably a concert and ridotto on the other two nights. Mr. Le Texier is to superintend the opera and all matters of spectacle." It was with such plans in mind that Sheridan and Harris had made their purchase, but obstacles they could not surmount lay in their way. On Midsummer Day, June 25, they took over the Opera House for £22,000, the annual rent being an additional £1,270, according to Michael Kelly (*Reminiscences*, 2d edition, 1826, II, 359-60). When the season began in November the plan for operas remained unchanged; the other entertainments were not held. As superintendent of the operas Le Texier seems to have been successful in all ways except one: the expenses were far greater than the receipts. Another venture, the management of a subscription fete at the Pantheon at the close of the season in 1779, was also a dismal failure. At the beginning of the 1779-1780 season, on Nov. 27, 1779, it was announced that Le Texier would no longer superintend the operas.

In his first four years in England, then, Le Texier had unsuccessfully attempted journalism and the management of opera. His journal, expensive and of limited appeal, might in less troublous times have had a greater chance of success. The need to show a profit at the Opera House made his sub-managership a disaster for the managers, although he apparently had a good eye for spectacle on the grand scale. Indeed, his connection with money matters was unfortunate from (or before) the time he left Lyons; what was said of his affairs there might be applied more widely, that he "had been *malheureux*, but not *malhonnête*." In those four years he had also started a pattern that would continue, that of making ambitious plans which would be unsuccessful or only partially realized. To counterbalance his failures, however, was his undisputed success in the reading of plays to fashionable audiences. Until the end of the century he would charm those audiences at his house in Lisle Street, Leicester Square, and be invited to fashionable houses in London and in the country, sometimes to act in amateur performances, sometimes to direct them. But he would come first to people's minds as a reader of plays. After Garrick's death Horace Walpole in a letter to the Countess of

Upper Ossory, February 1, 1779, compared Garrick and Le Texier. Garrick, he wrote, "was a real genius in his way, and . . ., I believe, was never equalled in both tragedy and comedy." Then he continued with an evaluation which is perhaps unfair to Garrick but which certainly states the case for Le Texier:

> I should shock Garrick's devotees if I uttered all my opinion: I will trust your Ladyship with it — it is, that Le Texier is twenty times the genius. What comparison between the powers that do the fullest justice to a single part, and those that instantaneously can fill a whole piece, and transform themselves with equal perfection into men and women, and pass from laughter to tears, and make you shed the latter at both?

With such a genius, or talent, he could afford an occasional failure.

NOTE

1. Biographical information in the introductory section, except as indicated in the text, is derived chiefly from Frank A. Hedgcock, *A Cosmopolitan Actor David Garrick and His French Friends,* London, [1912], pp. 267-74 and the references there cited. The French edition of this work appeared in Paris, 1911. Other sources are *L'Intermédiare des chercheurs et curieux,* LXXVIII (1918), 52-3, 223-4; *Notes and Queries,* 7th Series, XI (1891), 88, 214, 309-10. For Section II I have used the copy of Le Texier's *Journal étranger* in the Harvard University Library, the only copy listed in the *Union List of Serials.* Another copy is in the British Museum.

8

Playbills and Programs:
The Story of a Summer's Quest

R. W. BABCOCK

THE QUEST with which I am about to deal[1] really began in a Wayne University seminar in the spring of 1951, on the subject of eighteenth century drama. The problem I suggested to one rather clever boy in the class was to find out when playbills stopped and programs took their place in the English theater. All through the early history of English drama the audience had no programs, so the actors at the beginning of the play had to *label* each other for the audience's benefit. The arrival of programs would dispose of this sort of crude exposition that Shakespeare and even Sheridan and all the major and minor dramatists between them had to use. Hence we would be interested ultimately not merely in the isolated problem of finding precisely when programs got into the hands of the audience but also in relating the direct effect on dramatic structure that this new phase of the theater produced. The present paper will deal only with the first step, and the method here will be essentially historical, i.e., the chronological sequence of events that finally brought me step by step to the possible answer.

To return, that spring seminar in 1951 found both student and instructor ploughing through masses of dramatic source material in the attempt to pin down the arrival of the modern program. But neither student nor instructor got anywhere in particular, even in the copious material in the University of Michigan library. It looked like a perfectly barren, negative quest. Only one person, so far as we could discover then, ventured to assign a date to the beginning of programs; and that bold soul was Phyllis Hartnoll, the author of the *Oxford Companion to the Theater*.[2] She definitely referred to the problem and set "about 1850" as her guess as to when the program actually came in. She gave no very specific evidence to support this date.[3]

In the summer of 1956, when I got to England, I resurrected the problem. I think it was in Stratford when I was surveying the exhibitions in the Memorial Theater and in the Shakespeare Museum close by. The former was useless, but the latter contained two items that I decided must be programs. One was dated August 20, 1856 — for *The Winter's Tale* — and looked for all the world like a cut-down playbill, with merely the cast remaining, on paper about 3 inches by 4 inches. The other was for a "Royal Entertainment,"[4] dated February 2, 1854, and looked much more like a normal modern program: about 4 inches by 6 inches. Both were under glass, and for the moment I merely jotted them down.

From that discovery I went to the recently (1951) opened Hall's Croft, where another exhibition was presented on the top floor. There was nothing remotely resembling a program here, though there were two interesting playbills dated March 2, 1771, and June 16, 1824, with their regular, giveaway remarks: "The doors to be opened at half past five"; and "Doors to open at six." So in sheer disappointment I asked the young lady in charge of the book and postcard booth, Marjorie Mason, what she thought about it all.

Her answer was startling: "Sometimes they cut down the playbills to serve as programs. Then the original playbill was distributed in the cheaper sections of the theater, while the smaller playbill was sold to those in boxes and more expensive seats."

I thanked her and reflected immediately that she had answered the question I had just faced over the abbreviated playbill of 1856 now hanging on the wall of the Shakespeare Museum.

But she was not through yet. She told me to look up the research specialists in London, Messrs. Mander and Mitchenson, who would probably be able to give me further information. Here was a young English girl producing in five minutes more leads than I had dug up in five months!

The very day I got back to London I called up the famous firm. Mr. Mander himself answered the phone, and the moment he heard what I was after, he launched into a discussion over the phone that had me gasping. I took notes in pencil as fast as I could, and before he finished I had two 3 x 5 cards covered with notes on both sides (in handwriting that I myself now can hardly decipher). I tried to break in once or twice to tell him who I was, and ask him whether he objected to my using these notes. He hushed me up vigorously and continued his lecture, on a subject that must have appealed to him very deeply.

Some of his ideas were these. In the Haymarket Theater play-bills and programs appeared for the same performance (no date given); the cheap seats got the playbill, those in expensive seats could buy the program. (I recalled that Miss Mason said the same thing at Hall's Croft.) Playbills held on in the provinces, he continued, so no exact date can be set for their disappearance. In 1840, however, a small, leaflet program was in use in the opera houses; for Jenny Lind in 1847 programs were definitely used. (All of this, incidentally, predates the "about 1850" surmise Miss Hartnoll suggested in the Oxford Companion, but as yet, of course, we have not got to the regular theater itself.)

Then he jumped suddenly to 1867, when, he said, playbills and programs were used concurrently at the Haymarket, with a double-sheet leaflet for the program. Actually playbills, he continued, appeared as late as the 1870's. The paper used for play-bills was thin, that for programs much thicker. And of course the program was much smaller. He raced on and on, simply from memory apparently. I finally got in a question: "Did you ever publish some of this material?" Yes, he had — in The Theatre World,[5] but he did not know when.

Well, I made a rapid notation of this, but I felt very strongly that a new summary of this same material would be worth publishing over here, in America.

Then very casually he said: "Look up the Enthoven Collection in the Victoria and Albert Museum."

I said, "Yes, I will." (I should have thought of that long ago myself, for Miss Hartnoll referred to it.)

Off he went again.

Some programs, he said, were merely playbills, with the same type, but reduced in size to double-sheet leaflets, with the same flimsy paper as in the original playbill. The word, "program," he declared, was used first in the 50's. The nineteenth century, he added, produced playbills a yard long and two feet wide; the eighteenth century playbills were never as large as this.

And there my notes end. But I had his permission to use them over here if I wished.

The Victoria and Albert Museum was the next spot for investigation.

I walked in there late one morning in August and the minute the guard protecting the famous Room 132 heard my request, he unlocked two doors and turned me over to an assistant (both the curator and his secretary were out to lunch). This man never asked me who I was or where I came from. At my request for Drury Lane playbills from 1840-60 he just dumped on the table before me the 1840 file of Drury Lane playbills for the whole year — a file three or four inches thick!

All of these Drury Lane pieces were fairly long playbills (16 inches by 20), folded face up in the middle lengthwise. The biggest one was the January 13 issue — 16 inches by 26. Each was proved to be a playbill by the telltale words: "will be acted."[6] *Harlequin Jack Sheppard* ran from January 1 to February 8 (I failed to check it before January 1). The titles, of course, were larger. Now and then an actor was played up: P. G. Macready on March 6. There were no programs at all in this Drury Lane file.

Then the curator himself, George W. Nash, came in, and he promptly flooded me with excellent comments on more pertinent material. The change to program in the regular theater, he said, was gradual, with Charles Fechter leading the way with small programs at the Lyceum Theater in 1861-3. Playbills actually appeared as late as 1880. The first actual programs appeared at concerts in the 1840's (this corroborated Mr. Mander's idea).

The only concert programs he showed me were for May 31, 1856, and August 3, 1857, for His Majesty's Theater, "The Opera Box." They varied a bit in size — 6 by 9½ and 5½ by 9, respectively, but were both penny leaflets of four pages, sold outside the theater. Pages 2 and 3 were devoted to critical comments on the opera, and p. 4 gave advertising notice of forthcoming productions: all very modern. These operatic programs preceded and led to Fechter's regular theater programs, printed by Rimmel. The word "program" was not used in these concert programs.

The first definite regular theater programs apparently appeared in the Royal Lyceum Theater in 1863. Here it is possible to see playbill and program side by side for the same production of a regular play. On January 10, 1863, appeared *The Duke's Motto*, "under the sole management of Mr. Fechter." "This programme is supplied and perfumed by Eugene Rimmel."[7] On p. 2 is the cast: on p. 3 the acts and scenes, and on p. 4 Rimmel's ad, especially "Rimmel's Choice Perfumes." It is a 4½-by-7-inch leaflet. The same thing appeared on May 12, 1863.

The long 16 by 20 playbill for the latter production is here in the Victoria and Albert file and announces: "Monday, May 11, 1863, during the week." So *one* playbill served for a whole week. And the same combination of program and playbill keeps on occurring throughout this year. The word "programme" is now definitely used. On March 26, 1863, *The Duke's Motto* was still going strong — with both playbill and "programme" — and still "Mr. Fechter." But the program for February 24, 1863, was smaller: 3 by 5 inches.

I found nothing in the Lyceum files for 1861-2 that resembled this combination of playbills and programs in the 1863 file, though Mr. Nash seemed to think that such combinations existed for those years. Maybe the answer is that his file simply didn't include them, for both 1861 and 1862 are very small files, covering only a few performances each year. Obviously they were both very incomplete.

So now we have come, I hope, to a fairly definite answer to our problem, with definite evidence, 1863, at the Lyceum Theater. Both Drury Lane and Covent Garden produced their first playbills in 1737,[8] but the Garrick Club, Mr. Nash says, has a playbill of 1718. The most interesting playbill is the fake one of 1663, supposed for a long time to be the earliest of all (with a cast), but proved definitely spurious by W. J. Lawrence in *The Bookman*, October, 1920.[9] Thanks to Mr. Nash I saw and read Lawrence's letters to Mrs. Enthoven in the Victoria and Albert Museum about this playbill, and the article merely sums up his arguments written to her. The forger was John Payne Collier. Mr. Nash gave me a photostat of it.

The next step is to see whether the introduction of programs changed the technique of the dramatists in the matter of labelling for exposition. Actually Mr. Lawrence should have faced this problem in his chapter on the origin of the theater program, cited in note 1, with his playbill-program idea (1711 ff.).

I should here merely like to repeat my thanks to all the English who so graciously helped me in carrying out this quest.

NOTES

1. The basic historical study of playbills and programs appears in W. J. Lawrence's Chapter III, "The Origin of the Theatre Programme," of his *The Elizabethan Playhouse and Other Studies*, Second Series (Stratford-upon-Avon: the Shakespeare Head Press, 1913), pp. 55-91.

   Here Mr. Lawrence starts back in 1483 with the first oral announcements of *coming* theater productions and runs on down to 1711, when both newspaper ads and the *Spectator*, No. 141 (August 11, 1711) printed the full cast and thus "the theatre programme sprang into existence" (p. 85). No cast had been printed *before* 1700 (see his demolition of the forged playbill of *The Humorous Lieutenant* [April 8, 1663] on his pp. 74-77). He adds that from 1699 on "the name of the author of the play was to be regularly announced" (p. 82, but see note 8 below).

   The only trouble with all this is that such "programmes" were still strictly playbills, with the date of the actual performance due a few days later (i.e., August 11, for a play "to be performed on a future day" [p. 86], in this case August 14). How many of the audience had with them the "Bill of the Play" (a nineteenth century term used by both Mr. Lawrence and Miss Phyllis Hartnoll for the same day's entertainment)? How many of the audience bought such bills anyway? And why doesn't Mr. Lawrence apply this program idea to that play of the day to show how the author's labelling of characters was no longer necessary? Actually, in my judgment such labelling did not stop till nearly the end of the eighteenth century, at the earliest, in Kelly, Goldsmith, and Sheridan; and even then there is still some in *The Clandestine Marriage* (1766), *The West Indian* (1771), and *The Dramatist* (1789), to say nothing of *The Rivals* itself in 1775. That's why I set out on this quest. Besides, the above newspapers and the *Spectator* announcements implied taking into the theater the whole piece: not till 1737 did Drury Lane or Covent Garden provide separate playbills, with the full cast printed thereon (see my remarks below). And always the telltale mark of the playbill is the future tense: "will be presented." What Mr. Lawrence has chosen as a program was used essentially as a playbill.

"Once the programme [i.e., as playbill] was reached, very little alteration or extension of its character took place for over a century" (p. 87). The printer, he continues, had the "programmes" sold to pay for the rest of the posters (p. 89). The manager was then outside the venture, and perhaps the dramatist was too, as his constant use of labelling in the theater implies. Mr. Lawrence never faced this point. Finally he admits directly, in his last paragraph (p. 91): "In the London theatres of forty years ago [i.e., the 1870's], two kinds of programmes were simultaneously provided. In the cheaper parts of the house a replica of the ordinary folio daybill was on sale, thin in texture, and pungent to the nostrils with its heavy burden of undried printer's ink. This was the last relic of the old 'bill of the day.' No one could apply the term to the delicately perfumed programme of octavo size supplied at the same time to the occupants of the boxes." The appearance of the second — really first *modern* program — is the concern of this paper. For only with this really modern program, *supplied on the day of production,* could the dramatist afford to dispense completely with his labelling of characters in his play. When, then, did this program appear?

2. See "Playbill, Programme," *The Oxford Companion to the Theatre* (Oxford University Press, 1951), pp. 619-20.

3. This note will necessarily anticipate some of my exposition below.

Miss Hartnoll refers directly to the Enthoven Collection in the Victoria and Albert Museum as "the largest collection of London playbills and programmes in the world" (p. 619). She declares that by the end of the eighteenth century the playbill was serving as a program as well as "a theatre poster," and adds that "about 1850 the Olympic Theater, London, began to issue small playbills on a quarto sheet about 12 by 9 inches as well as the larger bills. These smaller bills were printed on one side and folded in the middle and were probably supplied to the occupants of the more expensive seats without charge. Drury Lane soon followed, and the other theatres came slowly into line." She never mentions the curator of the Enthoven Collection, George W. Nash, and though she knows the Rimmel perfumed programs "in the eighteen-sixties," she never mentions the manager, Charles Fechter, of the Lyceum Theater, who, according to Mr. Nash, introduced these programs. She never refers to the small concert programs that preceded all these in the 1840's, and what she calls a program is still a playbill in a transitional stage. ". . . folded in the middle" — How? Vertically, or horizontally? All the Drury Lane playbills of 1840, ten years before her "about 1850" were folded vertically, face up (except the big ones — cf. January 13, 16 by 26 inches, folded horizontally), apparently so they could also be used as programs, much as New York subway riders fold newspapers lengthwise to read them. She finally gets around to "a kind of magazine programme at the St. James's Theater [in 1869] called *Bill of the Play*," but all in all her account seems to lack something in definiteness and conclusiveness.

4. *The Tempest*, Shakespeare's play performed by royal command and directed by Charles Kean. Another type, apparently, of early program.

5. The date was March, 1948. Mr. Mander has very kindly sent me a reprint of his brief, three-page article on "The Story of the Theatre Programme." He starts with Lamb's essay in 1822 on "Some Old Actors" and then goes back to 1563. His next date is 1685, which he has written into the copy sent me, for that uses 1692 as the next date (his handwritten footnote mentions the discovery in the Public Record Office which wiped out his original date, 1692). He refers to a diary of 1712 but adds, "It was not, as we have said, till later that the casts were given on the bills" (p. 5). (Compare this with Lawrence's ideas in my note 1.) Then he goes to Chetwood in 1749, telling of the actors' quarrels over the size of the letters printing their names. He points out that the playbills of the eighteenth century "changed little in themselves" (p. 6), but that the nineteenth century bills were much larger. He notes two types of programs (without date — but he has handwritten into the margin, "late 1860's"), with the special boxes-program perfumed by Rimmel ("1870's" he has again written in the margin). So he concludes, ". . . the programme remains much as it was when introduced some eighty years ago" (p. 6). (Compare this again with Lawrence's remarks in my note 1.) Finally he refers rather indefinitely to the Victoria and Albert Museum as "a London Museum" and mentions his own large collection (it was put on exhibition in Birmingham in 1949 — apparently a very large one), "so that students in the future will have a source of reference . . ." (p. 6). Actually, I should add, his partner, Mr. Joe Mitchener, collaborated with him on this article.

6. Cf. the Shakespeare Museum playbill noted above.

7. Here the dramatic critic could actually and honestly say, "The evening's program 'smelled'."

8. It struck me as peculiar that the 1737 Covent Garden playbill should announce two plays, *The Funeral* and *The Cheats of Scapin*, without naming the author of either play anywhere. Cf. note 1 above.

9. The same arguments appear in his chapter, in *The Elizabethan Playhouse and Other Studies*, pp. 74-77.

9. City Life in American Drama, 1825-1860

GLENN H. BLAYNEY

Boston, Charleston, New York, Philadelphia — the great American cities of the nineteenth century illustrated so vividly the aspects of urban life that they attracted the interest of American writers. Plays about city life seemed a reply to the call for an American drama about native themes, such as James Kirke Paulding made in the introduction to *American Comedies* (1847): "Like every other people, we require a drama of our own, based on our own manners, habits, character and political institutions; and such a drama, it seems to us, if sustained with sufficient spirit by American writers, would take root and flourish in the United States" (pp. iii-iv). As early as 1787, the author of the prologue of the first social comedy about life in a city, *The Contrast*, realized that the type of play thus introduced was valuable for its use of native American material: "Exult each patriot heart!" the writer appeals and assures that the play to be shown "we may fairly call our own," for

Our Author pictures not from foreign climes
The fashions, or the follies of the times;
But has confin'd the subject of his work
To the gay scenes — the circles of New-York.[1]

Significantly, we then learn that the play is on "native themes" and that the faults and the virtues, too, are American.

In his selection of novels for consideration in *The City in the American Novel, 1789-1900* (1934) George Dunlap states: "Novels may be rejected for consideration because of deficiency in literary merit, that is, because of pronounced weakness in character portrayal, or in style, or because they indulge in cheap sensationalism" (p. 9). If we limit thus the selection of plays before 1860 to be used in a study of city life on the stage, many plays of small intrinsic literary merit would be excluded. And with the exception of the well-known landmarks of this period of American drama, *The Contrast* (produced 1787) and Anna C. O. Mowatt's *Fashion; or, Life in New York* (produced 1845), and a few other plays with interest not entirely dependent on the motive of city life, such as J. Murdock's *The Triumphs of Love; or Happy Reconciliation* (1795), R. M. Bird's *The City Looking-Glass* (MS, dated 1828), W. I. Paulding's *The Noble Exile* (1847), J. Brougham's *Temptation; or, The Irish Immigrant* (1856), E. G. P. Wilkins's *My Wife's Mirror* (1856) and *Young New York* (produced 1856), and D. Boucicault's *The Poor of New York* (1857),[2] such plays are artificial in action, weak in plot development, and full of ineffective caricatures. The dramatists found many stock incidents, themes, and characters typical of American city life, jumbled them, and combined as many as possible into a one-, two-, three-, or five-act play.

Why, then, consider such a large group of plays of doubtful literary merit? There are perhaps three reasons: to see what aspects of American city life before the Civil War were subjects of dramatic interest; to show the mid-twentieth century reader of these plays that the institutions of city life were exceptionally interesting to nineteenth century writers; and to add to our knowledge of the taste of the audiences of this period.

These plays about city life, most popular during the period 1825-1860, have even greater interest, if they are related to their predecessors and sources. When Royall Tyler wrote *The Contrast*, the first important American play with a city setting (New York), he established patterns for dramas with such a setting. These patterns were repeated many times in later plays — plays which up to 1860, however, never surpassed this first play of the type. Eight years after *The Contrast*, in 1795, Philadelphia became the setting for a clever comedy that showed many of that city's customs and manners. In *The Triumphs of Love* by J. Murdock, George Friendly, Jr. becomes the epitome of a fashionable urban life, the male counterpart of the interesting Charlotte of Tyler's play. *The Triumphs of Love,* like the other later plays about city life, is less unified than *The Contrast,* because Murdock introduces other aspects of life: the Quaker religion and its attitudes toward marriage, the slave question, the fates of the Irish immigrant and of the French traveler in a large city, the attacks on governmental revenue officers in the West. Yet again the play is valuable for this study because it illustrates on the stage certain aspects of city life repeated in many dramas after 1825.

These two plays are better as literary products than later plays with this theme: the dialogue is more clever and natural; and the characters, although they show many of the traits of human nature influenced by city environment, have some qualities which bring an audience's interest and sympathy.

The Man of the Times; or, A Scarcity of Cash, a farce written by John Beete and performed in Charleston in 1797, is set in Philadelphia and introduces a villainous city speculator, fraud, and oppressor of the poor: a character of the same general type is found in later dramas of urban life. The plot of this farce is slight and the character development is not strong enough to offset a weak plot structure. For its introduction of Screwpenny, the unscrupulous business man, however, the play deserves notice among the predecessors of city plays of the 1825-1860 period. In J. N. Barker's *Tears and Smiles* (produced in 1807), set in and near Philadelphia, the city atmosphere is distinctive. Several character types, such as Fluttermore, the traveled young fop, modeled on Tyler's Dimple, and Nathan Yank, a Yankee character brought to the metropolis, perhaps based on Tyler's Jonathan, appear, as do such activities as duelling and popular city amusements. The setting of the next early play of city life, *Love and Friendship; or, Yankee Notions,* by A. B. Lindsley, produced in 1807-1808, is Charleston, South Carolina; yet most of the characters have been brought there from northern cities — Philadelphia, Boston, New York, and Newport and in their behavior still retain the influence of their northern urban heritage. And the author seems not to intend contrasts between northern and southern urban manners or between the characters from the different northern cities. *Love and Friendship* ranks as an important contribution in the development of plays of city life, not because it has any special literary merit, but because many of its plot situations, themes, and characters foreshadow those in later plays. Lindsley joins in his play the motives of the ruin of a man of business by a scoundrel in business, the enforcement of the marriage of a daughter to a dissipated coxcomb with a huge, ill-gotten fortune, the addiction of fashionable society to foreign customs, and the struggle of the newly rich class for money. The title of *Wall Street; or, Ten Minutes Before Three* (1819), a farce written perhaps by a playwright named Mead, suggests its New York background. "Money" is a prominent motive in this play of city speculators, bankers, brokers, merchants, bankrupts, borrowers, store-owners, and fashionable wives and daughters. Even in an exaggerated and ridiculous way, a sense of the fast, confused, and not-too-scrupulous business life of the large American city is still present.[3] These plays show the interest of the American drama before 1825 in the theme of urban life.

These early American plays about city life did not include the motive of city low life. (This kind of motive dates back in English literature, of course, to the Elizabethan coney-catching pamphlets and the novels and descriptive tracts of Deloney and Dekker.) The year 1821, however, marked a change, with publication of the English novel *Life in London; or, The day and night scenes of Jerry Hawthorn, esq. and his elegant friend Corinthian Tom, accompanied by Bob Logic, the Oxonian, in their rambles and sprees through the metropolis,* by Pierce Egan. Tom, the most elegant, fashionable young fellow the town afforded, and Jerry, his rustic friend, in the pursuit of "seeing life in London," venture from the highest society at Vauxhall, Rotten Row, and Almack's, to the haunts of the lowest dregs of humanity in All-Max and the Beggars' back slums. In the 1869 edition,

J. C. Hotten claims that the book is our best picture of "Life, Fashion, and Frolic" or society in the reign of George IV.[4] A. Nicoll, in *A History of Early Nineteenth Century Drama 1800-1850* (1930), writes: ". . . a tale of eccentric humours, such as Egan's *Life in London,* could provide dramatic material for years" and notes ten plays (by no means an exhaustive number) based on this story in the British theater between 1821 and 1843 (vol. 1, pp. 96-97). The adaptation by W. T. Moncrieff was perhaps the most successful production; according to him, it "obtained a popularity, and excited a sensation, totally unprecedented in Theatrical History."[5]

With such an overwhelming popularity of both novel and plays in London, it is not strange that the American drama felt the influence of these descriptions of city life. Egan's book was read in the United States, and Moncrieff's play was produced in New York, Philadelphia, and elsewhere. It is from these English originals, then, that dramas of low life in American cities seem to derive, beginning with R. M. Bird's *The City Looking-Glass* (MS, dated 1828), the first extant American play to deal extensively with such life, and including the tremendous number of "fireman" comedies, climaxed by B. A. Baker's *A Glance at New York* (produced 1848). These plays of city low life, however, show changes and adaptations which give them a distinctively American flavor. The following dialogue from *Life in New York; or, Tom and Jerry on a Visit* (1856), John Brougham's American sequel to the English play and novel, seems to show a contrast between Tom's and Jerry's escapades in dens of vice in London and their activities in New York (although perhaps it is also a comment on the improvements in large cities between 1821 and 1856). We note the contrast between the frolicsome Tom and Logic of All-Max, the beggar's Holy Land, and the Green Room of Drury Lane, as conceived by Egan and Moncrieff for an English public, and the Tom and Logic presented by Brougham perhaps to satisfy a more puritanical American audience:

> *Tom.* Now, Bob, my boy, where shall we go to next? We've been to the High Bridge, peered through the City Hall, shook hands with his honor the Mayor, fraternized with Captain Rhynders, got nearly sun-stricken at a target excursion, lightened our pockets at faro, salooned at Niblo's, warmed ourselves at the summer garden, and cooled off at the Bowery. What have you to propose?
>
> *Logic.* Egad! there's very little else left — thanks to the increasing intelligence and self-growing respect of the people — the many dens of iniquity with which the city was at one time overrun, and which the unthinking kept alive by their injudicious visits, are to be seen no more: or, if they are visible, it is only to the doomed and degraded class by which they are sustained.
>
> *Tom.* I would not look upon such scenes even if I could, [*sic*] to me there is no amusement in degrading vice; there are plenty of stores from whence to draw wholesome and enjoyable fun without ransacking such filthy receptacles (p. 19).

It is also significant that, although both Egan and Moncrieff combine themes of low life and social satire, and Brougham merely follows their lead,[6] *Life in New York* emphasizes more the traits by these writers judged to be the follies of the newly rich "aristocracy" of the American city.

As the plays of the period 1825-1860 are discussed, the influence of these earlier American and English literary pieces will be clearer and increasingly significant.

In the plays of urban life from 1825 to 1860, playwrights in several ways emphasized the city setting as a leading force in dramatic development. They used typical stage sets from urban life; fashions, institutions, and other social forces in the city, not necessarily relating closely to the primary themes or situations, but merely establishing the urban mood; conventions of situation and theme significant of city life; and character types showing the influence of metropolitan environment. Necessarily, these methods overlap, but we will try to follow each and show the constant recurrence of these various settings, social patterns, situations, themes, and characters in the plays of city life from 1825 to 1860, the years of their greatest popularity.

Naturally, the most frequently occurring setting is the city street. In order to give realism to their urban environment, many playwrights have clearly described a street with the buildings or background people that mark at once the setting of a drama in the center of a large city.

The settings in *Wall Street* are given with a realism exceptional in so early a drama: Act I, scene i, shows part of Wall Street with a view of William Street and the Post Office with letter carriers delivering letters, etc.; scene iii is set in Pearl Street in the neighborhood of Wall Street, with auctioneers selling goods and newsmongers peddling papers in front of the Butler's Office; and Act II, scene i, is set in a city bank, where a great crowd is drawing checks, making deposits, and taking up notes. Similarly, the front of the Chestnut Street United States Bank in Philadelphia is the setting of the first scene in R. M. Bird's *News of the Night; or, A Trip to Niagara*. A city street setting in W. I. Paulding's *Antipathies; or, The Enthusiasts by the Ears* (1847) is closely related to the theme of his play: improvement versus conservatism. Jacob Changeless, returning to New York after forty years, with his mind already set against modern improvements of any kind, firmly asserts his dislikes, as from beneath the ground (unwittingly, on a dark, cloudy night, he has fallen into a hole in the city street where pipes are to be laid) he speaks his first lines in the play: "Heaven help me out of this cursed city! What infernal hole have I fallen into now? — The devil take the corporation — the devil take everybody — Watch! Watch! Watch! — No use calling watch! . . . And these are what you call your modern improvements, are they?"[7] In this way Paulding achieves a comic opening and states his urban theme. Similarly, Boston streets become the setting of three scenes of S. D. Johnson's *The Fireman* (produced, 1849): For Act I, scene ii, "Dock Square, Faneuil Hall. Lively Music" furnish the background. In Act I, scene iv, an alarm of fire is heard, several persons rapidly cross the stage (perhaps a fireman dragging a hose, a stock feature evidently greatly admired by the audience), and a bell rings as the action opens. A later scene occurs on the Mill Dam Bridge. Realism is the aim also in Brougham's street setting in *Life in New York:* "Tryon Row and part of Centre st. — Set market cart, apple stand, soda water, pop corn, weighing machine . . . every body in motion" (p. 20). For Tom and Jerry's arrival in New York, the playwright gives this setting: "Canal-street Wharf. — Crowd of Cabmen, Newsboys, &c., discovered. . . . Travellers pass across. — One lady drops her boa in the muss. — Newsboys cry, 'Herald — Extra Express, second edition'" (p. 4). In the last scene of the play, the audience sees the New York park, with an illuminated City Hall in the background; fireworks are displayed on the stage; and the curtain falls to the tune of "Hail Columbia." Certainly, Brougham thus encouraged realism in the theater of his day, if his lively stage directions were carried out by producers. Finally, we may notice a street scene in Boucicault's *The Poor of New York* (1857), which foreshadows such a modern experimental play as *One-Third of a Nation:* A tenement house burns down and partially crumbles on the stage in both plays. In Boucicault's drama the interior of this tenement house is shown; the playwright uses a vertically divided stage, thus showing simultaneously two rooms of the building.

Besides street scenes, which are by far the most prominent sign of city life in stage sets, tavern interiors are used in *The Triumphs of Love* (1795) by J. Murdock, *Calmstorm, the Reformer* (1853) by Cornelius Mathews, and *The Lottery of Life* (1867) by J. Brougham. In *The Lottery of Life* the tavern scene ends in a general row among the characters of low life: people stand on the tables, the bar-keeper jumps over the bar, and two girls faint in his arms. Interiors of stores were used in *Wall Street* and *Self* (1856) by Mrs. Sidney F. Bateman; fashionable gambling-houses in *The Road to Fortune* (1846) by Eugene Raux and *Wheat and Chaff* (1858) by D. W. Wainwright; New York wharves in *Life in New York, Ireland and America* (produced, 1852) by James Pilgrim and *The Lottery of Life;*[8] a dirty cook shop (with "dirty tablecloths" and newsboys) in *The Noble Exile* (1847) by W. I. Paulding; a sailor's dance hall in *The Silver Spoon* (produced, 1852) by J. S. Jones; a crowded retiring room of an opera-house in *The Musard Ball; or, Love at the Academy* by J. Brougham; and elaborately furnished rooms in which fashionable balls are being held in many of the comedies.

Thus, by the use of elaborate stage settings which must often have called for exceptionally ingenious stage designers or production managers, and which gave some realism to the plays, playwrights tried to recreate on the stage some of the physical environment of city life.

Plays of city life from 1825 to 1860 often described or represented phases of that life not always integral to plot or action but helpful to the spectators' or readers' impression of the reality of the life presented. Occasionally, besides adding to the realism of the play, these phases were used in advancing the social ideals of the dramatists.

One of the most interesting city institutions often described is the theater. Probably the best, and certainly the most delightful, example is Jonathan's account of his theater experiences in *The Contrast*, when he stumbled unknowingly into the playhouse and saw *The School for Scandal* and *The Poor Soldier*, an afterpiece. In *The Contrast*, also, actors are described in Dimple's remarks about the "miserable mummers, whom you call actors," who "murder comedy, and make a farce of tragedy" and at whose performance he sat with his back to the stage "admiring a much better actress than any there; — a lady who played the fine woman to perfection."[9] A humorous insight into the attitudes of audiences appears in Nathan Nobody's remarks in Bird's *The City Looking-Glass*, as he tells his employer Roslin what he wants for wages:

> *Nath.* A new suit when my old one decays, which may
> be monthly; pocket money when I want it, which must be daily;
> and a theatre ticket when I like it, which shall be nightly.
>   *Ros.* A theatre ticket! What would you do at the theatre?
>   *Nath.* Learn wisdom. Sir, I have learned much at the
> theatre; I have learned several speeches, which I can put you
> to sleep with; several songs, which I can keep you awake with;
> and above all, I have learned how a wise fellow can climb on
> the shoulders of fools.[10]

And in C. J. Cannon's *Better Late Than Never* (1857), a play
in blank verse and with no recorded performance, Windfall, the
main character, an actor, in telling of his being cast out by the
man to whom his father entrusted him as a child, shows the
attitude toward players[11] at the time: "I have found friends /
Where one would hardly think to look for them." And we learn
that as a starveling the boy was rescued and healed by a man
himself despised by society: ". . . shunned / By Priest and Levite,
a Samaritan — / Despised of both" and "That man was a poor
player."[12]

Attitudes toward the literary activities which the city fostered
are frequently expressed in the drama. In *Madmen All; or, The
Cure of Love* (1847) by W. I. Paulding, Garafelia Fizgig is
satirized as an ardent and extreme admirer of the new school of
romantic fiction. She quizzes Phil, a visitor to Philadelphia from
New York, "that literary emporium of cheap publications," about
the new novels just published in his native city. When she dis-
dains his mention of a new book by Cooper, he satirically invents
titles for two great new romantic masterpieces: "Azrael, or the
Deadly Huguenot Captain — a Romance of the times of d'Au-
bigné" and "The Bloody War-path of the Laughing Hyena — a
Tale of the Border Wars." Her ecstasies about these books bring
forth these remarks by Sam, one of her suitors: "Such works are
dispersed, like the seeds of disease, everywhere — they are like
their parent folly, ubiquitous. Published for a trifle, they find
purchasers in every village. Men who could write better, if

they met with encouragement, are forced to descend to such books as these, because they cannot obtain fair compensation for works that demand longer study and greater labour. The want of an international copyright law enables the publisher to grind the American author to the earth, and plunder the foreign author of the fruit of his toil."[13] Sam humorously satirizes his rival for Garafelia's love (or wealth), Pontefract Pinchbeck, a novelist of the new school: "He is never at home except under the shadow of a guillotine — his pulse never beats with any sort of alacrity, except when there is a current of blood flowing knee deep around him — and I verily believe that if all his works were subjected to a strong pressure, they would yield a hogshead of poisonous liquids!"[14] The slight plot of *Madmen All* ends as Sam realizes Garafelia's true nature (her tastes in fiction showing her shallowness) and leaves her to the "gorey" Pinchbeck.

In *Young New York* (produced, 1856), E. G. P. Wilkins similarly derides the cheap serial of the day. Adolphus Ten-percent comically relates the sensational events of a story he is composing for *Smasher* magazine. A few words of scorn are also aimed at the "namby-pamby female literature of the day," which, according to Rose Ten-per-cent, usually consists of "silly platitudes, abolition harangues, or disgusting personalities" (p. 29). And the writer himself is satirized, as we see when we recall the poet, T. Tennyson Twinkle, as a "fixture" of Mrs. Tiffany's New York drawing room in Mrs. Mowatt's *Fashion*. Other satirical references to the contemporary literature of the city may be found in J. N. Barker's *Tears and Smiles*[15] (produced, 1807) and J. Brougham's *Lottery of Life*. Sensational literature, fashionable in the city in the mid-nineteenth century, became the target of such dramatic satire.

Other amusements — gambling, drinking, and idleness on the streets — are also criticized in dramatic accounts of urban society. Even *The Contrast* stresses the loss by gambling of seventeen thousand pounds as one of Dimple's follies. And villainous characters, like the impostor Count Stromboli of Paulding's *The*

Noble Exile, Captain Dancer, the dishonest suitor of Pilgrim's *Ireland and America,* and Charles Sanford, who with his mother robs Mary of fifteen thousand dollars in Mrs. Bateman's *Self,* are shown as wretched gamblers. Yet perhaps the most sustained attack against city gambling in the drama of this period appears in *The Road to Fortune* (1846) by Eugene Raux. In this play Charles Legrand, led to believe that he is disappointed in love, rashly enters a sumptuous gambling house. But Legrand is still critical of his behavior and bitterly censures such conduct: "The world is right when it passes sentence upon a gambler . . . a deep-dyed knave, a black villain, a man without honor and principle, abandoned to all feelings of humanity, foreign to justice and integrity, a consummate scoundrel — aye, on the road to infamy and the gallows! . . . But here I am, a fool in the damning abyss, with a career of crime and infamy opened before me leading to ruin; aye to ruin, unpitied, a branded villain, a curse to society." Unsatisfied with this invective the author again moralizes in a speech by John Flitch, who sentimentally charges: "a gambler will not scruple to rob the last dollar of a victim, knowing that on it a wife and children depend for bread" (pp. 32-33). The literary merit of *The Road to Fortune* suffers greatly from such sermonizing.

Notable for scenes of drunken rowdiness in a large city are *Life in New York; The Triumphs of Love,* with a street brawl caused by intoxication; *The City Looking-Glass,* with the villain Ravin's drunken attack on Emily; and *The Musard Ball,* with the almost traditional drunken figure wrapped around a lamp post.

A fashionable amusement of young men in the city — promenading and observing the ladies — is also criticized. Such activity is suggested by Charlotte in *The Contrast* when she recounts the comments of the gentlemen when she flirted her "hoop to discover a jet black shoe and brilliant buckle."[16] In *The Musard Ball,* Polar calls Orlando Furioso Brown "one of those self-stultified Broadway loungers, who imagine that every good-looking woman that they meet is captivated by their passing

glance" (p. 5). In W. I. Paulding's three plays of Boston, New
York, and Philadelphia, his most likeable characters find fashionable strolling an amusing pastime. Phil of *Madmen All,* for example, declares, "I'll compound the matter, I believe, as I cannot
leave the house, by betaking myself to the front-door steps, and
staring the ladies out of countenance, as is the fashion of well-
bred strangers visiting New York."[17] In Wilkins's *Young New
York,* Washington Ten-per-cent enjoys similar recreation and
gives his account of the young ladies' attitude: "I'll take a walk
down Broadway, and look at the young women. Great fun, that
— they like it" (p. 22).

These motives from the fashionable urban life of the period
are not always significant in development of dramatic action,
yet they give these plays the detail the repetition of which is
characteristic of life.

Still another aspect of city life perhaps realistically portrayed
in these plays from 1825 to 1860 is the gangster life. Petty
criminals, pickpockets, molesters, harlots, and criminal gangs appear in *The City Looking-Glass,* G. H. Boker's *The Bankrupt*
(produced, 1855), *The Musard Ball, The Silver Spoon,* and S.
D. Johnson's *The Fireman* (produced, 1849). Outstanding in
this group are a notorious, ex-prison pickpocket, the brother of
the actual villain (*The City Looking-Glass*) and James Shorn,
head of an underworld gang (*The Bankrupt*). It is interesting
also that in Brougham's *The Lottery of Life,* Mordie Solomons,
alias Allcraft, with his Duffy, Dodgers, and other petty thieves,
seems to be patterned on Fagin, with his Artful Dodger and Bill
Sikes in Dickens's *Oliver Twist.*

Naturally, the catastrophes of city life cannot be fully shown
on the stage and their appearance is limited to descriptions of
railroad accidents in *Young New York* and *Self,* to references to
fires in *The Fireman* and *The Bankrupt,* and to the actual burning of a tenement house on the stage in Boucicault's *The Poor
of New York* and of a ship in *The Lottery of Life.*

Often the fashionable city folly of settling quarrels, mainly

over entanglements in love, with duels is ridiculed. In eight of
the plays before 1860 (*Love and Friendship, Tears and Smiles,
Madmen All, News of the Night, Life in New York, My Wife's
Mirror, Fashions and Follies of Washington Life,* and *The Musard Ball*), duelling is scorned or made ludicrous either because
of the slight provocation at which the parties are induced to
fight or because of the stupidity of the fashionable attitude toward
duels. With very slight provocation a duel is arranged between
Sam and Hodgson, the itinerant Englishman, in *Madmen All.*
While the duel is being supported madly by Garafelia, Hodgson
flees to avoid fighting.[18] In *News of the Night,* Bird hints that
duelling was then becoming a less fashionable practice in society.
When Eddybrain challenges Doubtful to a meeting, Doubtful
indicates that "duelling was getting out of fashion, and he be
cursed if he'd do anything that wasn't fashionable."[19] In H. C.
Preuss's *Fashions and Follies of Washington Life* (1857), the
only city play before 1860 set in the capital, Colonel Cecille, a
member of Congress, is at length persuaded to duel with a fellow member, but, in his reluctance, he gives practical and moral
reasons against the practice.[20] In several other later plays from
1856-1858, although duelling is still satirized, it becomes mainly
a source of humor. Brougham's character Logic, in *Life in New
York,* admits that duelling is "quite fashionable, but unnecessary" (p. 18). In another play also printed and produced in
1856, *My Wife's Mirror* by Wilkins, a threatened duel results
out of a comical situation in which a dog, owned by Racket, gets
between the legs of Peaceable, who, by treading on the cur's
tail, sends him running under a passing lady's hoop skirt.[21] So,
although, especially in the plays of 1856-1858, duelling may have
been shown as a phase of city life more than social practice war-
ranted, it remained a target for ridicule and a source of humor
in American drama.

City institutions and city social problems related to them — in
the diverse areas of law, politics, religion, journalism, industrialization and oppression of the poor, immigration, and general liv-

ing conditions — were also treated in the plays before 1860; but the period is not so striking for the strongly humanitarian interest prominent in the later American drama. With the exception of immigration, the city problems listed are shown in a closet drama that in part anticipates the expressionistic symbolic drama of the recent and contemporary theater. *Calmstorm, the Reformer* (1853), advertised on its title-page as "A Dramatic Comment," a loosely organized play in blank verse by Cornelius Mathews, set in "a City in America," is noteworthy as an attack on social problems of urban life. The life of Calmstorm, striving for immediate, forceful reform of existing ills, is contrasted with that of Umena, his wife, working for a more gradual improvement through Christian influence. The reformer's life was apparently suggested by the life of Christ;[22] the author clearly attempts symbolically to interpret Christianity and reform, but the symbolism is confused.

The first evil of city life shown in this play, the building of poor tenement houses, appears in a scene between a smith, a mason, and a carpenter, in which the mason complains of a ten-hour working day and a half-hour lunch break, but more significantly adds: "We're still at work on that great darkling pile,/ With pigeon-slips for human habitation" (p. 6). And as the three city workers pass on, Calmstorm, until now listening in the background, comments, "I wish the city would / But stop its din," and questions, "O, why forever, / In chains or grief, or silent sadnesses / Shall men toil on." And he begins the climax of the speech, "New Land of Hope! these things become not thee" (p. 8). Begging children enter in lament over their cold, underground apartments and rags. Calmstorm, as spectator, observes: " 'Tis clear the fountain whence they draw their life / Is muddied. One begs because its father finds / No work" (p. 12). A prisoner, accused of debt, who has failed because a city speculator sold him worthless land, is dragged across the stage. And in an attack on Slinely, the journalist, who, with Darkledge, plots against Calmstorm, the city newspaper is satirized by Waning, a weak, but devoted friend of the reformer.[23] To Calmstorm, Waning describes the man:

> The darkest Spirit of the city, Calmstorm!
> Who keeps a secret book wherein is writ
> In loathsome detail, all the city's vice,
> Each man's peculiar bias from the right,
> Who darkly with his neighbor's wife has erred,
> And who has clutched, with fingers lawless,
> The vaulted gold. . . .

Also described are other victims of Slinely who "keeps the evil count of all our deeds, / Avenging God in gloomy merriment" (pp. 26-27). Politicians as well appear and disclose their dishonesties; as one character says, "a perfect honest man's / Too great a monster for these difficult / Times in which we live" (p. 34).

Symbolic of the forces of evil, Slinely and Darkledge plot against the forces of good, Calmstorm and Umena. Calmstorm dreams of a Utopian world without the crushing of humanity by the machine and the long working day; in his Utopia men would work only six hours a day and spend the remainder in sleep, thought, walks, and honest pleasures. But a hopeless pessimism prevails: Umena dies, and Calmstorm's dreams evaporate:

> Who, who this knot will disentangle
> Of life, and weal and woe in life, for men
> In the massed city, in the crowded way,
> In links and ranks innumerable.
> Who break this net of meshes numberless,
> Where to be free is to be bound: where speech
> That should give hope, enmeshes more the foot,
> Than silence that consents to bondage! (p. 64)

The reformer dies: Calmstorm's lines, "I am a man of glass, and all men spy / My swiftly-running sands" (p. 61) foreshadow the final scene of the play in which Slinely and Darkledge approach and gaze on after his death.

Although *Calmstorm, the Reformer* may have small literary merit, it is unique as a blank verse tragedy about contemporary problems, as perhaps the first American play with clear, humanitarian social interest, and as a forerunner of some of the more recent experimental, expressionistic techniques in the theater.

American city law forces are satirized in several other plays before 1860. In *Wall Street* the City Council of New York is said to have "met on Monday, and adjourned to Saturday, without making any appointments, except a few sham commissioners and coroners" (p. 16). Another interesting satire against city government appears in *My Wife's Mirror:* here the character Mrs. Racket reads aloud" The Legend of the Devil's Mirror," in which Beelzebub, having decided to travel, "set out upon the subterraneous railroad and naturally visited New York, where some of his family had high places in the city government. He directed his steps towards the Park to pay his respects to Satan, who lived in a large building with a marble facade called the City Hall" (p. 6). Wilkins seems to have taken particular delight in caustic criticism of city law and politics in New York. In *Young New York*, Nutgalls, the newspaper editor, ironically comments upon the Board of Aldermen: "They do nothing but sit in a cushioned chair at City Hall, and say, yea or nay, as the party demands, and use up a great deal of stationery! much to the distress of the Comptroller, who refuses to pay for a package of envelopes, and winks at a fifty thousand dollar contract. New York has been taxed to death. . . . the people are waking up to a sense of their stupidity, and are preparing to administer the government themselves, instead of placing it in the hands of two or three hundred drunken rowdies, who bully voters at primary elections, and pack nominating conventions" (p. 9). In *The Noble Exile*, when Count Stromboli walks into the streets of Boston and is promptly fined five dollars for contaminating the pure Boston air with tobacco smoke, he characterizes not only Boston, but also Philadelphia and New York: "In de Philadelphie, dey wash de street all day long, and I believe *vraiment* half de night beside. In de New York, de omnibus splash de mud all over your pantaloon. — Mais en Boston, dey do noting but fine — fine — fine!"[24]

The problem of the immigrant, prominent in the city life of this period, as well as the poverty caused by unemployment, is used by J. Brougham in *Temptation; or, The Irish Immigrant* (produced, 1849). O'Bryan, the title character, comes for shelter to the house of Tom and Polly, two working class figures; to O'Bryan's inquiry about where he might find work Tom replies, "Anywhere — everywhere!" and O'Bryan continues: "Faith, sir, that's exactly the place I've been looking for the last three weeks, and there was nobody at home. I hunted the work, sir, while I had the strength to crawl after it" (p. 7). The Irish immigrant is also the central figure of J. Pilgrim's *Ireland and America* (produced, 1852). Jimmy Finnegan is followed to this country by his mother, sister, and sweetheart, who, by the plan of the gambling, villainous Dancer, are victimized in a special "den of iniquity," where newcoming immigrants are robbed. Another aspect of immigration appears in *Life in New York*, as Tom remarks, "as well as the honest, industrious immigrant, a treasure to any country, the offscourings . . . of the globe are shamefully let loose upon these shores" (p. 6). Equally unfortunate was the attitude of people of wealth toward the foreign settlers, as expressed by Airy Froth in *Young New York* — "railroad accident . . . smashed up a lot of immigrants . . . no fuss will be made about them. Detained a lot of Fifth Avenue people, though — they'll make a fuss" (p. 8) — and by the newspaper editor in the same play — "Send a reporter up to Dead Eye Creek, to see about that railroad accident — tell him he needn't spread on it much, as there were only twenty emigrants killed, and these things are so frequent as to be common-place" (p. 25).[25] Clearly, plays of city life from 1825 to 1860 show the problems of and attitudes toward the great numbers of immigrants then swelling the urban population.

Beyond the criticism in *Calmstorm, the Reformer*, industrialization in large cities is only mentioned in *Life in New York* and

Fashions and Follies of Washington Life.[26] Closely related are the incidents used by dramatists to show the oppression of the poor in the city, clearly illustrated in the early *The Man of the Times* and in *Life in New York*. In *Man of the Times*, Screwpenny distresses the poor, cheats poor soldiers out of their pay, refuses to recompense his servants, and desires his workmen to labor for little pay. In *Life in New York,* Codfishe's refusal to pay Fanny, the sewing girl, for shirts she has made, is condemned. Scenes of distress among the poor are shown in *The Poor of New York*. Gideon Bloodgood swindles a family out of their inheritance and dispossesses them of home and goods. Unable to find work, they are finally forced as beggars into the streets, and only kept from suicide. *The Fireman* shows the poverty of Mrs. Hawthorne and her daughter Alice, who lack money to procure food and medicine for the dying mother: at the deathbed, Alice reveals her problem: "I have tried at every place for labor, but in vain; hundreds, like myself, are suffering for want of employment" (p. 6). Other living conditions in American cities of the period are shown: the conditions of city streets in Boston in *The Fireman,* and in New York in *Self, Antipathies,* and *Young New York;* and the accommodations in city boarding houses and hotels in *Self* and *Young New York.*

Sometimes in close relation to their treatment of these city problems and institutions, dramatists repeatedly used in various and often confused patterns some stock themes of American metropolitan life.

The people seen most often in these plays are the newly rich whose respectability is built on wealth and not on the qualities known by others as signs of a more established merit. The plays show "a class, whose chief claims to eminence are that they are rich enough to be ostentatious, and insolent enough to set their feet upon the poor man's neck."[27] This city society believes as the French maid in *Fashion:* "Ah! Monsieur Zeke, de money is all dat is *necessaire* in dis country to make one lady of fashion."[28]

Such materialism appears as early as 1797, in *The Man of the*

Times, in the character of Screwpenny, who says, "Honesty, forsooth? — Money, money alone is honesty, honor, and every virtue that exists. — What! do you think I rose myself from a scrivener's clerk, to command half the ready cash of Philadelphia, by honesty?"[29] Thus the tradition of showing a materialistic American society dates from early plays and continues in later dramas like *News of the Night, Fashion, Better Late Than Never, Young New York, The Noble Exile, The Bankrupt, Self,* E. S. Gould's *The Very Age!* (1850), and C. Mathews's *False Pretenses; or, Both Sides of Good Society* (produced, 1855). One of the best expressions of such acquisitiveness in these plays appears in Boker's *The Bankrupt,* as Giltwood, after he is ruined, forswears his former master: "What has hope to do with dollars and cents? Their motion is like that of an inflexible machine, crushing all before them. . . . never whisper hope in connection with 'the almighty dollar'!"[30] The characters in these social comedies struggle to gain or keep money that will give them social respectability or to pretend possession of the vital passport to society.

Early marriage for money, entered into by a fashionable wife or marriage for money imposed upon a daughter by grasping parents; villainy in order to gain money, generally the defrauding of another man or his family; bankruptcy of a business man, usually plagued by a fashionable and extravagant wife — all these themes arise from the struggle to gain material advantage.

The marriage for money theme appears early in Van Rough's attempt in *The Contrast* to force Maria to marry Dimple, and in Mrs. Peevish's admission in *The Triumphs of Love* that she married early in life "allured by the wealth of Mr. Peevish." The pattern set in *The Contrast* reappears in the attempts of Campdon to marry Louise to Fluttermore in *Tears and Smiles;* of Marcene to marry Augusta to Dashaway in *Love and Friendship;* of Mrs Tiffany to marry Seraphina to Count Jolimaitre in *Fashion;* of Mrs. Waddletongue to marry Lucretia to Captain Heathcoat in *The Fireman;* of Mrs. Legrand to marry Miranda, her niece, to

Count Vonspoker in *The Road to Fortune;* of the Ten-per-cents to marry Rose to Needham Crawl in *Young New York;* of Mrs. Apex to marry Mary, her stepdaughter, to Cypher Cynosure in *Self;* of Mrs. Bradley and Mrs. Mathews to marry Eleanor and Martha, their respective daughters, to Count Stromboli in *The Noble Exile.* And following the example of Mrs. Peevish in her marriage for money in *The Triumphs of Love* are Mrs. Apex in *Self;* Mrs. Tiffany in *Fashion;* Mrs. Legrand in *The Road to Fortune;* and Mrs. Sunnyside in C. M. Walcot's *A Good Fellow* (produced, 1854), who deserts Sunnyside when he fails, because she thought he was a "man of fortune."

Wealth gained at the disadvantage of other men first appears as a theme in *Love and Friendship.* Old Dashaway has fled from Boston to Charleston after he has ruined the elder Seldreer by failing and fraudulently leaving Seldreer, his endorser, to discharge his notes. And Tiffany of *Fashion* is revealed by Snobson as a forger of note endorsements. Also, by a false will, Granite, the wealthy and unscrupulous merchant in *The Irish Immigrant,* has cheated Henry Travers out of his father's fortune. Crawl, issuer of fraudulent shares and forger of notes, ruins Ten-percent in *Young New York.* Bloodgood, a New York banker, enriches himself with the one hundred thousand dollars of Fairweather after the Captain's sudden death in *The Poor of New York.* Sir Wilton Downe in *The Lottery of Life* has been deprived of his business by the crafty Allcraft and his villainous wife.

Another favorite theme is the struggle of the newly rich businessman against ruin. In this pattern his bankruptcy is usually hastened by a foolish, fashionable wife, who is planning a grand ball while her husband fights his creditors. As Millinette of *Fashion* expresses it, "Monsieur make de money, — Madame spend it." Appearing still earlier in a short scene in *Wall Street,* this motive, illustrated in the following scene from *Fashion,* thus began its long course through the American drama:

Tif. Your extravagance will ruin me, Mrs. Tiffany!

Mrs. Tif. And your stinginess will ruin me, Mr. Tiffany! It is totally and *toot a fate* impossible to convince you of the necessity of *keeping up appearances.* There is a certain display which every woman of fashion is forced to make!

Mrs. Tif. Mr. Tiffany, I desire that you will purchase Count d'Orsay's 'Science of Etiquette,' and learn how to conduct yourself — especially before you appear at the grand ball, which I shall give on Friday!

Tif. Confound your balls, Madam; they make *footballs* of my money, while you dance away all that I am worth! A pretty time to give a ball when you know that I am on the very brink of bankruptcy!

Mrs. Tif. So much the greater reason that nobody should suspect your circumstances, or you would lose your credit at once. Just at this crisis a ball is absolutely *necessary* to save your reputation! . . .

Mrs. Tif. . . . If the Count was not so deeply interested — so *abimé* with Seraphina, I am sure he would never honor us by his visits again!

Tif. So much the better — he shall never marry my daughter! — I am resolved on that. . . .

Mrs. Tif. Mr. Tiffany, he is a man of fashion —

Tif. Fashion makes fools, but cannot *feed* them. . . .[31]

Only slightly altered, this scene is repeated in at least seven plays before 1860 — *Wall Street, Better Late Than Never, Self, False Pretenses, Life in New York, The Noble Exile,* and *The Road to Fortune.*[32]

These examples show how the desire of a materialistic urban society to gain fortune, increase it, and keep it gave useful subject matter to American dramatists writing about city life before 1860.

The ostentatious display of wealth is also mirrored in the drama of city life: dramatists used this popular motive to emphasize the effort to gain social respectability. Ostentatious fashion in all phases of life — house furnishings, clothes, conservatories, the imitation of foreign customs, the awkward conventions of visiting and receiving guests, some amusements, the entertainment of foreign "lions" (usually impostors) — is shown in many dramas.

The foreign nobleman eventually revealed as an impostor was a favorite motive for the development of plot: as the meek Mr. Bradley of *The Noble Exile* declares, "Mere people of fashion are more easily deceived by such characters than any other class of mankind."[33] First seen (as many of these devices of city plays are) in *Fashion,* in which Count Jolimaitre deceives the Tiffanys until the French maid recognizes him as a low-bred Frenchman, foreign scoundrels of the same type appear as key figures in *The Noble Exile* and *False Pretenses.* In the latter play Mathews has given his plot an original turn by allowing the Frenchman, Monsieur Boquet, to gain his position of eminence through the ignorance of the Mille-dollars and their friends, not through his own rascally premeditation. In *The Fireman* Captain Heathcoat, alias Stubbes, supposedly a wealthy Englishman, preys upon the ambitious Mrs. Waddletongue. And *Life in New York* (made typically American in tone, despite its general dependence upon Egan and Moncrieff) introduces the two servants of Tom and Jerry, who disguise themselves as foreign nobles, and as "lions" enter the society of the Codfishe family. And in Gould's *The Very Age!,* Charles Rodney, prompted by his mother, a villainess desiring revenge on a youthful lover (Charles's father), pretends to be Count de Bressi, is accepted in New York society, and proceeds unknowingly to woo his own half-sister and daughter of the man at whom the revenge is aimed. Easily, the reader of the city-life plays before 1860, accustomed to having the foreigner disclosed as an impostor, is puzzled when, in plays like *The Road to Fortune, Better Late Than Never, The Triumphs of Love,* and *Young New York,* a true nobleman emerges in the city. In *Young New York,* Signor Skibberini, a noble-blooded Roman opera-singer, becomes the hero of the piece. This noble Italian, in a complete reversal of the usual pattern, is actually *scorned* by society and driven from the country when he marries Rose Ten-per-cent, although he returns to claim his bride at the happy conclusion of this unusual play, in literary merit one of the best. Examples of the folly resulting from this addiction to other fashions than the "lionizing" of foreigners so crowd these plays that it is impossible to notice their full use. (Of the thirty-six plays discussed here, only five do not in some way develop prominently the fashions of city life.)[34]

If we look briefly only at the characters of this group of city dramas from 1825 to 1860, we see that many plays use caricature. In fact, a fragment like *Scenes at the Fair* (1833) is made up of only a group of social caricatures of urban people. Some types appear frequently as popular representatives of the metropolitan environment. Among these types are the fashionable and traveled fop (related to another type, the playboy), the Yankee servant brought to the city, the Irish servant, the fashionable wife and her daughter, the foreign impostor, the older person resisting city change, the Englishman who travels to the United States to acquire material for a book, the criminal villain of low life, and the fireman. (Some of these types and others have already been noticed in conjunction with the themes and situations in drama.)

The rustic brought to the city obviously provided contrast, as in the advent of J. S. Batkins into city life and politics in *The Silver Spoon*. Batkins refuses to pay the cab fare upon his arrival, declaring he has been victimized (as does country cousin Tabitha in *The Very Age!*). As part of Batkins's initiation to the strange city life, he is taken to the Sailors' Dance Hall, where he is lured to dance and then almost robbed, and to "high society," where he is fed sardines, made drunk on whiskey, and introduced to many beautiful "socialites." (Such scenes again remind us of Tom and Jerry.) And in *Fashion*, Adam Trueman enters city life in time to rescue his granddaughter from infamy and his old friend from ruin.

The Yankee hero and title character of *Ebenezer Venture*, a one-act farce by Lawrence La Bree, performed in 1841, objects to the amount of money asked by the porter upon his arrival and later describes his activities in the city. The play illustrates the contrasts between city and country life then used in drama: Ebenezer explains, ". . . you see I had a curious sort of a notion, to see things as they dew them up in New York, and so you see I thought to take a look round fust." He then notices the difference between city and country woman's attire, and Emma's remark, "It is the difference between the city and country" (p. 5), makes the point clear.

Numerous other plays link in some way with rural life: in Mathews's *False Pretenses*, the Crockery family, after financial loss, recall their happier rural days; in *Antipathies*, Changeless, returning to the city after forty years, resents modern changes; and in *The Noble Exile*, Nathan Willett, a youth from a country estate, arrives in Boston to join his fashionable young friends.

Finally, although we see that the literary merit of many of these plays is not remarkable, an extremely well-rounded picture of urban life, especially in Boston, New York, and Philadelphia, appears from them as a whole. Although all groups of urban society appear in the plays, we find the newly rich and the less respectable social elements more often and more successfully presented than the more settled, established social groups. Among the persons of the plays, typed characters, usually with tag names, appear, identified in the dramatists' and readers' or spectators' minds as types of city dwellers. Because of their repeated use, special themes illustrating city life may be seen growing into dramatic conventions of the period.

Although these early dramatists usually neither created lasting characters nor constructed plays of lasting dramatic interest, they at least achieved some realism and at times interestingly satirized some phases of urban life. Not in the characters or plots but in the creation of an urban atmosphere, these American plays of city life from 1825 to 1860 made strides toward realism on the American stage.[35]

124

STUDIES IN HONOR OF JOHN WILCOX

NOTES

1. A. H. Quinn, ed., *Representative American Plays* (6th ed., New York, 1938), p. 48.

Unless otherwise stated, as here, in this paper quotations, in which bibliographical accuracy (*e.g.*, distinctions of type) is not attempted, are usually from first or other early editions of the plays in the Library of Congress or the Library of the University of Pennsylvania. The dates in parentheses following titles of plays show dates of publication (unless described otherwise) from title-pages or from the list by A. H. Quinn, "A List of American Plays 1665-1860," in *A History of the American Drama from the Beginning to the Civil War* (2nd ed., New York, 1943), pp. 425-497. The first references here to play-titles are given as they appear in Quinn, "A List of American Plays." References will be omitted to differences between the titles given by Quinn and those on title-pages of editions used for quotation: *e.g.*, Quinn's entry of full title for Brougham's *Temptation* gives "*Immigrant*," whereas the title-page of Samuel French's edition (remarking John Brougham's entry of the play in 1856) gives "*Emigrant*." Later references are normally short-titles.

This study has been prepared in part by aid of a research grant from the Committee on Productive Work of Oberlin College.

2. This play, because of reliance on a French original, is not entirely true as a picture of American city life, although some American features introduced in it must be noticed.

3. The ill-natured, almost cankered character of the playwright makes it fortunate that his name has remained uncertain. The second edition of the play is dedicated to Major M. M. Noah (who criticized the play in *The National Advocate*): "Your *liberal* criticism on *Wall-street* . . . has induced me to dedicate the *second edition* to you. . . . you have made a *Book*, and I have made, as you say, '*A Thing*.' You have denounced without criticism, and I will do the same. Your Book is replete with bulls and blunders, your style is turgid, your language frequently ungrammatical, and your ideas badly expressed. You have thrown the gauntlet, and I accept the challenge. You edit a newspaper, and can, therefore, publish your folly. — You are a Jew, and I am a Christian. — You are a Major and I am a private. . . . You may write what you please, but I tell you, that mere assertion, without assigning your reasons, or proof, is evidence of a fool" (quoted from text of 1819 "Third Edition," pp. 3-4). The comments about Noah's grammar are perhaps merited; John Quincy Adams wrote of him: "He is an incorrect, and very ignorant, but sprightly writer" (I. Goldberg, *Major Noah: American-Jewish Pioneer*, 1936, quoted on p. 148). The author of *Wall Street* does not, however, here or in the play itself (where in Act I, scene iii, he introduces more comment about Noah), defend it convincingly.

4. J. C. Hotten, ed., *Tom and Jerry* by Pierce Egan (1869), p. 1. Thackeray, in a long discussion of this book in "Roundabout Papers," *Cornhill Magazine*, VIII, (October, 1860), 509-510, remarks: "As for Thomas and Jeremiah (it is only my witty way of calling Tom and Jerry), I went to the British Museum the other day on purpose to get it; but somehow, if you will press the question so closely, on reperusal, Tom and Jerry is not so brilliant as I had supposed it to be. . . . the style of the writing . . . was not pleasing to me; I even thought it a little vulgar . . . and as a description of the sports and amusements of London in the ancient times, more curious than amusing."

5. W. T. Moncrieff, *Tom and Jerry; or, Life in London* (1826), p. v. Moncrieff's version ran for many nights and was discontinued only because of the fatigue of the actors. By summer in 1822, ten plays on this subject were being given in and near London. See Quinn, *A History of the American Drama from the Beginning to the Civil War*, p. 304.
6. Quinn remarks, "Kate and Sue [wives of Tom and Jerry] follow their husbands to New York and their advent gave Brougham an excuse for taking Tom and Jerry to a ball at the Codfish mansion, thus linking this type of play with the social satire." — *Ibid.*, p. 307. Such linking of low life with social satire is no innovation with Brougham, however; a pattern of social satire having much in common with the tone of satire in many later American dramas of fashionable city life is plainly seen in Egan's and Moncrieff's descriptions of characters in Rotten Row and Almack's.
7. J. K. Paulding, ed., *American Comedies*, p. 239.
8. In *The Lottery of Life* (1867), Act V, scene ii, the detailed setting seems typical of city life around the wharves: "Ferry and boat house, — ship to burn on set waters up stage. Brooklyn heights at back. Night dark — moon rises during scene. Ferry boat in — people seen going on board. . . . the ship is discovered, which should be of a large size made of block tin, with transparent port-holes. To show fore sails furled, and rigging prepared with turpentine to burn. . . . Dock loafers around, one of them is sneaking off with . . . portmanteau."
9. Quinn, *Representative American Plays*, p. 70.
10. Quinn, ed., *The City Looking-Glass* (1933), p. 18.
11. Here we recall also the attitude toward concert artists, among a class of New York society not so much interested in encouraging the arts as in making money, which is evident in *Young New York* (produced, 1856) by E. G. P. Wilkins. When Rose declares that she will give a grand lyric concert, Ten-per-cent rages: "Going to have a concert, is she? Well, I never will forgive her, now. What an eternal disgrace — my daughter singing before every low fellow that can raise a dollar" (p. 31).
12. C. J. Cannon, *Dramas* (1857), p. 229. Some dramatists mentioned the theater to advertise or defend their own plays. The author of *Wall Street* (see note 3) defends his play against the attacks of Major Noah, the newspaper editor and playwright:

> *2d Wit.* He [Major Noah] cuts up the *"Thing, called a Farce, under the title of Wall-street,"* this morning, in fine style.
>
> *1st Wit.* That he does, and deservedly — it is a poor performance, and yet, I understand, it is attributed to some capable "pens."
>
> *2d Wit.* Yes, it is a poor thing — and it is not. If it is to be read and criticised as a regular dramatic composition, with its *unities,* and *plots,* and *catastrophes,* and so on, it is insignificant; but as a collection of natural dialogues, and every day occurrences, told just as they take place, in simple natural language, it is excellent. It is a happy hit at the times, as *Isaac Bronson* says. — Mead (?), *Wall Street* (1819), p. 17.

Another striking example may be found in *The Musard Ball,* in which Brougham even commends Burton, the New York theater manager:

> *Jones.* Many a laugh we've had, inside these doors, Fanny. . . . We must come to-morrow night out of gratitude. What are they playing? The Musard

> Ball; that's the contemporaneous drama. Fan. Ha! ha! cute fellow, that Burton; never lets a chance pass bye. Hallo! why that's strange, Fanny, look there, the name of that scamp, whoever he is, whose letter I found addressed to you, Mr. Orlando Furioso Brown.
>
> *Fanny.* Its only a coincidence, Jones. Why! there's your name and mine; they haven't dared to put us in a play? (p. 10).

In *The Silver Spoon*, J. S. Jones advertises his own play by letting Batkins, the comic central figure, hold up a huge play bill near the end, as he says, "I hold in my hand something of interest to the rising gineration" (1911, p. 65).

13. Paulding, *American Comedies*, pp. 184-185.
14. *Ibid.*, p. 177.
15. P. H. Musser, ed., *James Nelson Barker* (1929), pp. 161, 168.
16. Quinn, *Representative American Plays*, p. 51.
17. Paulding, *American Comedies*, p. 213.
18. Paulding here expresses satirically not only his attitude toward duelling but also his conception of the English tourist's view of the United States. Hodgson says: "No, I will leave as soon as may be, this accursed Philadelphia, which they call the city of brotherly love, (habitation of demons rather,) and will go home forthwith, to the quiet, peaceable, civilized, well-governed, happy land of my birth, where no impolitic exuberance of food makes men unruly and fierce — where no laxity of government makes the people democratic and ferocious — where a happy starvation keeps down the spirit of the unwashed — to merry old England!" — *Ibid.*, p. 207.
19. R. M. Bird, 'The Cowled Lover & Other Plays,' in E. H. O'Neill, ed., *America's Lost Plays* (1941), XII, 182. The gradually changing attitude toward duelling appears in an article in the *Democratic Review*, XI (October, 1842), 423, in which we read that no one was obliged to accept a challenge: "The public opinion will not only fully justify and sustain a noble and conscientious refusal in such a case, but it has little else than contempt, as well as severe censure, for the opposite course." Quoted from G. A. Dunlap, *The City in the American Novel, 1789-1900* (1934), p. 49.
20. The view set forth in the *Democratic Review* perhaps agrees with Cecille's reasons against duelling: ". . . one of the cardinal principles of this boasted code of honor is the idea of equality — 'open field and fair fight,' as the phrase runs. Now, in this case there is no equality at all — Blane is known to be a practiced shot — *I* am no shot at all — if I survive the fight, I will be publicly ostracised — doomed to my political grave — while he will but receive fresh laurels from his constituents. Again: Blane is encumbered with no immediate family ties — while I am almost on the eve of my union with one whose whole happiness, I solemnly believe, is centered in myself. One word more: This man has perpetrated a gross wrong upon me — must I, in addition to that wrong, allow him the opportunity of putting a hot bullet through my body?" (pp. 61-62).
21. We note also this amusing interchange in Brougham's *The Musard Ball* (pp. 6-7):

> *Dug.* We must meet, sir.
>
> *Brown.* As often as you please, hospitable creature.
>
> *Dug.* Pshaw, sir! I'm in no humor for such untimely jesting, [sic] One of us must die.
>
> *Brown.* Both, my good friend, according to the immutable laws of nature.

22. In his thirty-third year, Calmstorm foresees his death by martyrdom: "The hour, the hour is come" (pp. 56-57); he is betrayed to the citizen mob by a paid politician's taking his hand.
23. Peter is perhaps the prototype of this character, who momentarily deserts Calmstorm in the end. Again this is part of the vague symbolism of the play.
24. Paulding, *American Comedies*, p. 104. Satire against city politics is also seen in plays in which rather unscrupulous men try to gain some high political office. In *Better Late Than Never* by C. J. Cannon, Allsides, a New York merchant, striving for election to Congress, separately promises Tag, Rag, and Bobtail, ignorant leaders of three completely different city political parties, that he will uphold their ridiculous demands, all completely in opposition, if they will nominate him. Fizgig of *Madmen All*, described as "a political speculator and a speculative politician" of Philadelphia, commands his wife and daughter to call on a family that is "rolling in gold" and "has a good deal of political influence amongst a certain class." J. S. Jones, a Boston author who "grew up with the institutions which marked this city in his generation, and who contributed largely to its interest" (*The Silver Spoon*, 1911, Introduction, p. 5), gave the question of urban politics a novel turn in his popular comedy produced in 1852, revived regularly for many years, and finally adapted into novel form. The play has as its central figure Jefferson Scattering Batkins, member of the General Court of Massachusetts from Cranberry Centre, a man whose entire political philosophy might be expressed in four words: "agin the Boston klink [clique]."
25. In Mrs. Bateman's *Self* the same attitude is expressed by one of her shallow, fashionable women who has been held up by an accident in which some immigrants were hurt and "cluttered" up the way.
26. In *Life in New York* Logic says, ". . . everything in this steam power country is done by machinery, from stitching coat seams to manufacturing public officers" (p. 8). In *Fashions and Follies of Washington Life*, Smith remarks, "Progress in the mechanic arts? when thousands of human victims are being butchered by these new-fangled inventions . . ." (p. 65).
27. G. H. Boker, "Glaucus & Other Plays," in S. Bradley, ed., *America's Lost Plays*, III (1940), 69.
28. Quinn, *Representative American Plays*, p. 283.
29. Quoted from p. 23 of typescript of 1797 text supplied by the Library of the University of Pennsylvania.
30. Bradley, ed., *America's Lost Plays*, III, 64-65. These themes, like those in the plays discussed below, it may be added, are also discussed in the American novel of the same age. See, for example, Herbert R. Brown, *The Sentimental Novel in America, 1789-1860* (Durham, 1940). Professor Brown, moreover, has privately remarked on the striking "similarity of themes between popular drama and fiction of the time."
31. Quinn, *Representative American Plays*, pp. 295-296.
32. The following short excerpt from *The Road to Fortune* (p. 38) will show how closely many of these scenes parallel the one from *Fashion*:

> Peter L. This extravagance must be discontinued, wife; these endless follies must end at once. I have no idea of being cast into the street to give parties and entertainments to a set of idle acquaintances.
> Mrs. Legrand. We must think of the Count, husband; if Miranda marries him, we will be rich.

Peter L. Give to our niece a sober, sensible, and industrious man for a husband, if you desire her happiness. The Count ought to be forbidden the house!

Mrs. Legrand. Oh! husband, he is the type and pink of fashion, and such a great and rich man!

Peter L. Wife, shut your doors to the Count, and to every body, at once, if you value your husband's honor and integrity!

Mrs. Legrand. But I can't do it, husband. I should be the laughing stock of the world; I should be mocked by my friends; I have sent invitations for a ball; I could never bear the taunts and jests of the world.

Peter L. A ball, wife! at this time!

Mrs. Legrand. Why not at this time?

Peter L. When your husband is on the verge of bankruptcy!

Mrs. Legrand. Oh, dear!

Peter L. Yes, wife, and you squander thousands!

Mrs. Legrand. I would rather die than forfeit this ball; but it shall be the last; and, husband, you should keep up appearances — keep up your credit, although hypocritically.

33. Paulding, *American Comedies*, pp. 123-124.
34. These are *The Man of the Times, The City Looking-Glass, The Lottery of Life, Calmstorm, The Reformer,* and *Ireland and America.*
35. With these earlier plays as background, it would be interesting to show the use of realistic urban settings in American drama from 1860 to the present.

HERBERT M. SCHUELLER

IF, AS THE philosophers tell us, people's experiences are not comparable, then the works of art which occasionally are the source of experiences are not comparable either. Everyone seems to assume that what makes a masterpiece is an essence or uniqueness, a quality or series of qualities peculiar to it which make it stand out from other works. So *Hamlet* has qualities distinguishing it from other plays, as do *Othello* and *Macbeth*. But there follows an absorbing question: How can it be that one uniqueness influences or brings about another? I am thinking especially of works of art which belong to different media. How does the uniqueness of Mallarmé's *L'Après-Midi d'un Faune* inspire that of Debussy's work of the same name? Or Beaumarchais' *Figaro*, Mozart's? How are Rossetti's poems related to his paintings, and Rachmaninoff's *Isle of the Dead* to Boecklin's? How can the uniqueness of an opera derive from a drama? This last is a question which it should be not too difficult to answer since opera derives from drama and continues to be drama, or has little excuse for existing at all. A comparative study of Shakespeare's *Othello* as it is transformed into Verdi's *Otello* should tell us something. Both works are acknowledged masterpieces, each unique in its own way. It is a study of these works, then, and especially of Verdi's, which I undertake here, and if I cannot say how one "essence" has become another, I can at least show how much the transformed *Otello* is due to Verdi and how much is due to the conventions of opera.

The transformation I am to consider is of course only one of hundreds. No single dramatist has been so frequently the source of operatic works as Shakespeare. Loewenberg reports over sixty operas on Shakespearean subjects which saw production in Europe alone before 1900. This does not include incidental music to the plays themselves. It is probable that hundreds of operas on Shakespearean subjects were written before 1900, to be unproduced; and hundreds planned, to be unrealized. While Matthew Locke composed music for early revivals of *The Tempest* (1670) and *Macbeth* (1673), English composers were not the first to give birth to operas fathered by Shakespeare. One of the first *Midsummer Night's Dream's* seems to have been British all right (Purcell's *Fairy-Queen*, 1692), but the first *Hamlet* was probably Italian[1] and the first *Romeo and Juliet* probably German.[2] The first *Comedy of Errors* recorded by Loewenberg was by an Englishman, but it was first produced in Vienna.[3] The first *Tempest's* were German, both being produced in 1798.[4] The first *Falstaff* was Viennese,[5] and the first important *Otello* was Rossini's (1816, Naples), the outstandingly popular *Otello* until Verdi's in 1887. The first *Macbeth* was French.[6] The first *Measure for Measure* was Richard Wagner's,[7] while the first *Winter's Tale* was by an Italian, though it was produced in Prague.[8] The first *Merchant of Venice* was Italian,[9] and the first *Taming of the Shrew* German.[10] The first *All's Well*, though greatly changed, was French,[11] *Richard III* Russian,[12] and *Twelfth Night* Czech.[13] *Julius Caesar* did not become an opera until 1936,[14] though the other plays already mentioned had been used several times. All *Falstaff's* were of course made up of parts of *Henry IV, Part I* and *The Merry Wives of Windsor*. The best *Falstaff* was made up chiefly of the latter. It is Verdi's and is thought by some to be the best Shakespearean opera extant.

The dates of Shakespearean operas indicate that the operatic interest in Shakespeare was a phenomenon of the Romantic Movement and, as such, parallel to the interest in Shakespeare among creative writers, critics, and philosophers, not only in England, but throughout Europe. The most popular of all the Shakespearean operas have been Gounod's *Romeo and Juliet* (1867), Rossini's *Otello* (1816), Thomas' *Hamlet* (1868), Nicolai's *Merry Wives of Windsor* (1840), and three works by Verdi.

The Romantic and post-Romantic interest in Shakespearean opera was prompted, not only by admiration for an original genius, but also, as can be demonstrated (though not here), by the expectation that an opera will be a "total," an "organic" work. Verdi's own craft points always in the direction of the kind of "organic" work in which all parts are necessary to the totality which is the whole. His *Macbeth* (1887) is a respectable example of the Meyerbeer-Bellini type of Italian opera, but even here he is attempting to write "music-drama," in which, in contradistinction to the works of Rossini, Donizetti, and Bellini, music is only a medium for the expression of the passions of men in action. In later years he came close to becoming a member of the school of *verismo,* and the result was that the combination of realism (such as opera is capable of) and organic unity as found in *Otello* (1887) and *Falstaff* (1893) resulted in the best operas in Verdi's entire output, in the best Shakespearean operas to date, and, if Sir Sidney Lee is correct, in close and appreciative studies of Shakespeare himself.[15]

For Verdi, the shining light of Italian opera, Shakespeare was a veritable passion. He projected a *King Lear* and a *Hamlet,* but apparently his sense of operatic theater was so acute that he found insurmountable obstacles in the path of the translation of these plays to the operatic stage. Besides, one has the impression that he wanted his Shakespearean operas to be works of art. He wrote *Otello* and *Falstaff* as he wanted them to be, and the public might be damned. The result was works which are still separated by critics from Verdi's earlier ones: They are different from the earlier works, it is thought, as being more profound, more Wagnerian, more dramatic in the Aristotelian sense. But other critics have attempted to show that the Verdian style was an evolution and of a piece. Even so, the differences exist, and I think this is because Verdi concentrated, for once, entirely upon what his operatic art was to be without regard for public demands. He changed the plots, therefore, as his aesthetic instinct dictated; the characters are simplified and the action seems to have more logic than in the original plays; and the result is indeed dramatic composition on the grand scale but in keeping with operatic conventions.

I

In writing his two great Shakespearean operas Verdi had the assistance of Arrigo Boito (1842-1918), Italian composer, translator, and librettist. Boito, like Verdi, had adopted the ideal of psychological realism. Though his original text of *Othello* was French, he translated a *French* Shakespeare into an operatic Italian which is partly an equivalent of English blank verse, partly a free prose, each of which he used as it fulfilled his and Verdi's veristic requirements. The arrangement between the two men was a happy one, even though Verdi at one time suspected Boito of wanting to write both text and music to *Otello* himself. Verdi's interest in an Othello opera, his secrecy about his plans for the work, the manner in which his friends tempted him to write the opera — this story is readily found in published lives of Verdi and in his letters. The subject here is the changes Boito and Verdi made in the original, the most important of these changes being Verdi's.

And yet, as operas go, Verdi's *Otello* is close to its original. Rossini's practice was to forget the original play, if such forgetting was possible. His *Otello* departs from Shakespeare more than it follows him. The first act is strictly a new construction: Desdemona, a young girl living with her parents, is courted by Roderigo, whom her father forces her to accept. She loves Otello, however, and Otello has just returned from Cyprus to Venice. Otello is received with acclaim by the senate and people of Venice and is made a son of the Republic by the Doge. Desdemona is already secretly married to him, and at a betrothal dinner given by her father for her and Roderigo, Otello announces that he already has her hand. In Act II Desdemona confesses to Roderigo that she and Otello are married. She resolves to go to her husband, who has, however, already been so influenced by

Iago as to be transformed in one short scene from a trusting husband to a jealous one. Iago gives Otello a letter which Desdemona wrote to her husband in Act I and which Iago has filched; but he says it is written to Roderigo. Otello then challenges Roderigo and repulses Desdemona, who has come to meet him. In Act III, which takes place in Desdemona's bedroom, Desdemona retires overwhelmed by gloomy thoughts. She asks her friend Emilia to leave her alone. Otello enters, awakens her, and murders her in the fury of his jealousy. The news is brought that Roderigo, whom Otello thought to be dead, is alive but that Iago is slain, having confessed his treachery on his deathbed. When Brabantio arrives to make peace, Otello shows Brabantio his dead daughter and stabs himself. Thus Rossini's *Otello* is completely false to Shakespeare, it is unconvincing as psychology (especially in the rapidity with which Otello is made jealous), and it is totally removed from verisimilitude. Rossini shone as a composer, and his singers shone as vocal machines. But the drama was lost in the furthering of non-dramatic aims.[16]

What did Boito do to the plot of *Othello*?[17] The obvious change is the almost complete deletion of Act I. As librettist Boito had to decide about the form of the drama, and, according to report, Verdi himself, a practical man of the theater who knew about the time-limitations of opera, demanded the dropping of the first act of *Othello*. The opera therefore opens in Cyprus rather than in Venice. In the play the conflict begins late; in the opera it begins almost at once. Unconsciously both Boito and Verdi agreed with Dr. Johnson: "Had the scene opened in Cyprus," wrote Johnson, "and the preceding incidents occasionally related [as, one hastens to add, they would have been in Greek drama], there had been little wanting to a drama of the most exact and scrupulous regularity."[18] But Boito made an even more radical change than Johnson desired. He began the libretto in Cyprus, and he omitted the "relation" of the preceding incidents. Desdemona as daughter was patently less important to the drama than Desdemona as lover and wife. *Otello*, as sug-

gested by Boito's change, does not really begin until Desdemona
steps off the ship at Cyprus, and Cassio's line,

> O, behold,
> The riches of the ship is come on shore!

is the bell announcing the opening of the real action of the play.
Thus in effect Boito retained the love-interest which is the dominant theme of Act I without retaining the characters and actions
of Act I. The love-theme and the jealousy-motive are actually
brought closer together, are more concentrated in effect. Thus
also Boito set Verdi a greater problem than was Shakespeare's, to
make Othello's jealousy believable. In *Otello* it is Desdemona's
relation to her husband which carries the weight of the action.

The Viennese critic Eduard Hanslick thought it unfortunate
that Verdi should have omitted the first act of *Othello*. He saw
many attractive opportunities for the composer in it: the threatening crowd in front of Brabantio's palace, the meeting of the
senate to try Othello, Othello's narrative, and Desdemona's testament of love. But Boito and Verdi dispensed with the father-
daughter sub-plot of *Othello*, not only, as Hanslick suggests, because the nineteenth-century Italian would not tolerate operas
of more than four acts, but also because this omission is dramatically defensible. Coleridge, it will be remembered, did not agree
with Dr. Johnson about the deletion of Act I, though his exposition of the unity of *Othello* as it stands is neither thorough nor
convincing. Boito made the play one about love and jealousy in
marriage. The question of how Desdemona became Othello's
wife is another action for another play. The fact is that critics
have almost universally ignored the sub-plot of Desdemona's
betrayal of her father and her supposed perfidy with Cassio, the
former of which is supposed to augur the latter; few critics have
treated it as an integral part of the story of the disintegration of
a marriage. Thus with the omission of the Desdemona-Brabantio
sub-plot the opening scene may be Cyprus rather than Venice,

a change of which not only Dr. Johnson, but Thomas Rymer also, would have approved.

With the first act went the character of Brabantio. Omitted too are references to him: Desdemona's denial (*Othello*, IV, 2, 44-46) that he could have been plotting against her and her husband to bring them back to Venice, and a reference to him after Desdemona's death (V, 2, 204-205). Other characters disappear too: the count, Gratiano, and two senators. Gratiano, who appears only once after Act I in Shakespeare's play, is combined with Lodovico, who in both play and opera is an envoy from Venice. The clown is omitted (as he is also in the German version of *Othello* devised by Schiller). While Bianca plays a real part in *Othello*, she is merely mentioned (by Iago) in the opera. But her influence is felt in the action. The clown is omitted, and with him go the scenes between Emilia, Desdemona, and him. (In Verdi it is Iago himself who tells Cassio to go to Desdemona.) Since Bianca is not in the opera, neither are the Emilia-Bianca scenes.

All of the Desdemona scenes save the last one are omitted; and while the Verdian Emilia is quite different from the Shakespearean one, the difference is not as important as the increased credibility of the character itself. In the opera she does not have a chance to reveal what she supposedly knows. In fact, in the opera she never supposedly knows what, in the play, she is aware of. Her fate in the opera is more fortunate than that in the play: Iago does not stab her. Her scenes with Cassio and Iago are omitted, as are her scenes with Desdemona and Cassio. The result is little evidence that she is "in the know." Another result is that all of her salaciousness and rather "hard" and cold-blooded conversations about the relations of men and women disappear, to the increase in dignity of her own dramatic personality.

Most of these omissions result in a more "regulated" plot, as the neoclassicists would have said, and in a simpler plot better adapted to opera. There is yet another omission which is the result of the transfer from spoken to sung drama. This is the word in its full import. Taking first place in spoken drama, the word takes less than second in opera. Like the omissions already mentioned, the deletion of word-associations in their richness is made necessary by the different demands of the two art-forms.

In Shakespeare, Othello first tells Desdemona that he will deny her nothing, and later he changes his mind. This is too subtle a change for Verdi's purposes. At the end of the opera the introduction of a letter from Roderigo is omitted; it is included in the play, though, even here, it is a confusing and unnecessary detail. And since in the opera the revelations in it are to be sung in any case, it is just as well that Roderigo's confession of Iago's villainy becomes a matter of hearsay. But a more important result is the omission of Shakespearean poetry. Otello does tell his followers to keep up their bright swords (though he says it in Italian "after" the French), but he does not explain that the dew will rust them. Furthermore, the line that is retained finds itself in a new context. It is in Act I in Shakespeare, in the very act which Verdi omits. It is transferred to action which comes from Shakespeare's Act II. Though Otello's "crucial moment"[19] is better handled, is clearer and sharper, in Verdi than in Shakespeare, the words of Iago, so important to this scene, are usually robbed of their sharpness. Iago's character is revealed largely through his music. It is not necessary, therefore, for him to say to Roderigo that Desdemona loves Cassio. The lie in Shakespeare becomes a suggestion in Verdi. "Watch them," Iago says to Otello. He never makes the direct statement. In making such suggestions, however, Iago does not resort to the believable argument that she will tire of Otello in time (whether he is black or not). Such a suggestion is plausible in drama, but not in opera: It is too "rational" for the latter art. Therefore he does not work on Roderigo first as if to try out what he will later attempt with Otello. Similarly, Iago's taunting of Otello (IV, 1) is missing in the opera. The delicious playing with pictures of Desdemona's and Cassio's possible passionate encounters is gone, though a crucial speech, "I lay with Cassio lately," is included. Mind-play through word-play has no place in opera. Nor has the cynical-witty exchange of Desdemona and Iago in *Othello,* II, 1.

II

So much for the matter of Shakespeare's *Othello* which has been omitted in Boito-Verdi. There are other significant changes both in the nature of the characters and in the arrangement of the action. Let us allow Bernard Shaw the first word:

> . . . instead of *Otello* being an Italian opera written in the style of Shakespear, *Othello* is a play written by Shakespear in the style of Italian opera. . . . Its characters are monsters: Desdemona is a prima donna, with handkerchief, confidante, and vocal solo all complete; and Iago, though certainly more anthropomorphic than the Count di Luna, is only so when he slips out of his stage villain's part. Othello's transports are conveyed by a magnificent but senseless music which ranges from the Propontick to the Hellespont in an orgy of thundering sound and bounding rhythm; and the plot is a pure farce plot: that is to say, it is supported on an artificially manufactured and desperately precarious trick with a handkerchief which a chance word might upset at any moment. With such a libretto, Verdi was quite at home. . . .[20]

But Shavian exaggeration requires an analysis of the manner in which Verdi modified his libretto.

Otello

1. *His initial appearance:* Otello makes an impressive initial entrance. He comes as hero. Saved from the dangers of the ocean, he enters to announce in the most difficult kind of *tessitura* that he has conquered the Turks. Initially, the operatic Otello is more impressive than the dramatic one, whose marriage is under attack; and the opening declamation requires a singing-actor who can suggest Otello's vitality, power, and eloquence, and also an

animal vigor made noble by regality of mien and deportment. Is Otello a Negro or a Moor? The question is not as important for the operatic character as Lamb and Hazlitt thought it to be for the Shakespearean one. It is not important because opera admits easily and freely details off center, as it were: The eccentric, the picturesque, the exotic, the "oriental" are elements common in it.

2. *His crucial moment*: This is the initial moment at which Iago begins his planned campaign to arouse Otello's suspicions about Desdemona and Cassio. In Shakespeare, Iago and Othello enter the stage together, but in Verdi, Otello enters *by chance* and Iago turns this chance to profit by saying, apparently without intention of being overheard, "I like not that." Otello must think that Iago has not seen him. Boito-Verdi thus discarded the ambiguous elements of this moment.

In Shakespeare, the conversation between Othello and Iago is interrupted by Desdemona, who has just left Cassio. In Verdi, Desdemona and Cassio are *observed* in the garden; they are in conversation, Iago previously having sent Cassio to see Desdemona. Therefore both Otello and the audience can see them. The entire situation is at once clearer and sharper than in Shakespeare. Otello's suspicions can be aroused immediately because of Iago's remark about something Otello can see; and the audience understands immediately Iago's part in the situation, his plan, and Otello's response to it. The scene is eminently credible: Iago is able to vilify both Cassio, who is already in disgrace, and Desdemona. The basic irony is in Iago's *apparent* distrust of Cassio: To distrust Cassio is to raise the question, without mentioning it, of the degree to which Desdemona is implicated.

3. *His relations with Desdemona*: Otello is the dominant figure throughout the opera, and, as in the play (I, 1, 12), he loves "his own pride and purposes." From the beginning it is Otello's safety and triumphs in war and his safety and triumphs in love which form his theme, and to this theme the Iago-Cassio and the Iago-Roderigo relationships are subsidiary. The important

relationship is Otello's with Desdemona. But in Shakespeare there is no love-passage between the two. Othello expresses his love only in detached passages which have no intimacy because even Iago is present. In Cinthio, who was Shakespeare's source, the Moor (who is never named as Othello) watches his ensign club his wife to death. In Shakespeare and Verdi, he smothers her, but by himself, and in Shakespeare Othello is alone with Desdemona either as her murderer or as her torturer. But Boito took separate passages in Shakespeare and welded them together as one to form the love-duet at the end of Act I. Though Otello's brutality towards Desdemona is projected, greatly subdued, into the opera, it is his protective love towards his wife which is stressed in Act I. In the opera there is an intimacy between the two which the play does not suggest. Desdemona seems more a private than a public character, and the love-duet which completes Act I and which ends with the statement, "Venus shall guide us," carries with it a feeling of secret intimacy and perhaps also a secret dread of destiny.

4. *His credulity*: Certain critics have suggested that Othello's credulity was extreme, that it is an implausibility that he should have believed Iago's implied charges against Cassio and Desdemona. In the play, Desdemona had no time to be unfaithful since she arrived the day before Act II at Cyprus accompanied, not by Cassio, but by Iago. In the opera, however, she is already at Cyprus awaiting the triumphal return of her husband from the Turkish wars. She *could* therefore have been unfaithful: Cassio is already there and for how long is never said. Silence on this point makes for greater plausibility of the supposed adultery of Cassio and Desdemona and for a less facile credulity on Otello's part. In fact, Otello's blind trust is not intense to the point of probable stupidity; but in both play and opera he is wanting equally in self-knowledge. Each Othello is "perplexed in the extreme," however, and, as Dr. Johnson said, "inflexible in his resolution, and obdurate in his revenge."

Iago

1. *His revelation of his intent:* Boito, as his own *Mefistofele* testifies, admired the satanic as material for dramatic-operatic action. He wanted *Otello* to be an Iago-opera. But Verdi was the better interpreter of Shakespeare. He knew that Iago was merely the instrument of Othello's downfall, the seeds of which were in Othello's own credulity and in his own exalted estimate of himself. In the opera Iago reveals his true character to Roderigo at the beginning, the entire revelation being accomplished during the storm-scene. This takes much longer in Shakespeare, and the question of how Verdi could achieve this with the speed he did is a complicated one. But the essential fact is that the "villainous" intent of Iago is explicitly stated and that the storm scene serves to intensify his evil character, stronger here and less modified by an alloy of humor than in Shakespeare.

2. *His jealousy:* Othello is not jealous at the beginning of the play; neither is Otello at the beginning of the opera. The jealousy is Iago's. Iago is ambitious for high place, and in the play Cassio is given preferment because he has been a go-between for Desdemona and Othello. In the opera Iago is jealous because Cassio has the position he wants. He does not mention reported illicit relations between his wife Emilia and Otello. As realism, Iago's jealousy of Cassio and his desire to hurt Otello, who has slighted him, are sufficiently motivated. Sadism is supposedly a recognition of one's own insufficiencies, and Iago is nothing if not sadistic.

3. *His crudeness in conversation:* Since opera is less "verbal" than drama, entire conversations in *Othello* are omitted in the opera. The result is that Iago's speech is in general "cleaned up." Like the German dramatist Schiller when he translated *Othello* into German, Boito-Verdi struck out Iago's fulminations against women (beginning of Act II). The speeches are probably irrelevant to the action in any event, but they are clearly too "philosophical" to be convincing in opera. Iago's grossness is part of

the plot of *Othello,* but it can be shown in words recited better than in words sung. In the opera he becomes a kind of refined, elegant Renaissance villain as described by Jacob Burckhardt and John Addington Symonds. His "material" is contrasted with Otello's "ideal" attitude towards love. The famous *Credo,* which was Boito's creation and which many critics have called unnecessary to the action, has a reason for existing after all: It represents Iago as the whole man with his cruelty, his vileness, his falseness in his apparent honesty, his notion of human fate as worm-eaten death with nothingness thereafter. The *Credo* takes the place of Iago's lascivious and cynical speeches in the play. Here compressed in one statement of belief is Iago's conviction that man is mere animal, that his love is a loathsome thing, that death is the end of everything, and that all ideals are illusions motivated by the selfishness of men. His character is in large part revealed by statement in compression.

4. *His fate:* Boito avoided Shakespeare's rather cheap retribution for the sins of Iago; he lets Iago escape to an unknown fate, his reward, whatever it could have been, unmentioned, and poetic justice ignored.[21]

Desdemona

1. *Her character and action:* Johnson spoke of the "soft simplicity of Desdemona, confident of merit, and conscious of innocence, her artless perseverance in her suit, and her slowness to suspect that she can be suspected." Hazlitt called her gentle. Like Otello, Desdemona is fairly close to her Shakespearean model. Yet she is not quite such a nagger (*Othello,* III, 3). Nor is she so complex: She is not a daughter, though she is a wife. She is naturally less addicted to rhetoric and speechifying (I, 3). She is more direct and less enigmatic.

In *Otello* it is her naïvete which seems to be stressed. She relies on her own judgment, but she suffers from a kind of myopia, from an inability to see what is going on except when violence or near-violence is an element in it. She is an innocent despite the worldliness around her. She cannot see the results which may come of her persistent suit for Cassio. Her increased directness in Verdi is partly due to her public character as an operatic heroine: Her supplication to her husband on her knees is private in Shakespeare, public in Verdi. She is not the self-deceiver in Verdi that she is in Shakespeare (Act IV, 3, conversation with Emilia). Her secretiveness is not underlined in Verdi. Like her husband, she supposes men to be what they seem. In Verdi she does not need to prevaricate when Otello asks for her handkerchief. She is more immature in Verdi. But she is undeniably the lady wronged. Otello's "Venus stands high" symbolizes the quality of his love for her, and like her husband she is an instrument for the purging of terror in the audience, that emotion which arises when one sees how the universe works against one's best interests.

2. *Dramatic decorations to her action:* These are mostly additions to the play and involve the chorus. Boito-Verdi here added material for musical effect: In Act II Desdemona enters with her attendants, who sing a song to her. This song is dramatically unimportant and as part of drama was a mistake. There are other additions, however: The "Willow Song" is through-composed, as it should be, and respresents one of Verdi's most masterly strokes. An *Ave Maria* is added in the last act before Desdemona goes to bed, later to be smothered under a pillow. This addition is dramatic in the structural sense and comes in naturally, though a similar kind of addition to action was a staple of nineteenth-century Italian opera. Verdi himself was opposed to the Church, but he used such an obviously Catholic song whenever it was useful. Anticlerical in feeling, Verdi was still a practical man of the theater living in a Catholic country.

3. *Dramatic compression of her action:* This involves chiefly her request of Otello for Cassio's pardon. Here two separate Shakespearean scenes are fused, both the refusal of Othello and the handkerchief scene being brought together. Furthermore,

Cassio is less attentive to Desdemona in the opera than in the play. He never talks to her except to ask for something, and these talks are seen or reported, never heard. Thus Desdemona's possible guilt is reduced in importance, her naïvete increased, and her helplessness made consonant with a notion of uncontrollable fate.

Other Characters

The Verdi Desdemona seems less operatic than the Shakespearean one according to Shavian description. Even the Verdian Otello seems so, the Shakespearean "music" for him being more magnificent, I think, than that of Verdi. Yet the totality which is Verdian has a magnificence and uniqueness, too, which are undeniable. And the final effect is partly in what happens to the minor characters who are retained.

Emilia has already been mentioned. She gains nobility in Verdi. Her coarseness disappears and her cynicism about marital faithfulness with it. Her secretiveness disappears, as does her ambiguous responsibility in the handkerchief episode. She has less "personality" in Verdi than in Shakespeare because her rich vulgarity is gone. She is part of the great "quartet," but she is not a leading character.

In the dramatic action Cassio is more important than Emilia. But he is no tragic hero. He is a mediocre person who must hold on to his job; he is brave probably, honest certainly, but essentially unseeing. In this respect he is like Desdemona. Shakespeare absolves Cassio from all suspicions by causing him to pray for the safe return of Othello (II, 1, 77-82) so that Othello can find love in Desdemona's arms. This is not necessary in the opera. At the same time, Cassio's greeting of Desdemona and his charge to the men of Cyprus (II, 1, 83-88) are operatic in the Shavian sense. Cassio is less colorful in Verdi than in Shakespeare, though he is the cause of drunken fun during the drinking scene. In Cinthio he had a wife. In Shakespeare the wife is ambiguous, being "fair" in the first scene and non-existent thereafter. In Verdi she is simply non-existent. In Cinthio Cassio refers to a courtesan he is about to visit. In Shakespeare and Verdi he has a mistress. This does not make him especially daring or interesting. In *Othello* his mistress appears on the stage; from *Otello* she is absent, but in a comic-ironic scene with Iago, Cassio speaks of her. Not the least of the ironies of *Otello* is that a mediocrity should unwittingly help destroy the marriage of his leader.

Roderigo is not in Cinthio. He is Shakespeare's invention. In Verdi he has little character, little individuality, though he is an important item in the plot. Like Emilia, Desdemona, Otello, and even Iago, he is less coarse in the opera, and the audience cannot conceive a prejudice against him, as it can against the Shakespearean character. He is less a potential villain than a gull. In *Othello* (I, 1, 110) he calls himself a simple and pure soul, only to have Brabantio dispute his word; in *Otello* he is what in *Othello* he describes himself to be. In fact, his innocence and simplicity seem to be extended to all characters of *Otello,* except for Iago. Iago alone is crafty and sophisticated; the rest are misled by people and events.

If, then, as Shaw says, Verdi was quite at home with "such a libretto" as *Othello,* he showed no hesitancy about altering some of the furniture or, indeed, the very structure of the house itself. *Otello* even seems less "operatic" than *Othello,* but, as Shaw further points out, Verdi often rises fully to his source: The libretto is enhanced by a return to "the simplicity of real popular life in the episodes of the peasants singing over the fire in the storm in the first act."[22] But one finds it hard to agree with Shaw about the attractiveness of the people's serenade to Desdemona in the second act of *Otello;* it helps to give *Otello* a public setting, but the guitars and the trappings of Italian opera choruses cheapen the work.

III

Verdi's transformation of Shakespeare's *Othello* can be analyzed into a number of types of changes. Whatever the "essences" of the two works may be, there are demands which singing-drama makes of speech-drama to satisfy its own requirements. Everything, of course, turns upon the taste of the transformer; but in general, if *Otello* may serve as an example, the following are changes that can be expected of any transplanting of a work from the spoken to the singing stage:

1. *Scenes pictorialized:* An example is the storm-scene (Act II of *Othello*, opening of the opera). Fewer things are described in words, the scene is pictorial rather than "literary," a spectacle rather than a speech. It of course contains fewer images. Boito probably took his cue from II, 1, 53-54:

Messenger: The town is empty; on the brow o' the sea
      Stand ranks of people, and they cry, 'A sail!'

2. *Scenes compressed:* As has been pointed out, the omission of Shakespeare's Act I brought about a unity of place which Shakespeare's play lacks. Also, certain scenes are brought together because of a character they have in common. Even better (and this is something opera can do, as drama cannot) two scenes are sometimes dovetailed. In the quartet of Act II, *three separate actions occur* (or two, if the words of Otello and Desdemona are counted as one conversation). Otello and Desdemona separately, as it seems, soliloquize about their fate, while Iago and Emilia struggle over the handkerchief, which Iago eventually gets. *A greater simultaneity* seems possible in opera than in drama, and in consequence a greater irony. Operatic quartets and quintets antedating *Otello* had combined actions into a unity. No matter how crude aesthetically this simultaneity may seem, it is blood-brother to similar technical devices in literature, the scene at the agricultural fair in *Madame Bovary*, for instance, and in painting,

such as the *Nude Descending a Staircase,* which presents simultaneously different moments in time.

3. *Properties more directly relied upon:* Though Bianca is not necessary to the action of *Otello,* Desdemona's handkerchief is. What is more, Boito saw to it that both Otello and the audience observe the handkerchief, once in Cassio's hand and twice in Iago's, first when Iago gets it from Emilia and second when he has taken it from Cassio to wave it behind himself for Otello, who is hiding behind a column on the stage, to see. In opera there should be no ambiguity about properties. They cannot be sufficiently talked about to convince an audience that they are there. Therefore they should be seen, a principle which explains the ineffectiveness of the smaller properties (the ring and the toad) in the *Ring des Nibelungen.*

4. *Time-scheme simplified:* Verdi's *Otello,* because the plot is more "rational" than Shakespeare's, requires no complicated explanation of time-sequence like Christopher North's theory of "long-time" and "short-time" in Shakespeare.[23] Extensions of time are suggested when the audience sees, at a distance, Cassio and Desdemona speaking together, as they are not so observed in Shakespeare. Furthermore, the scenes in which the chorus plays a major role involve a psychologically slow time, opera being a kind of art which, like the world of dreams, seems to exist in a kind of time slower than mathematical time; or which calls up in the minds of the audience a credibility so uncritical that real time is hardly a point of reference. The action of opera exists in a world of illusion more dense than that of spoken drama, in the sense that realistic time is almost alien or irrelevant to it. Only the most romantic of dramas, like Maeterlinck's *Pelléas,* for instance, approximates opera as embracing psychological dream-time.

5. *Characters simplified in terms of stereotypes:* When dramas become operas, the protagonists lose their individualities and frequently become types. They do not do so in Verdi's *Falstaff,* and, if Shaw is right, neither is there any need for their doing so in *Otello.* The people in *Otello* are exceptions proving the rule;

they are operatic characters in the play itself. They are more like people in the English "heroic" drama of Davenant, for instance, or Dryden, than like people in realistic plays. In the opera, as in the play, Desdemona is helpless, sweet, lovable, and patient in suffering. Her character is relatively simple in both. Similarly, the dramatic Othello is almost, if not quite, identical with the operatic Otello. But these identities are the exception: The dramatic Hamlet and the operatic one cannot be the same, however much certain critics may try to simplify the former into the stereotype which the latter must be.

6. *The "chorus" more extensively utilized:* It is a commonplace in the history of opera that the form resembles ancient drama in a number of respects. In fact, the origin of opera at the home of Giovanni Bardi in Florence, Italy, in the sixteenth century was the consequence of an attempt to revive the style of musical declamation peculiar to Greek tragedy. The chorus in *Otello* serves as the social background against which the dominant action is played. The chorus of modern opera serves a function similar to that of Greek tragedy.

7. *"Spectacle" and music sometimes used for their own sakes:* The temptation of the opera composer is to let the spectacle and the music run away with him, even when both are dramatically irrelevant. The "fire" scene and Iago's drinking song are examples in point, though both contribute to the social background of the action. Spectacle has always been an element in opera because opera tends to become pageant, and Aristotle himself can be quoted in support of its use. The "fire" scene is not really dramatic in the structural sense; it interrupts Iago's conversation with Roderigo, which is not taken up again but seems to "resolve" itself into the scene in which Iago gets Cassio drunk. And yet it serves the function I have mentioned.

Musical elements in *Otello* which are undramatic are few in number. There is the chorus of the children sung for Desdemona and there is the *Ave Maria*. But, as Shaw suggests, the opera is less "operatic" than the play. Some people think of a Shakespeare play as a concatenation of poetic speeches, as others think of operas as concatenations of arias. The great speeches are in *Othello* all right, but there are no arias in the usual sense in *Otello*. Even Otello's soliloquy at the end is more a declamation than an aria. Verdi denied himself the temptation of making up a good song in *Otello;* the *whole thing* is song, and the whole work is, in the metaphorical sense, more through-composed than the play. Highly lyrical moments like the love-duet at the end of Act I seem to be songs separate from the action; but they were not composed that way.

8. *The symbolical import of certain words in certain situations, and of certain situations themselves, frequently enhanced:* This results from the alliance of words with music and from the ability of the latter to call up associations.[24] Close analysis of Boito-Verdi's handling of III, 4, beginning with Desdemona's query, "How is it with you, my lord?" and containing the scene in which Othello asks for the handkerchief — such analysis shows that Boito-Verdi expand the scene in time, as they must since it is set to music, and that the result is a symbolical richness which does not lie in the words themselves. Throughout the scene, the melodic lines of Otello and Desdemona are distinguishable as to quality. Hers sounds clear, calm though pleading, graceful, and feminine; his is obscure, distressed, mysteriously threatening, awkward, impulsive, and impatient. But the first lines of the scene are divided between them, and Otello sounds as courtly and gracious as Desdemona herself (*Otello*, III, 2):

> How is't with you, my husband,
> My heart's sole lord and master?

And he answers:

> Well, my good lady.
> Give me your hand as virgin snow so white.
> Hot yet and moist; which argues
> A frank and liberal heart.

There is naïvete and straightforwardness in her manner and there is concealed irony in his. After a long passage in which Otello accuses her of infidelity and calls her a strumpet and whore, he repeats in the same calm, measured words the statement about her white hand. Now she too recognizes, as the audience has previously done, that he is both ironical and bitterly sarcastic. The symbolical significance of the entire passage is far richer than it is in Shakespeare, where it is rich indeed. But only close analysis of both words and music as Verdi handles them can demonstrate what I cannot make clear here. Of even more power and more symbolical significance is the entire fourth act of the Verdian work, sometimes called the perfect act in opera. Here the atmosphere of murder, Desdemona's cries, and Otello's despair and suicide are supported by a musical symbolism surprising from a man who never pretended to be a conscious "symbolist" and whose dramatic works were not, as were those of Richard Wagner, thought of as models of the total work of art. The French Symbolists never took him up. But then, unlike Wagner, he was no theorist and amateur metaphysician. He was merely a practical man of the theater who in *Otello* and in *Falstaff* hoped to realize his own artistic ideals.

IV

The works I have been comparing are both dramas of passion. But the passions are presented, not analyzed. Neither Shakespeare nor Verdi approaches psychological states with the intention of achieving Proustian detail. Both Shakespeare and Verdi are synthetic, not analytic; creative, not critical. They present and represent; they do not explain. The psychologically subtle has little place in drama, and it has none in opera. In both play and opera a passion is thoroughly treated; but it is not minutely and microscopically drawn. It is wrung dry. It is exhausted. And it requires of the audience, not intellectual, but emotional participation. If the passion is exhausted, so in another sense is the audience.

Though Otello falls into only one "fit" in the opera (he has two in the play), he is no less a victim of passion than his dramatic original. Like the heroes in medieval romance, the heroes of tragedy can succumb to their intense and overwhelming passions, those idealizations of the emotions of the everyday man. Otello's remorse is as intense as the passion which caused him to murder his wife. But Otello's passions lead to Otello's demoralization. The opera, like the play, shows us men and women covertly watching one another; they almost become peeping-Toms in the moral world.

And yet *Otello* is a tragedy in the Aristotelian sense. Even more, it is a heroic play. Both opera and play depend on spectacle, the opera more so than the play. In both, the main characters undergo violent emotional upsets in keeping with their "epic" proportions. But the opera is more like a heroic play than is the play itself for the reason that its plot is based upon an idealized kind of love. This is the love of heroes, of idealized men of honor. Though Otello admits the total destruction of himself and of his honor through the degradation he has undergone, his love remains. Fame, glory, his profession as a soldier, all are important to him and all are destroyed because of sexual jealousy. For *Otello*, more than *Othello*, is a drama of sexual passion, but the love in the play is "Christianized" in the opera: The idealization in the opera is constant, though in the play Iago pokes fun at it. The Shakespearean Iago cynically plays with the idea of sex; the Verdian is not allowed to do so. The Shakespearean Iago is revolted by sexual love in the manner of the inverted puritans who find only disgust for themselves in the sexuality of others. Nor is Emilia allowed to be the worldly materialist in the opera that she is in the play. But in the opera Iago's powerful negative attitude does not deny the fact that deep sexual passion is made ideal in Otello and Desdemona. To be sure, their love-night suffers by an interruption caused by a quarrel outside their windows; but the love-duet takes away the sharpness in the contrast between the commonness of ordinary men and the heroic nature of the love of this hero and his bride.

The "kiss" motive, enunciated as if spontaneously, in Act I and repeated, as if to recall the spontaneity of the passion, in Act IV, makes the love-theme more "human" in actuality as well as more conventional. It achieves a symbolism of its own which is *not* the property of Wagnerian opera alone, or even the invention of Wagner himself. This symbolism reveals itself in two ways: It emphasizes the overall quality of a stoicism at once Christian and pagan. And it points up the factors in the action which are of personal importance to the characters. But, of course, like literary symbolism, the operatic type is vague, and in its vagueness lies its power to say many things to different men.

Though Boito, with Verdi's approval, cut out of the opera Othello's cogitations about immortality and death in the first part of V, 2, and though Verdi's *Otello* contains no reference to immortality, it leaves a more conventional Christian effect than does the play. The Christian elements are intensified over the pagan: Verdi retains the Christian *amen* of Othello (II, 1, 197) in the love-scene; he adds it, blasphemously, to the revenge scene of Otello and Iago, though it is not in Shakespeare; and he adds a lyrical *Ave Maria,* a Roman Catholic prayer, to Desdemona's preparations for bed. These *amen*'s and prayers temper the stoicism of the original play and turn the minds of the audience towards Christian symbolism.

But the symbolism of both play and opera expresses a fatal irony with which both are interpenetrated. This is not merely the dramatic irony couched in terms of contrasts in personality. It is, rather, that irony caused by differences between man and the universe, between man and his fate, between truth as man thinks it to be and truth as it probably is. The "universal" symbols in both play and opera fuse with the dramatic ones, and Iago's use of the symbol of the web (*Othello*, II, 1, 169), his naming of jealousy as a green-eyed monster, his use of the handkerchief, all relate to the great irony of the play, the irony that people are not what they seem, honesty being the focal point of the dramatic action. The question of honesty is not Iago's alone. It is Desdemona's too. Has she been honest with and faithful to Otello? And in the course of dramatic events, when Iago's work is succeeding only too well, the audience asks of Otello if he really can tell honesty from dishonesty and, more important, if he can be true to his own ideal and to his own nature, which are an open honesty with which Otello was ostensibly born.

The lyricism of *Othello* remains in *Otello* and is intensified. The lyricism I mean is the subtle fusion of emotion, dramatic situation, and expression, sometimes symbolical and sometimes nonsymbolical, by means of sound and sight. As for that which is heard, repetitions of themes (the "kiss" motive, statements of Iago's "honesty," Iago's use of the symbol of the web) are "musical," in the metaphorical sense, without the music. The lyrical and dramatic are interfused; the *sounds* of the words and the *sounds* of the music are intertwined with their dramatic source. In *Othello* there is recurrence of the motives of sword-suicide, of Othello's greatness in the past, of his reputation in the future. Shakespeare's art of repetition is itself like the first principle of musical form upon which opera is based. Repetition is essential to intelligibility in music, even among the "atonalists." But repetition is an element in all lyrical art. Apart from repetition, however, the lyrical elements of Shakespearean drama, among which are classified some of the soliloquies and of course the songs, are musical in the sense of the word as used by Mallarmé, because they are based upon a dramatic situation. Desdemona's "Willow Song" is not just a song in a play or in an opera; it is part of the dramatic context in which it appears. My point is that Verdi took advantage of the "musical" quality of Shakespeare which, by Professor E. E. Stoll and Granville-Barker, has been called his "orchestration," and has intensified it in the manner of operatic composers; or, as Coleridge might have said, he brought about the "interfusion of the lyrical — that which in its very essence is

poetical — not only with the dramatic, as in the plays of Meta-
stasio . . ., — but also in and through the dramatic. . . . [T]he
whole of Midsummer Night's Dream is one continued specimen
of the dramatized lyrical." And if Coleridge mentioned Meta-
stasio with the respect he did, one wonders what he might have
thought of Boito and Verdi, who together interpreted Shakespeare,
not in the words of criticism, which is an attempt at a science
of axiology, but in a new artistic creation, which is a transformation from one medium to another.

Verdi achieved a fluidity in the succession of his materials in
Otello which allows the lyrical and the dramatic to be one. His
opera is not divided into bits of recitative and aria as are many
operas, "Italian," as well as French and German, before the *Fly-
ing Dutchman*. In *Otello* Verdi reached a degree of technical
mastery which allows him to retain his amazing melodic quality
without his having to make a sharp differentiation between exposition and song. Action *is* the backbone of his opera, and song is
an integral part of the action. The opera proceeds like a play,
though necessarily at a slower pace. Scenes follow scenes without
a "formula" to distinguish them from one another: The static
character of Italian opera has been replaced by the dramatic
character of drama. Verdi has fewer formulas for scenic divisions,
even, than Shakespeare; he has used in *Otello* nothing comparable
to the couplets which designate the ends of scenes in Shakespeare.
The duets and trios of conventional, "static" opera *become* di-
alogues, not "concerted" numbers. Even quartets further the
dramatic action, as does the quartet during which Iago gets the
handkerchief from Emilia. *Otello* might well be the model of
dramatic action which Shaw had in mind when he wrote the
passage introducing this paper: Song follows thought, feeling,
and word to an extent that, especially for an incident like Iago's
account of his sleeping with Cassio, requires technical analysis
of the most searching type, like that which the play itself has had
at the hands of G. R. Elliott (*Flaming Minister*, 1953) and
Robert B. Heilman (*Magic in the Web*, 1956). The result would

be a long book and a complicated one. Music in *Otello* is less independent than it is in most opera: It follows mood in the manner of operatic realism and it follows the words. There are technical matters of importance to analysis: Chromaticism is common and an uncertain shifting back and forth between major and minor tonalities gives the opera its character and suggests a musical symbolism too abstruse to be examined here. Each character has his own personality, and this is revealed as much through the music as through the action. Each character has his own type of melody. But since melody is tied to character, and character to dramatic action, and music to words, the opera can be said to have reached the ideal of Count Francesco Algarotti, who in his work on opera in 1755 indicated that good opera should have a further unity, that between poet and composer. The poet is Shakespeare, and the composer is Verdi. The man who helped them to work as one was Boito. On November 1, 1886, Verdi wrote to Boito: "I have finished! All hail to us . . . (and to *him* too!!)." Verdi had finished *Otello*, and when he was satisfied with his *dramma per la musica*, it seemed that Shakespeare had indeed been faithfully interpreted though undeniably transformed.

NOTES

1. My facts here come chiefly from Alfred Loewenberg, *Annals of Opera 1597-1940*, with an Introduction by Edward J. Dent (Second edition, revised and corrected, Cambridge, England, 1955). Loewenberg's lists are selective, but one may safely assume that he has mentioned every opera of note produced during the period he covers. The *Hamlet* referred to here is Francesco Gasparini's *Ambleto*, 1705.
2. G. Benda's *Romeo und Julie*, 1776, produced at Gotha.
3. Stephen Storace's *Gli Equivoci*, 1786.
4. G. F. Reichardt's *Die Geisterinsel*, produced at Berlin, and J. R. Zumsteeg's *Die Geisterinsel*, produced at Stuttgart.
5. Salieri's of 1799.
6. H. Chélard's of 1827, produced in Paris.
7. *Das Liebesverbot*, 1836, produced at Magdeburg.
8. C. di Barbieri's *Perdita*, 1865.
9. C. Pinsuti, *Il Mercante di Venezia*, 1873, produced at Bologna.
10. H. Goetz, *Die Widerspänstigen Zähmung*, 1874, given at Mannheim.
11. E. Audran, *Gillette de Narbonne*, 1882.

12. G. Salvayre's, 1883, at St. Petersburg.
13. K. Weis, *Viola*, 1872, produced at Prague.
14. Malipiero's *Giulio Cesare*.
15. *A Life of William Shakespeare* (New York, 1924), p. 626.
16. As usually given, Rossini's *Otello* is even further from Shakespeare. The Italian audience of 1816 disliked the final scene: It was too gruesome. Rossini therefore substituted a "happy" ending. *Then* Desdemona said she was innocent, Otello threw away his dagger, and their reconciliation ended in a duet out of another of Rossini's operas (*Armida*, 1817). To supply such happy endings was not rare in the eighteenth and nineteenth centuries. Remember the end of Gluck's *Orpheus*.
      I suppose that the most popular of the Shakespearian plays for operatic transformation was *Romeo and Juliet*. Besides the version by Benda, there are operas on this play by Steibelt (1793), Zingarelli (1796), Vaccai (1825), Bellini (1830), Marvhetti (1865), Gounod (1867), d'Ivry (1867), Barkworth (1916), and Zandonai (1922).
      Certain Shakespearean plays have not been used for opera. These are *Antony and Cleopatra*, *Coriolanus*, *Cymbeline*, *Henry VIII*, *Henry IV* (except for the Falstaff sections), *Henry V*, *Love's Labour's Lost*, *Much Ado*, *Pericles*, *Timon*, *Titus Andronicus*, *Richard II*, and *Troilus* (at least before Britten).
17. The question has been answered in part by Edgar Istel in a series of articles called "Verdi and Shakespeare," which are to be found in *Die Musik* (1913) and in *Musical Quarterly* (1916). The original article on the two Othellos appeared in the *Shakespeare Jahrbuch*, LIII (1917), 94-118. I have used this article, but I have gone beyond it in interpreting changes in the Boito-Verdi version of the play. Istel discusses chiefly the plot, though he did make mention of changes in characterization.
18. *Edition of Shakespeare* [1765], VIII, 473; reprinted in D. Nicol Smith, ed., *Shakespeare Criticism: A Selection* (Oxford World's Classics: Oxford, 1936), p. 142.
19. See John Wilcox, "Othello's Crucial Moment," *Shakespeare Association Bulletin*, XXIV (July, 1949), 181-192. Has Iago been talking about his suspicions to Othello *before* this scene? Professor Wilcox thinks so. Verdi changes the plot to make the question irrelevant.
20. *Shaw on Music*, A selection . . . made by Eric Bentley (Doubleday Anchor Books: Garden City, 1955), p. 142.
21. Not that Iago goes "unpunished" in Verdi. He disappears as if ostracized, a fate bad enough. Boito apparently agreed with Dr. Johnson about the characters of *Othello*: Othello has a "fiery openness" and he is "magnanimous, artless, and credulous, boundless in his confidence, ardent in his affection, inflexible in his resolution, and obdurate in his revenge." By contrast Iago has a "cold malignity" and is "silent in his resentment, subtle in his designs, and studious at once of his interest and his vengeance. . . ." Verdi gives no reason for Iago's desire for revenge except the advancement of Cassio, a sufficient reason dramatically. But Iago himself is changed: Shakespeare can show him as furtive, dishonest though apparently honest, and deliberately concealing what he knows; and these are subtleties possible in drama. "In opera you must be graphic," Verdi once wrote. And yet he thought his Iago should be acted as if he were vague, nonchalant, indifferent to everything, skeptical, repugnant: "He should throw off good and evil sentiments lightly, as if he were thinking of something quite different from his actual utterances."
22. *Op cit.*, p. 143.

23. North's theory is discussed in detail by A. C. Bradley, *Shakespearean Tragedy,* 1904. The most recent reprinting is in Meridian Books (New York, 1955). See pp. 341-344.

24. Since musical tones and phrases are not intrinsically allied with content, many minds grope for associations, sometimes merely for the love of associations themselves and sometimes because of a subjective state or feeling of insufficiency when associations are not present. Therefore a great deal of music criticism, based as it is on a desire to make cognitive what is not in the usual sense cognitive, or emotional what is not emotional, is made up of matter to fill the proverbial vacuum. An opera composer skilfully fills this vacuum and satisfies the everyday desire to give significance to tone whose own significance can be nothing but tone.

Billy Budd as Moby Dick: An Alternate Reading

VERN WAGNER

It seems to me that in *Billy Budd* Melville continued to ask what he had asked in *Moby Dick*, *Pierre*, and *The Confidence Man* nearly forty years before: "What *is* it all about anyway, evil and good and all that?" He tempered the view by eliminating the italics — thus giving the thoughtless the comforting suggestion that he had quieted down.[1] But he enriched his picture of disharmonies in this story by pushing further into why's than ever before. Seventy years of living refined, subtilized, and deepened his speculation. The more than thirty years that followed the publication of his last prose work, three decades of silent fermentation relieved only by poetic bursts that seldom hit the mark, this long period of time did not end in any craven conclusion. I am sure Melville never forgot his ideal Bulkington in *Moby Dick* who saw glimpses of

> . . . that mortally intolerable truth; that all deep, earnest thinking is but the intrepid effort of the soul to keep the open independence of her sea; while the wildest winds of heaven and earth conspire to cast her on the treacherous, slavish shore. . . .
>
> But as in landlessness alone resides the highest truth, shoreless, indefinite as God — so, better is it to perish in that howling infinite, than be ingloriously dashed upon the lee, even if that were safety! For worm-like, then, oh! who would craven crawl to land! Terrors of the terrible! is all this agony so vain? Take heart, take heart, O Bulkington! Bear thee grimly, demigod!

Of course *Billy Budd* deals with democracy, naval law, history. Of course it presents on one level an admirable young hero done in by a black-hearted villain — who is aided in his act by a good man manacled to "social justice." But all these things are minor. A man like Herman Melville, writing his last testament, seeking to reveal his final recognition, aiming at posterity or maybe only personal clarification alone (there is no evidence he planned to publish this piece) — such a man will deal with the ultimate question: the true mysteries of iniquity. I believe Melville kept the open independence of his sea of thought. I think he bore himself grimly to the last in the consideration of Lucifer and of God, of crucifixions and the deadly Serpent, and of the ambiguities of white and black.

The writing of *Billy Budd* is dishabille. Nowhere else does Melville write with so relaxed, so humble, so scattered an air. The story is stuffed with digressions, historical flotsam, bits and pieces. The sentences are casual. The paragraphs are entirely tentative, full of "perhaps," "it may be," and "presumably." It hardly ends — and the author apologizes for this. The narrative drags. It is garrulous. *Moby Dick* wanders, too, but there is such vim in the asides, such vigor in the digressions, the reader knows it to be the work of an intense young man at the height of his powers who feels with excruciating force the storms and gales of wide-ranging thought. *Billy Budd* seems to be the work of a tired old man who is more tolerant and more careless. It is all very disarming.

But the writer of *Moby Dick* is still fully evident, and this undress, distant style is nearly all deception. The final manuscript was improperly punctuated, as F. Barron Freeman found, but it was complete enough. Melville had spent nearly two and a half years on the various versions of it, short story, revisions, and final novel. This was a time equal to that which had long before covered nearly all the writing of *White Jacket, Moby Dick,* and *Pierre.* Melville was crafty to pretend senilities, I think, for by means of such tactics he penetrated to greater depths of probabilities than ever before. He did not cry uncle and seek the safety of the lee shore. He exhibits the lowering rage of that aged bull whale in *Moby Dick,* who, an isolato suffering from penal gout, his admiring harem lost, spends his final time regretting final truths. In *Billy Budd* Melville was forced into more devious indirection than ever before, but not this time by the demands of a tender-minded public; rather, the terrible complexities and agonizing suppositions of his own mind compelled him to try this gentler tack to get it said.

So, for example, he comments simply on the chaplain of the warship *Indomitable,* a "minister of the Prince of Peace serving in the host of the God of War — Mars":

> As such, he is as incongruous as that musket of Blucher etc. at Christmas. Why then is he there? Because he indirectly subserves the purposes attested by the cannon [canon?]; because too he leads the sanction of the religion of the meek to that which practically is the abrogation of everything but brute force.

And with "quiet" sardonic wit he explains that "if that lexicon which is based on Holy Writ were any longer popular," it would explain such a man as Claggart; but (he sighs), "one must turn to some authority not liable to the charge of being tinctured with Biblical element." So he turns — or so it seems — to Plato the pagan.

Must such passages because quietly written be taken as quiet acceptance? I think the old wounds ached increasingly at the end and that Melville persisted in being Bulkington, still the very man who, his friend Hawthorne said so memorably in 1856, was one who "can neither believe, nor be comfortable in his unbelief; and he is too honest and courageous not to try to do one or the other." A thicker, more steady view of this final work shows that Melville finally smites the sun as Ahab said he would do if the sun insulted him. Let us examine the record.

Consider Billy. He is a curious figure.

1. When impressed by Lieut. Ratcliffe from the *Rights of Man,* "To the surprise of the ship's company, . . . Billy made no demur. . . . Noting this uncomplaining acquiescence, all but cheerful one might say, the shipmates turned a surprised glance of silent reproach at the sailor." This is odd. Billy is devoid of loyalty, without roots, and a mere chip on the wave.

2. When Billy says, "And good bye to you too, old *Rights of Man!*" Melville quickly declares that Billy intended no satire — he lacked the "sinister dexterity" satire requires. "To deal in double meaning and insinuations of any sort was quite foreign to his nature." How then could we tell Billy a joke? We can't get close to him, for he's another, simple-minded beyond compare.

3. Transferred to the more complicated life of the *Indomitable,* he remains "unaware." He "scarce noted" the subtleties of this new world.

4. Billy has no background. His father? "God knows." He evinced "noble descent," though, and with God as his father and nobility his lineage, he is separated from nearly everybody else.

5. He exists without yet having been proffered "the questionable apple of knowledge." He lacked any of "the wisdom of the serpent"; though "nor yet quite a dove," he had no self-consciousness. He was an "upright barbarian," Adam before the fall. He is mindless, a *tabula rasa* on which no experience had written. He is "very harmlessness itself."

Billy's appearance is that of a blank, empty vacuum; and this is a state of non-being we all know nature abhors. Human growth and development are always a darkening of some sort, and *Billy Budd* fully deals with this particular fact of life. What I think Melville sought to do with Billy was to beat the dusty darkness out so that we can see his content of real humanity. All this was an intricate undertaking and a daring one, for Melville sought to show that the beautiful Billy Budd, nature's boy in truth and in fact, was only another manifestation that nature "paints like the harlot."

Of itself blankness bothers all of us, for it is nothing. An object that is pure, innocent, virgin, ignorant, naive, disturbs the soiled, the corrupt, the experienced, the knowing and the sophisticated — disturbs because we envy and admire simultaneously. A magnet, such a thing cries for substance; it is an irresistible challenge, and we are all like mischievous brats who would throw mud balls on the drying sheets. Are we really supposed to accept the notion that Billy's appearance is a Melvillean ideal? Such a belief implies, then, that Melville also held the Wordsworth-Emerson idea that innocence is godliness since trailing clouds of glory do we come. Melville believed no such thing. Calvin, Schopenhauer, and self study had taught him otherwise.

Human suspicion confirms the validity of this notion. A freshman student of mine recently wrote this: "I don't trust Billy Budd. Something — intuition, or doubt, or something— tells me he's a phony." This boy has never read *Moby Dick* and "The Whiteness of the Whale," for if he had he'd see that in all likelihood Melville thought so too. I think Melville saw that Billy's real attraction was that he was a target with all that unsullied blankness. His only redeeming feature was his stutter, a "flaw" we can feel since it exists — a hint that probably Billy existed too, underneath.

What is made only too evident about Billy is his blindness and willful deafness, his "instinctive" insistence on retaining nonentity. He neither saw Claggart for what he was nor really heard the old Dansker or listened to the mutinous plot. The deaf mute in *The Confidence Man* heard nothing either as he exhibited his signs of "Charity endureth all things" to his fellow passengers aboard the *Fidele*, and he would not see the "No Trust" sign over the barber shop door. Lucy in *Pierre*, blind and deaf by her own virgin dream, does not heed the existence of Isabel's dark fascination as she journeys to New York to join Pierre Glendenning. The admired Jack Chase of *White Jacket* was oblivious too, steeped as he was in beauty. And there is Moby Dick.

What all these figures have as a common appearance is color. They are white, which to Melville at its most extreme was inscrutable blankness but still a hint that "the invisible spheres were formed in fright." It is this "mystic" aspect of white that so infuriated Ahab and so frightened Ishmael: whiteness "when divorced from more kindly associations, and coupled with any object terrible in itself, [serves] to heighten that terror to the furthest bounds," he wrote in "The Whiteness of the Whale." At

162

first no one can see Billy Budd as an object "terrible in itself," for he is a Christ-like "hero," a beautiful golden boy. He lacks even in the old Dansker's sight "any touch of defensive ugliness." But like similar golden lads he too must come to dust, for this is the rule of God.

In the concluding paragraph of "The Whiteness of the Whale," Melville says that light which is white and colorless in itself "if operating without medium upon matter, would touch all objects, even tulips and roses, with its own blank tinge." Billy's horrible quality is that he seems to provide no medium, and when light strikes his matter it hints at a palsied universe that is intolerable. Melville provides a final stop by explaining when he ends the section describing Billy's refusal to dig deeper into the mutiny scheme because he wants to protect himself against the possible consequences of being involved, "But something more, or rather, something else than mere shrewdness is perhaps needful for the due understanding of such a character as Billy Budd's." He does not tell us what the something is — not directly at any rate. Rather, in the paragraph immediately following the remark he shifts to Claggart's monomania ("if that indeed it were"), saying in effect that by watching the dark Claggart we will get that understanding of Billy Budd's character his blankness prevents. This is the decisive moment in the story when the whole account turns to action. The paragraph ends with the foreboding statement, "Something decisive must come of it."

What of this Claggart to whom our attention is thus directed? "What was the matter with the master-at-arms?" What is the matter *of* the wicked John Claggart? — whose "portrait I essay," says Melville, "but shall never hit it." Claggart is likened in one place to "the man of sorrows" when his glance followed the gorgeous figure of that "sea-Hyperion" Billy Budd. This is an odd business since he is so black a villain. He yearns for Billy, "but this [yearning look] was an evanescence, and quickly repented of, as it were, by an immitigable look, pinching and shrivelling the visage into the momentary semblance of a wrinkled walnut." This relationship seems clear. But "Claggart's envy struck deeper" than mere homosexual attraction, and it is here, I think, that the basic explanation of Claggart lies — as Melville wrote earlier, "The point of the present story [turns] on the hidden nature of the master-at-arms," and Melville says that to comprehend Claggart we must pass from normal nature, crossing "the deadly space between." We can understand this, for Melville says specifically that Claggart is a man "in whom was the mania of an evil nature . . . born with him and innate, in short 'a depravity according to nature.'" It is easy to see, therefore, that Claggart must be the Serpent to Billy's Adam, a serpent who possessed "a peculiar ferreting genius" that is becoming to both the infamous snake and a master-at-arms. On this basis the story is to be read as a war between good and evil in which Billy as God's son is pitted against a Lucifer who is filled with "pale ire, envy and despair" and persists eternally (for he is immortal) in battling God by continually destroying God's chosen creature.[2]

The trouble here is that since Billy's emptiness repels, too, we cannot altogether despise his enemy, and a close look at John Claggart's "matter" shows he has a good deal of "medium." Throwing a light on him gives us something.

First, though, there is the question whether natural depravity is a reality in human beings. A modern instance of the naturally depraved is Cathy Ames in Steinbeck's *East of Eden* who was a moral monster, bereft of a sense of good, born without it. She burnt her parents alive at twelve, deserted her twin children at their birth, and ran the most vicious whore house in Salinas — after poisoning her patroness. And had no regrets. Cathy is an extreme example of the cankered born, a romantic imagining of what can be being here. And like all extreme picturings, she is unacceptable since Steinbeck drew her as apart from human kind.

Claggart was no moral monster like this. He was a human being whose abnormal base was "perhaps" monomaniac antagonism. He existed past the deadly space beyond "normal" nature all right, but this is not to say he is absolute evil. What he possessed

— here we take Melville's own "indirection" in order to assess him — was something of the "mysteries of iniquity" which is to say "gross injustices" — and which is probably to say further a sense of inequality. Unlike Cathy he is not pure viciousness but a doubled soul, halfway here and halfway there, helpless to prevent antipathy from lunging forth against "very harmlessness itself." I don't think it is so hard to see why at this point. Claggart's nature could not abide the persistence of the white. Billy's purity detonated his animosity, and though able to apprehend the good he was "powerless to be it." He wept tears of recognition and regret, for he had a "disdain of innocence," and his complaint against Billy was the groan, "to be nothing more than innocent!" That gravelled him. Melville quietly ends this passage by explaining,

> . . . a nature like Claggart's surcharged with energy as such natures almost invariably are, what recourse is left to it but to recoil upon itself and like the scorpion for which the Creator alone is responsible, act out to the end the part allotted it.

And finally, when he looked at Billy for the last time his glance was "the hungry lurch of the torpedo-fish," for his look had sunk to the pre-human, to that of "certain uncatalogued creatures of the deep."

At this point, if we stop, we must decide to condemn Claggart despite our sneaking sympathy with his position. But my main point is not just that he did Billy in to the distress of all kind readers. I think Claggart is meant for much more, for he ruined Billy beforehand by tarnishing his white, or rather, by seeing through it to something else. He forced the astonishing revelation that Billy was a masked man, that his white gold was fraud and deception, that his stutter was by no means only a gimmick designed to disarm the simple but was an opening to Billy's blacker beyond, to his humanity. "Handsome is as handsome does," Claggart said of Billy, and what he meant was that as Billy did nothing his handsomeness was nothing but a blind.[3]

In making his charge against Billy,

> With the measured step and calm collected air of an asylum-physician approaching in the public hall some patient beginning to show indications of a coming paroxysm, Claggart deliberately advanced. . . .

And he won the necessary knowledge he gave his life to find: the knowledge that Billy no more than any other human creature was able to "endure all things." Claggart's sophistication, his sense of iniquity, if you will, taught him the fact that innocence does not truly exist and that its appearance is only pasteboard. In getting Billy to strike him he got Billy to do the unfortunately unchristian human thing in that he made him retaliate a tit for a tat. It was Billy's undoing; it was Claggart's victory; and it was Melville's deep intent.

Much earlier in the story Billy's dark interior had lunged forth in exactly the same way. Aboard the *Rights of Man* he had quelled Red Whiskers, the one holdout among that crew who "out of envy, perhaps" mockingly designated Billy like Claggart later such "a sweet and pleasant fellow." Penetrated too deeply by Red Whiskers, Billy sucked him into position by reasoning with him in a "pleasant way." Then one day "quick as lightening Billy let fly his arm" and converted Red Whiskers into a staunch supporter. How? By giving Red Whiskers the assurance the latter's nature demanded — the evidence of Billy's dark humanity.

Is my interpretation strained at this point? What then of Billy the night before his execution when Melville speaks of "the prone sailor's exterior apparel ["exterior" was a word added to the extended version of the short story], white *jumper*, white duck trousers, each more or less soiled, [that] dimly glimmered in the obscure light of the bay like a patch of discolored snow in early April lingering at some upland cave's black mouth"? Is this not the master's clever stroke, proof that Claggart knew all along Billy's white veiled a blacker beyond? It is not idle to emphasize this. Billy's position at this time is curiously described. Billy himself does not show through the soiled white in "the dirty yellow" light of the lanterns polluting the moonshine "ineffectually struggling." As ever, light striking no medium reveals no substance. Billy's genuine darkness again lay hidden behind the mask of white he had reassumed after killing Claggart.

But we have not done with John Claggart. He does more yet than I have indicated. He exposes Captain Vere too, the half-innocent, middle-blond man who did not shy at Billy's white gold but in his starry way resented Claggart's declaration that "a man-trap may be under his ruddy-tipped daisies." Vere should have called for Claggart's proof of Billy's mutinous behavior. If the false-witness risked the yardarm, in the interests of building good feeling in the crew of his ship, as well as supporting the naval law and etiquette for which he was such a stickler, Vere should have quietly sought out other witnesses to support or ruin Claggart's charges. But no. Since Vere was Starry Vere, mutinous parlous times or no he would do the idealistic, the innocent thing, by skipping the obvious and hasting toward a romantic solution in "practically" testing the accused alone. So Melville adds to his deeper theme: He shows Vere's Budd-like innocence and consequent ignorance ("struck dead by an angel of God," Vere says) and emphasizes Claggart's wisdom in properly assessing Vere's character as well as Billy's. Claggart knew this man, too.

It is not easy to type *Billy Budd*. All Melville says is that it's not a romance.[4] Regardless of type, however, its special value lies in the peculiar Melville context, especially as it elucidates the greatest American novel, its author's own *Moby Dick*, and ultimately as it reveals more "Melville" than anything that had gone before.

In the first place, the similarity between Billy Budd and Moby Dick is striking. At first thought it is ridiculous to equate a pure and lovable young man to a monstrous, man-eating whale; but a slower consideration reveals that if Billy Budd *is* a man-trap as Claggart suggests, then he is cousin-german to the tremendous fish.

We can begin this slower consideration by noting that the

pre-eminent quality in both Billy Budd and Moby Dick is whiteness, the quality that meant the most appalling things to Melville. In Billy the white indicates innocence and goodness to the simple-minded since Billy is no "object terrible in itself." But since the corollary of innocence is unfortunately not only goodness but ignorance too, it is clearly a lack. To Captain Ahab, heaven-bent or hell-bent, he cared not which, the most heaping, the most tasking, of all Moby Dick's characteristics was the completely impenetrable fact of his white. How can you get hold of nothing? And the nothing masks — well, what can it mask? It is inscrutable. Damnation: "Sometimes I think there's naught beyond," says Ahab, and such a possibility was totally intolerable to this very sophisticated man. I must proffer here the reminder that sophistication may be knowledge, but that it is also a worldliness which implies a kind of corruption. Melville fully realized this; in Billy Budd he wrote, "A child's utter innocence is but its blank ignorance, and the innocence more or less wanes as intelligence waxes." Is corruption so awful then? A nurse reminds me it is not per se, for we should witness fleshly wounds wherein corruption through concentration permits cleansing. Nor can it be altogether bad otherwise if we believe in the superior power of reason since corruption is the inseparable corollary of waxing intelligence and *the very contrast that supplies matter to reality*.

I interpret *Moby Dick* here with Ahab as the protagonist. It is what I think Melville meant after all. There is no doubt we can reverse these roles and should for richer reading; so Ernest Hemingway chose to interpret *Moby Dick* when he rewrote it as *The Old Man and the Sea*. (But more about that in another place at another time.) Ahab is a hero. He is classic, tragic, admirable, compelling, magnetic, terrible. We thank God he has loaded the weight of all man's protesting, questioning, resentful mind onto his own back, a human Atlas. Thus burdened he sets himself to solve a Promethean problem, thinking that blankness, masks, and the monstrous Moby Dick himself are possible opponents for human beings.

The full quality of Ahab's monumental anger will never be

fully assessed: What really provided the fuel for his fiery temper? Not the loss of a leg. Not the blasting thunderbolt of God that blistered a line all down his steely length. Ahab had been at schools. He had explored the deep-most sinks of man's inequality. Evermore he had met non-explanation and more iniquity. So he resolved at last to strike at iniquity itself. The depths of the midnight provided no answers; the brightness of noon therefore must. So we see he thought when he looked at the doubloon and saw the sun and the flashing peaks as spurs to his activity. So we know he believed because of Fedallah, the worshipper of the sun, the fire, and the light. So we have it impressed upon us while he adopted Black Pip in order to set him aside and increased his enmity at Moby Dick.

The insulting irony was that Ahab found man can thrust and thrust his penetrative sword into a dark and meaty resistance but never to a final answer. If the dark would yield no ultimate, only further deeps of dark, then the light must, and the lighter the better for his purposes. Hence Ahab's violent and entire rage toward Moby Dick, who was an enemy that should be black by all reasonable law, but who roamed the world as a white Leviathan of mockery. But how can man fight the light, the white, the blank? Starbuck reproached Ahab by crying, "Violence on a dumb brute!" and Ahab was set aflame by the adjective. It is the very dumbness Ahab can't abide because he knows it is deception and fraud.

Just so Claggart identified Billy's dumbness. Be the dumbness agent or be it principal both men sought to wreak their hatred on it, the greatest strength they had. Did Ahab love? As much as Claggart did, I think: They both loved answers, and the whiteness of both Moby Dick and Billy Budd barred the way. Ahab finally drove Moby Dick to retaliation too, and in so doing made Moby Dick show himself to be *not* dumb, not utter white and not blank. Ahab won this much for human kind: He found that white is a lie, for behind its polar, blizzardy veil beats a life not so dissimilar to our own that it will not strike back. Just so much did Claggart win in revealing the "matter" of Billy Budd, for when he accused Billy to his face, Billy did not turn merely pale: ". . . his cheek looked struck as by white leprosy." Ishmael pointed out in *Moby Dick* that the ultimate aspect of white is that it reminds us, when we consider, that "the palsied universe lies before us a leper."

The white is a damnable puzzle to be sure, but Ahab discovered its weakness when it was attached to natural objects: It is only a mask, after all, over existent substance. It is agent, it is not principal, it is not real in itself. Behind it lie the facts of truth. Is virgin virgin? White white? Blond blond? Not unless these things are nothing, and the mind can envision nothing no more than it can infinity. Space must have a stop as time must too, or we are totally adrift. Such a concept is almost inconceivable — or was before 1900. Time did not bend for Melville, nor did space explode, and atoms did not disappear under the most powerful microscopes. So Ahab found only a terrifying hint of the "existence" of nothing. He *had* to rip through the mask, he *had* to find something there, and he did: He found that Moby Dick was only a deceiver after all, and that the universe was real if it was malign.

What then of Claggart? I suggest he is in most respects an exaggerated version of Captain Ahab. Melville gave the screw another turn. A study of Claggart is a study of Melville at seventy — a greatly developed thinker. *Clarel* only served to improve the time from *Moby Dick* to *Billy Budd*. If a man thinks hard for a lifetime, try as he will he can hardly escape from himself unless he *is* a mystic, and Raymond Weaver notwithstanding, Melville was ever the mariner and never the mystic when it counted. It counted in *Billy Budd*. Melville remained Bulkington. He had sailed ever farther from shore into even more perilous infinities.

What then is Claggart? A "sensitive spiritual organization" in contrast to his opponent whose "innocence was his blinder." Both characters, as men, are at opposite extremes of the human scale, but both are still human, nevertheless. Claggart is part Lucifer, a "peculiar human creature the direct reverse of a saint." But Billy

Budd is a peculiar human creature too, though the direct reverse of a devil. Claggart focussed his purple glance on Billy, discovered the truth, and perished for it. Milton did not mean that Lucifer should dominate his poem and be heroic. But he does and he is. We can know him when we can't know God — except in Satan's reflected light — and Satan gets our grudging admiration for his stoutness of heart in fighting Omnipotence. He is, finally, more human than not. So Ahab, that "grand, ungodly, god-like man," is a hero after our own limited human hearts, a protestant against the imperial will of the Father, discontented to accept, to believe, and to knuckle under.

Melville says Billy is no conventional hero. Indeed, he can be no hero at all because he has no content and is "nothing more than innocent." Moby Dick can not be a hero either for he is only a dumb brute. Both lack medium. Both are pristine. Melville says Billy had "one thing amiss in him," his vocal defect. "In this particular Billy was a striking instance that the arch interferer, the envious marplot of Eden still has more or less to do with every human consignment to this planet of earth." It is a "striking instance" because this is Billy's only defect by means of which he can be subverted.

In the never flagging war of immortal Lucifer against God and of Man against mysterious iniquity, such stout warriors can only take advantage of that defect which God in the pride of His own perfection allowed His prime creature, the blemish that would keep human beings from like godliness. Lucifers know this and attack God's vanity — they strike at the sun by forever and forever aiming darts at the weak spot.

Claggart like Ahab could not abide the white mask because he was convinced it covered something else. He sought to tear it off and he did. Beneath the mask was no blankness, no purity, and no blondness. Billy was an artificial blond.

The sealing proof is Billy's famous valedictory, "God bless Captain Vere!" These were his final words as he felt the hemp around his neck, "his only ones, words unobstructed in the utter-

ance." Melville had said earlier that "under sudden provocation
of strong heart-feeling [Billy's] voice . . . was apt to develop . . .
a stutter." Are we supposed to think, then, that there was no
heart in Billy's words? Presumably. At any rate, this line pierced
Vere to the heart because of the unconscious derision of such a
truly Christ-like benediction. It needed no "low laugh from the
hold" for emphasis, but Claggart could have supplied it from his
ocean grave.

Melville's irony here is overwhelming and it capped the climax,
a subtle arrow. As Billy "ascends," an additional signal, a

> preconcerted dumb one was given. At the same moment it
> chanced that the vapory fleece hanging low in the East, was
> shot through with a soft glory as of the fleece of the Lamb of
> God seen in mystical vision. . . .

All the last of the story, five more sections, all these are irony,
too. Like a real symphony, not that one in *Moby Dick,* Melville
stills and quiets the clamor he had aroused by supplying quiet
explanation. He digressed to present the discussion between the
Purser and the Surgeon about Billy's curious absence of muscular
spasm at the moment of death. He added the passages on the
dispersal of the crew, the distorted newspaper report of the case,
the death of Vere, and the sailor's ballad "Billy in the Darbies."
All this is no softening, though, but irony on irony. Melville
quietly apologizes in the midst of these final sections — or so
it seems:

> The symmetry of form attainable in pure fiction cannot so
> readily be achieved in a narration essentially having less to do
> with fable than with fact. Truth uncompromisingly told will
> always have its ragged edges; hence the conclusion of such a
> narration is apt to be less finished than an architectural finial.

What he must mean is that there is no real end because truth is
without an end, residing as he had said long ago "in landlessness
alone . . . shoreless, indefinite as God. . . ."

One other passage requires final mention. Melville writes that after Billy's burial:

> And now it was full day. The fleece of low-hanging vapor had vanished, licked up by the sun that late had so glorified it. And the circumambient air in the cleanness of its serenity was like smooth white marble in the polished block not removed from the marble-dealer's yard.

This is the conclusion of the narration. Melville "quietly" informs us of the frightful fact that frightful white remains, untouched in its immensity. But he implies that it is still assailable because it still remains. It still calls forth from Ahabs, Claggarts and all of us an unresting antagonism and an active protest against what may lie beyond. If naught, says Melville, then let us know. But if something, let us see. At least, let us continue to try to see.

NOTES

1. I have examined some twenty studies made of the story, beginning with E. L. Grant Watson's "Melville's Testament of Acceptance," in *New England Quarterly*, VI, (1935), 319-327. The current interpretation of *Billy Budd*, with little variation, is represented by this comment in one of the newest anthologies of American literature for college students, S. Bradley, R. C. Beatty and E. H. Long, *The American Tradition in Literature* (New York, 1956), I, 709:
   > This testament of reconciliation provides a clarifying contrast with the novels of the earlier period, with the young novelist's heartbreaking rebellion against the overwhelming capacity of evil in man and the universe, and the inescapable doom, as in *Moby-Dick*, of those who pit themselves against the implacable Leviathan of God. In *Billy Budd* the author has made a truce, perhaps a peace. He is at least reconciled to the enigma represented by Captain Vere's ordeal in sentencing Billy to death for killing, in Claggart, the festering "depravity according to nature." By "natural law," Billy is guiltless, but not by "law operating through us. For that law and the rigour of it, we are not responsible."

   Another recent textbook, J. D. Hart and C. Gohdes, *America's Literature* (New York, 1955), p. 514, describes the novel as
   > . . . a controlled tale of an eighteenth-century sailor, symbolic of the passive and pure Christian who, though led to execution by the ways of the world, triumphs in death as his virtue wins him salvation in the hearts of man.

   The first of these interpretations declares that the "horological vs. chronometrical" conflict of *Pierre* is dealt with in the last novel merely as an admitted though sad fact of human life. The second view fails completely to see anything below the surface story of *Billy Budd*, assuming far too easily that Billy must be viewed as a pure hero defeated by evil society but triumphant in man's eyes. Both interpretations fail to suppose Melville kept to the open seas for the last thirty years.

2. It is fit that in his present guise as chief of police Claggart should cause "mysterious discomfort" to the ship's crew. It is ironic of course to note that the policeman ostensibly serving the rule of order should so discommode the sons of Adam. As we know, Satan carries with him a smell of Tartarean smoke, and Claggart like Satan was one deposed, living *incog*, fallen on hard times, no longer a quarter-deck figure, but forced to prowl the bowels of the ship and of existence.

3. Richard Chase in "Dissent on Billy Budd," in the *Partisan Review*, XV (1948), 1216-1217, says:

> The weakness of *Billy Budd* is the central character himself. The trouble is that he is not in any meaningful way what Claggart says he is: "deep" and a "man-trap." He *ought* to be "deep" and in some inescapable human way a "man-trap." Otherwise he cannot function meaningfully in a tragedy which tries to demonstrate the opposition between human nature and the heart on the one hand and law on the other.

Chase also says that Claggart has a claim to sympathy. He notes that Claggart's complaint about Billy, "To be nothing more than innocent!" is somewhat beguiling. But Chase goes no further than this. He concludes: "The fact is that Billy Budd is the final, and almost the first — first *crucial* — self-indulgence of a great intelligence." Chase almost had it here, but failed to think far enough.

Another study of depravity is in *The Scarlet Letter* — with which Melville was of course quite familiar. The depravity is in the character of the black Roger Chillingworth. But who gets sympathy in this novel? Hester Prynne, the predominantly red and human? Arthur Dimmesdale, the palely white and loitering? Only D. H. Lawrence asserts that Chillingworth has a case, but his argument is impressive, for aside from his shocking attack on Hester as a man-eater, he made very clear that the villainous Roger, who is also filled with pale ire, envy and despair, fulfills a necessary human role in exposing the blond fraudulence of Dimmesdale.

4. It is easy to call *Billy Budd* a tragedy. In most interpretations Billy is a tragic hero in classical, Aristotelian terms. The explanation is that Billy is a good man whose flaw is the stutter that caused his last minute of passion. Catharsis is achieved in the pity Billy excites, the fear his unjust execution arouses; purgation comes from our realization of his apotheosis, his "triumph in the hearts of men," when he forgives Vere, the unwilling executioner. But Billy never recognized the flaw, and the flaw itself is unacceptable since the stutter is only physical and the moment of passionate temper was accidental in its result. Billy thus fails to be a tragic hero because he has no mind and no real will.

Captain Vere can be suggested as the tragic hero, too. He fits the classic pattern better in some ways, especially in that he is a good man who comes to full recognition of what his achieved position in the world has forced him to do. But no or little catharsis is possible with Vere as hero, since even his defeat in wanting to save Billy, "the angel of God," was only academic, so to speak.

No definition of tragedy is apt, of course, unless it is founded on the realization that pride is the essential base of the tragic hero. Thus Arthur Miller's contemporary definition has merit:

> The tragic feeling is evoked in us when we are in the presence of a character who is ready to lay down his life, if need be, to secure one thing — his sense of personal dignity.

Applying this definition to *Billy Budd*, the curious result is that only Claggart fits the formula — if we believe that Claggart's "essence" was a sense of personal dignity or pride that demanded Billy's destruction.

The final result of my speculation is that I have decided *Billy Budd* is no tragedy in any ordinary formulistic sense. It is nothing so romantic. It may well be a parody of tragedy, however, for the wicked Claggart is genuinely heroic in both Aristotle's terms — and Arthur Miller's. The final question is whether Claggart is a "good" man, good enough to elicit the reader's admiration and sympathy.

12.   *The Development of*
Frank Norris's Philosophy

ARNOLD L. GOLDSMITH

Henry James once wrote that "when vigorous writers have reached maturity, we are at liberty to gather from their works some expression of a total view of the world they have been so actively observing."[1] Benjamin Franklin Norris was certainly a vigorous writer whose powers of observation were acute, but his premature death kept him from attaining that total world view of which James speaks. That Norris was always groping towards such a philosophy is evident to any student of his writing, but Norris was not a systematic thinker, and it is this very groping with its many inconsistencies which has led most critics to reproach him.

Underlying the genetic growth of his world view is Norris's constant questioning the place of man in a universe of natural law and order. Like many another author fifty years ago, Norris wondered whether man is the master of his environment and destiny or the victim of forces beyond his control. The problems of fate, chance, free will, hereditary and environmental determinism fascinated him, and his ideas sometimes changed from year to year, story to story, and book to book. Several critics have pointed out inconsistencies in his individual works, but none, it seems, has tried to trace the development of his philosophical views throughout his writing career.

I shall outline four general stages in the evolution of Norris's philosophy and suggest reasons for his changes of opinion. The dates of the four stages are somewhat arbitrary and are not intended to be restrictive. Writers do not throw open their bedroom windows on January 1 and proclaim, "This year I will be a naturalistic pessimist; next year I'll be a romantic optimist."

The first of the four stages covers approximately the years 1891-5.

175

Only three works from this period merit serious attention in the evolution of Norris's philosophical ideas. The first is the short story "Lauth," which appeared in the *Overland Monthly* in 1893. The theme of this tale about a medieval doctor's attempt to bring back to life a student-warrior, Lauth, killed in battle is that "life cannot exist without the soul any more than the soul, at least upon this earth, can exist without life. Body, soul, and life, three in one; this is a trinity."[2] Lauth's atavistic decline after being brought back from the dead proves that man's soul "is the chiefest energy of his existence; take that away and he is no longer a man. . . ." It is the soul which makes "the difference between man and brute. . . . There is no . . . life half human, half animal. The most brutish man is still immeasurably higher than the most human brute."[3]

Less optimistic but equally concerned with the nature of man and the brute is Norris's first novel, written when he was a student at Harvard. There he wrote a full length study of atavism called *Vandover and the Brute*. This is the story of the disintegration of an art student who, unable to control his sensual appetite, temporarily thinks that he has turned into a wolf. His downfall is brought about by chance, animal intuition, and lack of will power. That he did have, at the age of twenty-one, both a soul, "the chiefest energy" of man's existence, and will power can be seen when Norris writes, "Vice had no hold on him. The brute had grown larger in him, but he knew that he had the creature in hand. He was its master and only on rare occasions did he permit himself to gratify its demands, feeding its abominable hunger from that part of him which he knew to be the purest, the cleanest, and the best."[4]

Unfortunately, the young artist loses this control and becomes much lower than "the most human brute." Vandover, says Norris, became another victim of ". . . life, . . . the great mysterious force that spun the whole of nature and that sent it onward like some enormous engine, resistless, relentless: an engine that sped straight forward driving before it the infinite herd of humanity, driving it on at breathless speed through all eternity, driving it no one knew whither, crushing out inexorably all those who lagged behind the herd and who fell from exhaustion, grinding them to dust beneath its myriad iron wheels. . . ."[5]

Though not ground to dust, by the end of the novel Vandover is ruined. His fate distressed some critics like Professors Walker and Marchand, who felt that Norris was guilty of sympathizing with Vandover, giving him free will and then condemning him for doing wrong. But there is nothing inconsistent in giving a character freedom of will and a sense of moral responsibility and then blaming him for not using it. At this early stage in his literary career, Norris did not have the objectivity and amorality of the other naturalists who had such a marked influence on his later writing. Norris simply wanted to illustrate rather graphically what happens to an individual who allows moral turpitude to govern his actions rather than free will. Although he felt sorry for Vandover, that was no reason for his softening what he thought would be the tragic results of such behavior.

The third major work of this period is a novel which was not published until 1899, but since Norris's biographers believe that he wrote most of it at the same time as *Vandover and the Brute,* it will be treated here. It is, by far, the most pessimistic of the three literary works of the first stage and anticipates the pessimism of the next period. Nor is this growing pessimism about the efficacy of free will hard to understand when one remembers that in 1894 Norris's father's divorce cut him off from an inheritance of almost a million dollars. The elder Norris's remarriage must have caused Frank, accustomed to a gentleman's mode of living, considerable unhappiness, particularly since he was earning only fifty dollars a month from *McClure's.* Added to these problems was his ill health brought on by severe attacks of African fever.

Whatever may have been the cause, *McTeague* reflects Norris's characteristic opinion that man is a victim of forces beyond his control. It is his most naturalistic novel and the only one in which he unequivocally denies free will to his characters and portrays them as victims of heredity, environment, and chance. The protagonist, a dentist with an enormous build and brute strength, acts only by instinct and impulse, a trait he holds in common with the bull, horse, bear, ape, elephant and other animals with whom he is constantly compared. The brute in him lies close to the surface. Once, when he shrieks in pain after having been bitten in the ear in a fight, the sound is described as "something no longer human; it was rather an echo from the jungle."[6]

It is chance that brings Trina and Mac together and wins Trina $5000 in a lottery. When Trina debates whether she really loves the dentist and chooses him of her own volition, Norris makes it perfectly clear that no choice was involved. "It is," he says, "a spell, a witchery, ruled by chance alone, inexplicable."[7] And Mac, in love, is "like some colossal brute trapped in a delicate, invisible mesh, raging, exasperated, powerless to extricate himself."[8] This point is bluntly made again and again: "Neither of them was to blame. From the first they had not sought each other. Chance had brought them face to face, and mysterious instincts as ungovernable as the winds of heaven were at work knitting their lives together. Neither of them had asked that this should be — that their destinies, their very souls, should be the sport of chance. If they could have known, they would have shunned the fearful risk. But they were allowed no voice in the matter. Why should it be?"[9]

Not only does chance govern the destinies of Mac and Trina, but also "mysterious instincts." One of these is "the evil of an entire race [which] flowed in Mac's veins."[10] This he has inherited from hundreds of generations before him. Another of these "instincts" for which he cannot be blamed is his love of liquor inherited from his father, who drank himself to death. As long as Mac drinks harmless steam beer he is all right, but when anxiety drives him to whisky, he becomes vicious. Nor is Trina really responsible for her miserliness, which is also inherited, as the following passage shows: "A good deal of peasant blood still ran undiluted in her veins, and she had all the instinct of a hardy and penurious mountain race — the instinct which saves without any thought, without idea of consequence — saving for the sake of saving, hoarding without knowing why."[11]

Environment completes and dominates the triumvirate of forces which produce McTeague's downfall and impel him to murder Trina. Although many of Norris's contemporaries did not see this, Isaac Marcosson did, as literary editor of the *Louisville Times*. In his review of the book he calls McTeague "a coarse, prosaic creature, who was the product of those early, semi-savage days" in primitive California. "The man is a great, coarse grained hulk, the elements of his life as a driver boy at a mine ever dominant in his make-up and his actions." As a dentist in a poor neighborhood "he is the creature of his environment. There is scarcely any variety in the monotony of his life. The cable cars trundle by his door by day and at night the ducks and geese cackle in the market near his office. He drinks more beer, pulls more teeth and becomes more stupid."[12] Marcosson's emphasis on McTeague's being a victim of his environment is all the more significant in the light of Norris's own statement that Marcosson "saw every point I tried to make in *McTeague* and didn't misunderstand where many other critics have been thick-witted enough."[13]

As the novel progresses, environmental determinism becomes even more important. With Mac out of work and unable to adjust himself to his new situation, the McTeagues move to a succession of cheaper apartments, each one more gloomy and dismal than the one before. As Orrington Cozzens Ramsay points out, "This decline in environment both reflects and hastens the degeneration of their characters."[14] Mac's downfall comes swiftly. He robs and deserts Trina, who becomes a charwoman in a school. One night, Mac enters the school and kills her. From that moment on he becomes a hunted beast until his luck gives out when he is handcuffed to Marcus's corpse in the middle of Death Valley.

While Norris was writing *McTeague* and *Vandover* at Harvard, he was obviously moving away from the romantic idealism expressed in "Lauth." The years 1895-1899 saw his pessimistic naturalism expressed in two short stories, an important dialogue, and *McTeague,* which was finally completed and published one year before the twentieth century.

The stories, "A Reversion to Type" and "Son of a Sheik," dramatize Norris's belief that man's freedom is strictly limited by heredity and environment. Paul Schuster, the respectable department store floor-walker in the former, would never have committed highway robbery and murder if he had not got drunk one day and thrust himself "under the dominion of unknown, unknowable impulses and passions."[15] Poor Schuster was not to blame for his crime because "like all the rest of us, [he] was not merely himself. He was his ancestors as well,"[16] particularly his grandfather who had served a life sentence in San Quentin for highway robbery.

The hero of "Son of a Sheik" is Bab Azzoun, a French government official who is the son of a Kabyle sheik. One day, when his fierce countrymen attack the French military expedition to which he is attached in North Africa, he suddenly remembers his youth spent in his father's tent among his Arab brethren. "In an instant of time all the long years of culture and education were stripped away as a garment. Once more he stood and stepped the Kabyle."[17] Shouting the shrill battle cry of his countrymen, he leaped upon a riderless horse and disappeared never to be seen again by his French friends. Thus Norris implies not only that environment is a latent determining factor in human behavior, but that the memories of *early* environment (the first ten years of Bab's life) might motivate a sudden change in action even if they had remained dormant for many years under much different conditions such as Bab's nineteen years of education and governmental work in France.

More significant than both of these stories as a statement of Norris's philosophy is a dialogue first printed in *The San Francisco Wave,* May 22, 1897. For some strange reason it has been almost completely ignored by all of Norris's critics and biographers. This is especially surprising since it is basic to any understanding of the development of Norris's philosophy. Called "The Puppets and the Puppy," it is a satirical allegory in which the philosophical problems of free will, determinism, and mechanism are debated by the following characters: a lead soldier, a doll, a mechanical rabbit, a chessman (queen's bishop) and Japhet, a wooden figure from Noah's Ark. The scene is a child's playroom and the time is the night after Christmas.

In the first part of the dialogue the queen's bishop denies the existence of God ("There is no boy, except that which exists in your own imaginations"[18]) but acknowledges that "there is, perhaps a certain force that moves us from time to time — a certain vague power, not ourselves, that shifts us here and there. All of us chessmen believe in that."[19] However, he makes it clear that "this force, is not omnipotent. It can move us only along certain lines. I still retain my individuality — still have my own will. My lines are not those of the knight or the pawn, or the castle, and no power in the room can make them so. I am a free agent — that's what is so terrible."[20] (Here Norris again refers to the mysterious life force which had been mentioned in *Vandover* and was to be an important part of almost every serious work he wrote, but his concept of man's degree of free will within the framework of this force was to change from period to period.)

The other toys disagree with the queen's bishop, the mechanical rabbit presenting the teleological argument to prove the existence of God (someone had to wind up his mechanism to make him play his cymbals). The toys also dispute the probability of immortality, with the lead soldier defending reincarnation. Once again, the queen's bishop disagrees with all, arguing that nothing comes after death. When we die, he says, our bodies disintegrate and are "finally absorbed by the elements."[21] His theory of mechanistic atomism (or what Edwin Arlington Robinson aptly called "a blind atomic pilgrimage") must have been convincing because the rabbit is won over.

The toys then dispute the merits of "falling-down," apparently an action symbolizing suicide, or more likely, fear to stand up and live realistically in a world marked by a fierce struggle for existence. The queen's bishop argues that "falling-down" capriciously is terrible because "it would disarrange the vast, grand plan of events."[22] He insists on staying upright because in so doing "we are only helping on the magnificent, incomprehensible aim of the room."[23] In other words, the individual must exercise his free will within the limits of the natural order of the universe.

The conversation at this point turns to the relativity of moral standards. The lead soldier refuses to accept an absolute moral law applying to everyone, since some unfortunate individuals are "twisted and bent" by forces beyond their control, such as heredity and environment. The queen's bishop admits that it is hard to understand how some people can be blamed for moral deficiencies when, as the soldier points out, "They were doomed before they were cast, and were thrown away afterward."[24] Admitting that such things are incomprehensible, the chessman insists that "there must be a reason in them."[25] (This kind of Browningesque faith and optimism will be seen more fully developed in the controversial ending of *The Octopus*. There, Norris tries to rationalize and explain individual suffering in terms of the ultimate betterment of the entire race, a theory which he had not fully arrived at in 1897.)

Suddenly, while the toys are discussing the mystery of their origin, Sobby, a fox terrier puppy, enters the room and makes short work of them. The queen's bishop is slightly more fortunate than some of his friends, who are annihilated, and as he disappears down the register to oblivion, he mutters vaguely "something about the 'vast, resistless forces of nature.' "[26]

What does all of this add up to in Norris's mind? The puppy (a small scale Moby Dick) obviously symbolizes the capriciousness and omnipotence of nature and natural law, which does not always follow the orderly lines claimed by the queen's bishop. Like a hurricane or an earthquake, the capricious puppy sweeps away his helpless victims. Therefore, the toys (men) are but puppets in the hands of the mysterious natural forces which govern all human activity. Although the queen's bishop insisted that "this force is not omnipotent" and that he is a free agent with limited free will, he soon finds out how limited it really is as he plummets helplessly down the register. This ironic ending, undercutting all of the chessman's arguments, had been foreshadowed by the epigraph at the beginning of the dialogue: "There are more things in your philosophy than are dreamed of in Heaven and Earth."[27] This amusingly distorted quotation is a satirical barb aimed at all of the puppets, especially the queen's bishop and all such people who think that they have any degree of control over their destinies.

"The Puppets and the Puppy" ends the second period of Norris's groping for an understanding of man and his place in the universe. The third period is probably the most surprising since Norris, like a pendulum, swung almost to the opposite extreme and literally celebrated man's freedom of will with only minor limitations. Here he let loose all of his boyish romanticism and allowed himself to be swept along emotionally by the popular intellectual current of the times. This was the era of Anglo-Saxonism and supermen, of the Leonard Wood's, Teddy Roosevelt's, Andrew Carnegie's, and J. P. Morgan's. This kind of romantic idealism had always appealed to Norris, though in *Mc-Teague* his realistic, scientific observations had kept his emotionalism pretty well under control.

And he had more reason to be optimistic now. His literary reputation was growing. As a reward for his articles and stories in *The Wave*, especially his romantic novel *Moran of the 'Lady Letty,'* *McClure's Magazine* had invited him to come East. Writing *Moran*, a two-fisted tale of adventure and love on the high seas, had been ridiculously easy, and *A Man's Woman* (1900) was in the same romantic vein. In private, Norris apologized for this book, saying that "it's a kind of theatrical sort with a lot of niggling analysis to try to justify the violent action of the first few chapters. It is very slovenly put together and there are only two real people in all its 100,000 words."[28] Though this was obviously a potboiler written simply to make money and enhance his popularity, it merits serious attention here because it represents Norris's third stage, which lasted about a year.

Ward Bennett, the hero of *A Man's Woman*, is the antithesis of Vandover and McTeague. If ever a man had almost unlimited free will, it is this commander of the Freja Arctic Exploring Expedition. Despite prodigious Arctic obstacles, he firmly writes in his journal, "I am no whit disheartened. Succeed I must and shall."[29] Nature (which in *The Octopus* is described as being indifferent to man, not hostile) is Bennett's bitter enemy. Conditions become desperate, and "the nearness of the enemy strung Bennett's nerves taut as harp strings. His will hardened to the flinty hardness of the ice itself."[30] Men die, dogs are eaten, the elements seem insurmountable, but "for a last time that iron will rose up in mighty protest of defeat. No, no, no; he was not beaten; he would live; he, the strongest, the fittest, would survive."[31] That Norris refers here to Darwin and Spencer and their deterministic philosophy in the midst of a passage describing Bennett's dynamic free will is especially significant because it reveals his rooted belief that the life force is an engine which works inexorably. Unconscious of any inconsistency or contradiction, Norris emotively accepts Bennett's freedom within this framework. Thus, the philosophical ideas in *A Man's Woman* differ from those in the other novels mainly in Norris's shifting the emphasis from the inhibiting forces to man's freedom despite them.

Bennett is not the only strong willed character in this book. There is also Lloyd Searight, a nurse, and a clash between the two is dramatically inevitable. The opportunity arises when Bennett is determined to make Lloyd leave a typhoid fever case which might endanger her health. "The force of his will," says Norris, "seemed brusquely to be quadrupled and decupled. He would do as he desired; come what might he would gain his end."[32] Lloyd is equally determined to remain at her post of duty despite the danger. She wonders to herself, "Where under the blue sky was the power that could break down her will?"[33]

The crisis is intensified when Bennett learns that the victim is his own best friend, Ferris. He must now make a momentous decision. If he forces Lloyd to leave, Ferris will probably die; if she stays, she will probably succumb to the disease. He decides to make her leave. Despite her frantic pleas and revelation that she loves Bennett, he blocks her way when she is needed upstairs. Lloyd sinks into a chair and weeps violently. Ward has won — "his will remained unbroken. . . ."[34]

The loss of Ferris, who dies, and the end of his romance with Lloyd are accepted by Bennett as his own fault. He refuses to blame fate or chance but laments that he was defeated "by his very self's self, crushed by the engine he himself had set in motion, shattered by the recoil of the very force that for so long had dwelt within himself."[35] The two lovers are brought together again when Bennett now comes down with typhoid fever and when Lloyd, who has *voluntarily*[36] confessed to the other nurses that she had committed the cardinal sin of deserting a patient, is assigned to this new case. This time when he insists upon her leaving the sickroom, his weakened body does not have the strength to enforce his will. Lloyd is the stronger of the two and for the first time she begins to "understand that the mastery of self, the steady, firm control of natural, intuitive impulses, selfish because natural, was a progression. Each victory not only gained the immediate end in view, but braced the mind and increased the force of will for the next shock, the next struggle."[37]

Ward finally recovers and both he and Lloyd renounce their careers, get married, and settle down to a quiet life. But Lloyd soon sees that Bennett is unhappy writing books and longs for the strenuous life of an explorer. She realizes that "some great engine ordained of heaven to run its appointed course had come to a standstill, was rusting to its ruin, and that she alone of all the world had power to grasp its lever to send it on its way."[38]

Norris repeats his favorite figure of speech in expressing this philosophy; however, its importance this time lies not in its mechanism or predestinarianism but in its emphatic acceptance of limited free will in the natural order of things. Lloyd has the will power Vandover lost. Only she can make the decision which will take her husband from her. She pulls the lever. As the novel ends, Bennett's ship leaves for the North Pole.

The fourth and final period of Norris's philosophical groping covers the years 1901-1902, when he died. To some critics, the two sociological novels of this period — *The Octopus* and *The Pit* — are his most important works. Norris said this himself. While working on *The Octopus,* he wrote to Isaac Marcosson that it was "the best thing far and away I ever did." He added that he was going back to the style of *McTeague* and that the wheat trilogy would be "straight naturalism, with all the guts I can get into it."[39] Did this mean that the characters of *The Octopus* and *The Pit* would be the absolutely passive victims of chance, heredity, and environment the way Trina and Mac were? A close analysis of both novels proves that there is a significant difference. This same analysis will reveal the final — though probably tentative — conclusions Norris arrived at in formulating the answers to the questions which had disturbed him for so long. As might be expected, the new view is a mixture of the philosophical ideas he had been expressing in the three previous periods. In fact, it is one that had been repudiated in "The Puppets and the Puppy," almost ten years earlier.

In 1901 an anonymous reviewer of *The Octopus* felt that "the final impression on the reader is that the individual will has no sway or freedom, but is beaten down by inanimate force."[40] Ernest Marchand agrees and considers the characters of the novel mere "pawns" caught between two impersonal forces, nature and economics. On the surface this seems to be true, but even though free will is strictly limited in *The Octopus*, it is not completely denied as it was in *McTeague*. Nor are the characters mere pawns as were the toys in "The Puppets and the Puppy," who were all destroyed through no act of their own but by the inexplicable capriciousness of nature. On the contrary, though Buck Annixter is killed and Magnus Derrick loses his mind, each man is endowed with the volition to make certain limited decisions crucial to his future. These decisions might be influenced by antecedent causes, but the individual finally makes a definite choice, not acting on uncontrollable impulse or animalistic instinct. He acts, and is not just acted upon, as are McTeague, Vandover, Paul Schuster, and Bab Azzoun.

Among Norris's notes for *The Octopus,* there is the following sketch of Buck Annixter: "Obstinate, contrary, dictatorial, wilful." He has "great executive ability," is "very shrewd, far-sighted, [and] suspicious."[41] The word *wilful* is significant and immediately distinguishes this rancher from the San Francisco dentist. Annixter, by the end of the novel, might be the victim of relentless forces, but unlike Vandover and McTeague, he fights his oppressors every inch of the way. Furthermore, he has the strength and will power to change his character. Whereas at first he is egotistical, selfish, and contrary, his love for the dairymaid Hilma converts him to a life of altruism. Where Vandover and McTeague are unable to improve themselves, Annixter is able to and does. He makes a respectable home for Hilma and gives food and shelter to Mrs. Dyke and her grand-daughter Sidney, letting them live in the house that Hilma's folks used to occupy. He is no fatalist, no puppet, no passive spectator as he struts on the stage of life.

Limited free will is also illustrated in the life of Magnus Derrick, who is faced with a bitter dilemma. On the one horn is the upholding of his incorruptible honor and the resulting economic ruin; on the other is the loss of his honor and the protection of his wealth. The farmers in the San Joaquin Valley look to him for leadership in their struggle against the railroad. They form a ranchers' league, the executives of which, unknown to the other members, plan to use legislative bribery as their only means of combating their enemy on equal terms. Since

188

Magnus will automatically share the benefits of the reduced railroad rates if their plan succeeds, they plead with him to pay his share of the expenses and take a chance along with the rest. But Mrs. Derrick, intuitively sensing the disastrous outcome of their plans, tries desperately to stop her husband from joining.

The night of Annixter's big barn dance, when the news suddenly comes that the road has put up the ranchers' land for sale at a ruinous price, Magnus finally decides to join the league. It is true that economic necessity influenced this choice, but it is the kind of clear headed decision that McTeague was incapable of making. Once Magnus *voluntarily* accepts the leadership, his conscience begins to bother him. At this point, however, it is too late. Like a man who decides to cross a street on the wrong light and then finds himself trapped by the oncoming traffic, Derrick is "hopelessly caught in the mesh. Wrong seemed indissolubly knitted into the texture of right. He was blinded, dizzied, overwhelmed, caught in the current of events and hurried along he knew not where. He resigned himself."[42]

In *The Octopus*, then, Norris no longer denies free will as he did in "The Puppets and the Puppy," nor does he exalt its almost unlimited powers as he did in *A Man's Woman*. Here he has arrived at the belief that though the individual has free will, it is strictly limited in a universe governed by certain natural and economic laws. The most explicit statement of this philosophy is found in Norris's description of Mrs. Derrick's thoughts, as she tries in vain to keep her husband from joining the league. She

> felt vividly that certain uncongeniality which, when all is said, forever remains between humanity and the earth that supports it. She recognized the colossal indifference of nature, not hostile, even kindly and friendly, so long as the human antswarm was submissive, working with it, hurrying along at its side in the mysterious march of the centuries. Let, however, the insect rebel, strive to make head against the power of this nature, and at once it becomes relentless, a gigantic engine, a vast power, huge, terrible; a leviathan with a heart of steel, knowing

no compunction, no forgiveness, no tolerance; crushing out the human atom with soundless calm, the agony of destruction sending never a jar, never the faintest tremor through all that prodigious mechanism of wheels and cogs.[43]

These ideas and the imagery in which they are expressed are by now annoyingly familiar to Norris's reader. Here once again is the machine of life governed by natural law. This natural law is indifferent to man: winter follows summer whether or not man is provided with warm clothes, fuel, and shelter. Sometimes nature is even *kind* and *friendly* to man: sunny skies, fertile soil, and adequate rainfall yield bountiful crops. Mrs. Derrick feels that as long as man works and plays within the limits of natural laws and keeps pace with nature, its goodness and bounty will help him thrive. However, should man forget his place in the order of things and try to cross nature as though he had unlimited free will, nature's indifference and kindliness will turn to relentless hatred and destroy him.

The San Joaquin ranchers have, according to Norris, rebelled against the natural laws of supply and demand. To the reader's surprise, Norris is naively sympathetic towards Shelgrim, the president of the railroad, who tells Presley that

> Railroads build themselves. Where there is a demand sooner or later there will be a supply. Mr. Derrick, does he grow his wheat? What do I count for? Do I build the railroad? You are dealing with forces, young man, when you speak of wheat and the railroads, not with men. There is the wheat, the supply. It must be carried to feed the people. There is the demand. The wheat is one force, the railroad another, and there is the law that governs them — supply and demand. Men have only little to do with the whole business. Complications may arise, conditions, that bear hard on the individual — crush him maybe — but the wheat will be carried to feed the people as inevitably as it will grow. If you want to fasten the blame of the affair at Los Muertos on any one person, you will make a mistake. Blame conditions, not men.[44]

In this way, the smooth talking Shelgrim has convinced not only Presley but the confused Frank Norris as well that building the railroad is one of the mysterious forces of nature just like growing wheat, both of which are governed by the ageless law of supply and demand. Though free will and human effort are minimized ("Men have only little to do in the whole business"), they are not denied completely.

As *The Octopus* ends, Norris obtrusively introduces a new idea which was to dominate his philosophy in this final period. It is expressed by Vanamee, who tells Presley that in life, "The individual suffers but the race goes on . . . the larger view always and through all shams, all wickedness, discovers the truth that will, in the end, prevail, and all things surely, inevitably, resistlessly work together for good."[45] This comes as a stunning, unconvincing, and disappointing revelation to the reader. After having aroused great sympathy for Annixter, Magnus, and all of the other ranchers who fought against the railroad, Norris blames nobody for their destruction and even feels that out of all this evil will come good. Probably Norris intended to dramatize this theory in *The Wolf,* the third volume of his trilogy which he never wrote, but the injection of this idea here is as illogical and contradictory as having *Cinderella* or *Snow White* conclude with a theory concerning the omnipotence and inevitability of evil in this world.

The last novel Norris wrote was *The Pit,* the second part of his proposed trilogy, the epic of the wheat. It is a good illustration of Norris's philosophy of this final period. Here again is his determinism with its acceptance of a limited free will in a world of immutable natural laws.

Curtis Jadwin is more wilful than any of Norris's previous creations. He is an opportunistic, self-centered, merciless businessman intent on amassing a fortune and power. His battlefield is the Board of Trade Building in Chicago. There "he was a being transformed, case hardened, supremely selfish, asking no quarters; no, nor giving any. Fouled with the clutchings and grapplings of the attack, besmirched with the elbowing of low associates and obscure allies, he set his feet toward conquest and mingled with the marchings of an army that surged forever forward and back; now in merciless assault, beating the fallen enemy under foot, now in repulse, equally merciless, trampling down auxiliaries of the day before, in a panic dash for safety, always cruel, always selfish, always pitiless."[46]

Jadwin amasses a great fortune through his own initiative and industry, but, like the ranchers in *The Octopus*, he tries to circumvent the inexplicable force of natural law and is ruined. His mistake is trying to corner the world's wheat market. His early success fans the embers of his obsession into a monomania which consumes him. When his wife, Laura, complains that he is completely neglecting her since he has become so absorbed in his business, Jadwin answers passionately, "You think I am wilfully doing this! You don't know, you haven't a guess. I corner the wheat! Great heavens, it is the wheat that has cornered me. The corner made itself. I happened to stand between two sets of circumstances, and they made me do what I've done. I couldn't get out of it now, with all the good will in the world."[47]

Like most sufferers from excessive selfhood, Jadwin blames forces beyond his control for his madness. In his attempt to corner the market, he rides the summit of a gigantic wave until he learns that a large new wheat crop is about to ruin him. As the wave breaks and he goes under, he realizes that he has rebelled fruitlessly against the universal natural order which is omnipotent. He realizes that "the wheat had grown itself; demand and supply, these were the two great laws the wheat obeyed."[48] It was the mysterious life force, not any single man or group of men, which had beaten him. What he does not admit, however, is that his dynamic will made the crucial decision to try to corner the wheat market in the first place, and this decision had its share in bringing about his downfall.

Norris obviously admires Jadwin's dynamic, free-willed rise to power and even suggests at the end of *The Pit* that this titanic figure, after being nursed back to health by Laura, will start all over again in business. Laura, too, has the free will to reject the tempting offer to run away with the artist Courthell and instead remains faithfully by the side of her husband. She comforts him with the optimistic reminder that "the world is all before us where to choose."[49] Once again Norris finds it impossible to accept a complete denial of the efficacy of human will.[50]

The Browningesque optimism which was so inappropriate at the end of *The Octopus* is found in *The Pit,* too. Sheldon Courthell tells Laura that "a little good contributed by everybody to the race is of more, infinitely more importance than a great deal of good contributed by one individual to another."[51] Laura finally sees this, too, and says:

> The individual — I, Laura Jadwin — counts for nothing. It is the type to which I belong that's important, the mould, the form, the sort of composite photograph of hundreds of thousands of Laura Jadwins. . . . But the type Laura Jadwin, that always remains, doesn't it? One must help building up only the permanent things. Then, let's see, the individual may deteriorate but the type always grows better. . . . It began good . . . and can never go back of that original good. Something keeps it from going below a certain point, and it is left to us to lift it higher and higher. No, the type can't be bad. Of course the type is more important than the individual. And that something that keeps it from going below a certain point is God.[52]

The Pit was the last full length book Norris wrote. His death ended the philosophical probing found throughout his writing. Having denied free will in "The Puppets and the Puppy" and *McTeague* and accepted it with minor reservations in *A Man's Woman,* Norris finally arrived at a realistic, empirical compromise: in a universe governed by a mysterious life force, man has only limited free will. Though men may frequently be the victims of chance, heredity, environment, and life itself, mankind evolves steadily upward, and good will ultimately prevail. Thus, ten years after writing "Lauth," Norris still had optimistic faith in the infinite perfectibility of man. It is this optimistic world view which places his complete works on the literary bridge between romanticism and naturalism.

NOTES

1. "Ivan Turgenev," in *Henry James: Representative Selections, with Introduction, Bibliography, and Notes,* ed. by Lyon Richardson (New York, 1941), p. 34.
2. "Lauth," *Collected Writings* (New York, 1928), p. 145.
3. *Ibid.,* p. 147.
4. *Vandover and the Brute* (New York, 1928), p. 25.
5. *Ibid.,* p. 202. In this and other quoted passages, I have altered Norris's excessive capitalization.
6. *McTeague* (New York, 1914), p. 54.
7. *Ibid.,* p. 89.
8. *Ibid.,* p. 54.
9. *Ibid.,* p. 89.
10. *Ibid.,* p. 32.
11. *Ibid.,* p. 86.
12. "The Story of McTeague," *Louisville Times,* March 13, 1899, p. 6.
13. Isaac Marcosson, *Adventures in Interviewing* (New York, 1923), p. 225.
14. See the unpublished dissertation, University of Wisconsin (1950), by Orrington Cozzens Ramsay, "Frank Norris and Environment," p. 62.
15. Frank Norris, "A Reversion to Type," in *The Third Circle* (New York, 1928), p. 45.
16. *Ibid.*
17. Frank Norris, "Son of a Sheik," in *The Third Circle,* p. 74.
18. *Frank Norris of "The Wave"; Stories and Sketches from the San Francisco Weekly, 1893 to 1897* (San Francisco, 1931), p. 175.
19. *Ibid.,* p. 176.
20. *Ibid.*
21. *Ibid.,* p. 177.
22. *Ibid.,* p. 178.
23. *Ibid.*
24. *Ibid.,* p. 179.
25. *Ibid.*
26. *Ibid.,* p. 180.
27. *Ibid.,* p. 175.
28. *Adventures in Interviewing,* p. 237.
29. *A Man's Woman* (New York, 1928), p. 14.
30. *Ibid.,* p. 24.
31. *Ibid.,* p. 38.
32. *Ibid.,* p. 103.
33. *Ibid.,* p. 117.
34. *Ibid.,* p. 133.
35. *Ibid.,* p. 170.
36. *Ibid.,* p. 162.
37. *Ibid.,* p. 182.
38. *Ibid.,* p. 218.

39. *Adventures in Interviewing*, p. 238.
40. *The Independent*, LIII (May 16,1901), 1139.
41. Franklin Walker, *Frank Norris, A Biography* (New York, 1932), p. 260. Professor Walker says that he is quoting notes in the possession of Charles G. Norris.
42. Frank Norris, *The Octopus* (New York, 1928), II, 8.
43. *Ibid.*, I, 173-4.
44. *Ibid.*, II, 285.
45. *Ibid.*, II, 361.
46. *The Pit* (New York, 1928), p. 59.
47. *Ibid.*, p. 270.
48. *Ibid.*, p. 358.
49. *Ibid.*, p. 397.
50. Two short stories written in the last few years of Norris's life also illustrate this point. In "Toppan," the famous explorer has the free will to renounce his career for the woman he loves. In "A Lost Story," Rosella Beltis, a manuscript reader, "deliberately" rejects a good novel which coincidentally is so much like her own manuscript that its publication would wreck her future.
51. *The Pit*, p. 234.
52. *Ibid.*, pp. 234-5.

13.

John Galsworthy: Aspects of an Attitude

WOODBURN O. ROSS

I

The reputation of John Galsworthy seems to continue a steady decline, a decline which probably began somewhere around 1928. Partly, of course, he has suffered for being a Late Victorian; partly for being sentimental; partly for resisting extremism, an -ism to which the twentieth century seems attracted more than to most -isms. But I think that no small part of Galsworthy's eclipse arises from the fact that he has been unhappily labeled. Galsworthy was known as a social critic by a generation of readers who had little notion of the possibilities of systematic, rational, and informed inquiry into the nature of the social structure. To many of them Galsworthy's partial and emotional revelations resembled illumination. A technically better-informed kind of social criticism, however, has become standard in fiction and drama — was, in fact, winning the day through such men as Wells and Shaw while Galsworthy was still writing — and the very application of the term "social critic" has come to arouse expectations which he does not fulfill. As a matter of fact, Galsworthy had few vantage points from which to preach an elaborate social gospel. He was the son of a wealthy attorney and had himself been educated for the law. I know of no evidence that he ever undertook to inform himself concerning the dismal science of economics or the new science of sociology. What he wrote he wrote to a startling extent from immediate personal experience, as I propose to show. From this experience he did gain, however, particular kinds of social insight which he put to excellent use.

A purpose of this paper is to show succinctly what kind of

situation Galsworthy was primarily concerned with in his fiction, to explain why he was thus concerned, and to trace the development of private tragedy into social interest. It is also a purpose of this paper to deny that Galsworthy's work should ever be considered as if it should contain significant analyses of the structure or general dynamics of our society. His work is highly personal, it is intelligent, it is moving. But it is limited in scope.

In proceeding to this interpretation of Galsworthy I have no new facts to offer; though it is true that I cannot remember seeing any previous discussion of his first three volumes. My purpose is to arrange the facts in a comprehensible fashion to the end that Galsworthy's achievement may stand for what it is, with all its limitations but without the weight of the excess baggage hung upon it by those who would have him be what he was not. I shall confine my attention almost exclusively to his early novels. The total volume of Galsworthy's writing is enormous; but I do not believe that lengthening this study to include consideration of his dramas and essays and careful analysis of the late novels would alter the results.

II

In 1897 Galsworthy published his first volume, a callow affair called *From the Four Winds,* a collection of short stories. No one who reads the book is likely afterwards to challenge Galsworthy's assertion that he was a made and not a born writer, for in his first effort he shows practically no insight into the nature of serious fiction. He displays the unsophisticated layman's interest in plot — plot distinguished by sentimentality or by improbable, adventuresome action. Hardly a character lives, hardly a moment of insight into the real life of man disturbs the flow of time in the incredible land of his immature fancy.

Yet one story, "Dick Denver's Idea," no more distinguished in the manipulation of its contents than any other, no more intelligently conceived, marks Galsworthy's first use of a theme which was to be fundamental to a large number of his subsequent works and which is analogous to the themes of most of the rest. The story goes as follows: Dick Denver, an American gambler aboard a ship in the West Indies, meets the tearful and beautiful Mrs. Massinger. Attracted by her but unnerved by his recognition of his unworthiness, he is incapable of pressing a personal acquaintance upon her. He understands what her difficulty is: she is married to a cad, an English major — "a large, bull-necked man with eyes like a cod fish" — with whom Dick is accustomed to carry on gambling bouts. The heart which beats beneath Dick's uncouth exterior is touched, and he determines to do something. Somewhat familiar with the geography of the land about the port which the ship is approaching, he makes Massinger a proposition: he bets him his total winnings on the trip that he will go to a certain dangerous location that he knows and remain there longer than Massinger will. The major accepts, though as it turns out he should have thought twice. Together the two men go to a dark cavern in the hills. In its floor is a large, apparently bottomless, hole, whose edge the beams of the brightly shining moon are slowly approaching. Dick explains. They are on the brink of a periodically erupting geyser. When the moonbeams reach the crater, the cavern will be filled with boiling water. Massinger tries to get out, but Dick declares that only one of them will leave. The two of them shoot it out. Massinger falls, and Dick, first making sure that his enemy is indeed dead and will not be parboiled alive, takes to his heels. Later that night he creeps into Mrs. Massinger's room at the hotel. She lies before him, the very picture of feminine beauty and innocence, her hair cascading over her shoulders in the moonlight. He tiptoes to her bed and pins to her pillow an envelope containing all the money he has won from her husband and a note assuring her that the rascally fellow will trouble her no more. The next morning he sails away without a word.

This story, no doubt a reader will agree, is striking from more than one point of view. Our present concern, however, is with the fundamental situations: a gallant man falls in love with a married woman; the woman's husband is a brute; the marriage constitutes no genuine spiritual union; the woman herself is beautiful and lovable. Together these make up a kind of crude defense of the third party of the eternal triangle. Dick is never overtly justified in the story; the total situation is simply of such character that a man normally attracted by female beauty, moved by feelings of human sympathy for outraged and helpless virtue, believing in the propriety of human dignity, is likely to be tempted to intervene. True, law stands in the way; but are there not values which transcend man-made law? Does not all decency itself demand that one intervene to defend human dignity, and outraged innocence, and beleaguered integrity? Is marriage entitled to respect when it is based on barren law instead of love? Here, in this crude little story, are contained many of the fundamental questions which the mature Galsworthy was to ask of life; here appears by implication the gravamen of his charge against his society. In 1897 such questions were revolutionary.

Galsworthy's first novel, *Jocelyn*, published in 1898, marks a surprising improvement. Herein a married man, Giles Legard, who lives a life of leisure on the Riviera, and whose invalid wife has never been a true companion, falls in love with the beautiful and virtuous Jocelyn. Moved by a torturing passion, he seduces her and involves himself in a tangle of events through which he becomes partly responsible for the death of his wife. Jocelyn, tormented by guilt and love, leaves him and returns to England. He wanders through foreign parts, and finally, almost out of his mind with longing, goes to England to effect some kind of definite resolution of the affair. He sees her and begs her not to ruin both their lives because of a past that can never change. Upon her refusal to marry him he tells her that he is taking passage for the Far East and will end his life there, unless she changes her mind before he sails. She does not and he leaves, broken hearted. His life seems to him to have lost all possible meaning; but happily Jocelyn, having taken a faster boat, meets him at Ismailia and they are united forever.

This book is superior to *From the Four Winds*. Though Jocelyn and Giles are to some extent puppets of the action, they are convincing as human beings. Galsworthy takes time to describe in detail the complexities of their situation and their feelings. The subject is, for 1898, courageously treated. I should guess that, considered as a whole, *Jocelyn* is somewhat better than the average novel written then. But notice that the book consists, essentially, of a rewriting of "Dick Denver's Idea." Here again is the triangle, with the insignificant change that the male and not the female protagonist is married and in a difficult situation. Again the marriage has no inner significance; again the lady is beautiful and, at first, virtuous. Again no overt attempt is made to justify the setting-aside of law, but the situation is developed in such a manner as to enlist the reader's sympathy with the sinners and arouse him against the rigidity of the conventional order.

III

That the case of unwed lovers should be argued eloquently twice in Galsworthy's first two books will surprise no one familiar with his life. Let me say a word to those who are not.[1] John Galsworthy's first cousin Arthur married, in 1891, Ada Cooper. This couple seems to have been genuinely incompatible. Naturally enough John met his cousin-in-law with some frequency, but unnaturally, in the eyes of the late nineteenth century, he fell in love with her and she with him. In the autumn of 1895 they began an intimacy which was to be permanent. The obvious thing to do was run away together and let Ada be divorced; but it is not surprising that they were unable to accept this solution. In the first place, divorce was much more rare and more psychically and socially destructive then than it is now; and in the next place they had to consider the condition of John's father. He was an old man, and devoted to a rigid code. Their elopement, they thought, might well mean his death. Thus they felt that there was but one possibility before them: unable to part, they must pursue a clandestine and illicit affair until his death. When the Boer War broke out, Arthur went to South Africa. Ada moved then into quarters of her own and lived there until the death of John's aged father made an elopement possible. The couple were promptly served with divorce papers, and they passed through a pitiless early twentieth century divorce trial. As soon as the law made it possible for them to do so, they married.

The story can be told coldly enough. But one can imaginatively embellish the bare outline of fact with some insight into what the daily lives of two sensitive people caught among society's regulations must have been. Ford Madox Ford furnishes actual reminiscence. "The long excruciation of waiting years for the opportunity of happiness had made him sensitive beyond belief," he writes. "The anticipation of possible future grief for his wife rendered him at the time almost out of his normal mind and the emotion was rendered all the stronger by the thought of the suffering that for years before she had had to endure . . . with, as it were, Soames Forsyte. I really thought that, at about the time when he had just received those divorce papers, he might have gone mad. . . . And that note of agonized suffering at the thought of oppression or cruelty became at once the main note of his character and of his public activities."[2]

There can, I think, be no reasonable doubt that Galsworthy's private life was the background of the early stories of his which we have just discussed. And as he matured, he constantly made use of variations of the same theme.

IV

In October, 1900, appeared Galsworthy's second novel, *Villa Rubein*. The amatory triangle itself does not appear; but conditions within the social organization which keep young lovers apart are attacked. The situation is of the simplest: a young English girl living on the Continent falls in love with an artist, impoverished and of peasant stock. Her upper-class step-father opposes the match, naturally; and only after very considerable difficulties are the young people united in happiness. Here the sympathy for the unfulfilled member of a mismated couple, which Galsworthy has previously expressed, is simply altered slightly. It becomes sympathy for the couple who could, presumably, form a fulfilling union if they were not prevented by social prejudices against poverty and low birth. Society, as represented by the immediate human environment of the lovers, is not wholly unsympathetic: Nicholas Treffrey, the uncle of the English girl, does help them; but the holders of social power are unimaginative, myopic, and custom-ridden. Galsworthy is definitely casting accusing glances at society.

The Island Pharisees (1904) marks a fresh modification of Galsworthy's theme. It represents, as it were, a triangle with one of the sides missing; or, to put the matter otherwise, it develops a situation which was sure to become a conventional triangle and then breaks off the foredoomed love affair short of marriage. The hero of this book, Shelton, becomes engaged to the beautiful, conventional, and, because of her conventionality, frigid, Antonia. She is afraid to see the life of people outside her own class or to think about a social organization which leaves many destitute and functionless. Galsworthy succeeds here in blending in a convincing fashion the social attitudes and the general personality of a character, as he was to continue to do later in a distinctive way. On the one hand, Antonia is gracious, normally intelligent, conventionally warm-hearted. But the simple fact that she is unable and unwilling to inspect the rules of life of her class vitiates all. The poor are of interest only so long as they are no threat; love is stifled in the name of chastity; ideas which blur her simple pattern are terrifying. Thus the Antonia who might have been never develops. In her place is an empty and misleading outline. Shelton, meantime, becomes an exponent of the open mind and finds that marriage with Antonia will be impossible. There is no doubt where Galsworthy's sympathies lie. "What can you expect in a counthry where the crimson emotions are never allowed to smell the air?" asks one of the characters. "And what'sh the result? My bhoy, the result is sentiment, a yellow thing with blue spots, like a fungus or a Stilton cheese."[3] Shelton reflects concerning his own class, "They were the best-bred people of the sort who supported charities, knew everybody, had clear, calm judgment, and intolerance of all such conduct as seemed to them 'impossible,' all breaches of morality, such as mistakes of etiquette, such as dishonesty, passion, sympathy (except with a canonized class of objects — the *legitimate* sufferings, for instance, of their own families and class)."[4] Shelton's attitude is thus generally challenging; but it is particularly challenging to the marriage laws — their proprietary and their compulsory character. "I can't understand any man wanting to live with a woman who doesn't want him," he says.[5] Manifestly in *The Island Pharisees* Galsworthy's complaints are an indictment of the social rigidity which he thinks is largely to blame for the frustrations he describes. The isolation of social attitudes as significant determinants of the characters of Antonia and Shelton is an achievement of some importance. The attitudes involved, however, all have clear relevance to Galsworthy's own troubles.

By this time Galsworthy had developed his techniques and had practiced the manipulation of his theme to the point where the writing of *The Man of Property* (1906) was possible. He had learned to subordinate a simple rehearsal of facts in a case like his own — *Jocelyn* is such a rehearsal — to a criticism of qualities of human character and of certain aspects of society which, he thinks, caused many of his difficulties. In *The Man of Property*, it will be remembered, the beautiful Irene is married to the repulsive Soames Forsyte, when there appears on the scene the artist Bosinney, at first certainly intending no harm. But he and Irene fall in love, are tormented by their passion, become lovers. Bosinney dies, by accident or suicide, and Soames, heart-sick but triumphant, closes his house about the wife whom he still possesses. What causes of this tragedy does Galsworthy find? First of all, just as in *Villa Rubein* and to a much greater extent in *The*

Island Pharisees, unimaginativeness and conventionality of mind. No Forsyte dares attempt genuine knowledge of another human being; no Forsyte dares question the code of his class. But there is a particular aspect of the code which Galsworthy here brings into a salient position for the first time, and it comes close to being the making of the book. The Forsytes believe in property; they measure their entire environment in terms of the relationship of each item to their possessive urges. This need to possess is at once a psychological and a social quality. Galsworthy's psychology at this point probably strikes a modern reader as curious; but at least it is clear. He has no recourse to depth psychology; indeed, such analysis was hardly available to him in 1903-6, when he was writing the book. He finds his explanation in heredity. Soames is acquisitive and possessive because the whole family is; and the family is because for generations acquisitiveness paid, until somehow this abstraction, acquisitiveness, merged into the concrete reality of genes and chromosomes. But at the same time this possessiveness is socially relevant because, as Young Jolyon explains, the Forsytes are typical. They represent half of England, the upper half, the propertied half. Their virtues and their faults are reflected throughout the governing class of the island. This is Galsworthy's charge against his society now: the governing classes are Forsytes, who, in turn, because of habit hardened into heredity, and because of their limited insights, are unable to transcend the concept of property as the most significant form under which they apprehend their environment. They are imaginatively dull, they are provincial, they are selfish, they know how to drive a good bargain, and they usually mean to be virtuous, in their limited understanding of virtue.

The Man of Property, though, it seems to me, a masterpiece, does not quite represent the end of Galsworthy's formation of himself, although his next novel, *The Country House* (1907), is essentially *The Man of Property* in a new locale and with some alteration of action. Here George Pendyce, heir to the estate of Worsted Skeins, is in love with the beautiful Helen Bellew, who is separated from her husband. The best that can be said for this woman, who is distinctly atypical among Galsworthy's female characters, is that she is true to her own nature: first she gives herself to George and then, tiring, breaks off their affair. Gregory Vigil, an idealistic philanthropist and guardian of Helen, whom he loves and does not understand at all, brings about the fundamental entanglement of the plot when he undertakes to induce Helen to sue her husband for divorce. But the husband sues first, naming George as co-respondent. George, Helen, and her husband are all tough and tenacious, capable of withstanding the shock of the suit. It is not so with George's provincial, unimaginative, fundamentally stupid, but equally tenacious father. He has no mind for anything but the conventions, which he habitually applies with unintended cruelty. Again Galsworthy attacks the divorce laws. "I mean to say," says the Pendyce attorney, "that she must not ask for a divorce merely because she is miserable, or placed in a position that no woman should be placed in, but only if she has been offended in certain technical ways. . . . To get a divorce . . . you must be as hard as nails and as wary as a cat."[6] But there is more to the matter than this. The laws are absurd, but they are absurd because of the nature of the men who make them and whom they govern. Again the attorney speaks: "It's this disease, this grudging narrow spirit in men, that makes such laws necessary. Unlovely men, unlovely laws — what can you expect?"[7] And this is exactly the point of the book. It is George's father and the local clergyman whose insensitivity and provincialism are pilloried — and they are specifically represented, as were the Forsytes, as typical of their class. This is the elder Pendyce's creed: "I believe in my father, and his father, and his father's father, the makers and keepers of my estate, and I believe in myself and my son and my son's son. And I believe that we have made the country, and shall keep the country what it is. And I believe in the Public Schools, and especially the Public School that I was at. And I believe in my social equals and the country house, and in things as they are for ever and ever. Amen."[8] These men are not monsters; despite their rigid attitudes toward human beings, they are genuinely kind to animals. For their own security they have subscribed to an impossible code of human conduct — impossible because it is based on the narrowest of interpretations of human needs and behavior.

The remedies for these conditions which Galsworthy dislikes may be inferred, in part, at least. Let men be kind; let them try to understand each other; let them distrust mechanical, generalized solutions to human problems. Where possessiveness and provincialism have become hereditary qualities of character, there is need for new dominant personalities in the society to supplant the old ones — gradually, of course; Galsworthy was no revolutionist. It is in *Fraternity* (1909), the novel which in a sense rounds off Galsworthy's notions, that his solution is overtly stated, though in a very curious fashion. The book contains two marriage triangles — not, after all, a surprising fact — and a description of slum conditions upon which young social workers seem to have little effect. But much interest is focused upon the father of two sisters in the story, one Professor Stone, now in his dotage but writing a book such as has never been written before about human life, a book of universal brotherhood. He is a character straight from H. G. Wells. In his book, he is writing about contemporary life, but everything is in the past tense, thus: " 'To take life,' went on the old man in a voice which, though charged with strong emotion, seemed to be speaking to itself, 'was the chief mark of the insensate barbarism still prevailing in those days. . . . They did not stop to love each other in this life; they were so sure they had all eternity to do it in. The doctrine was an invention to enable men to act like dogs with clear consciences. Love could never come to full fruition till it was destroyed'."[9] Here, of course, is the answer — love — insofar as Galsworthy can see an answer. He utters the Christian injunction, "Love one another," but he does so in a fashion which indicates his pessimism. The man who preaches this gospel is aged, semi-insane; and nobody in the book gives his observations a second thought. Certainly no one considers seriously the possibility of cultivating his powers of loving his fellow man.

After he had written *Fraternity* Galsworthy had nothing significantly new to say to readers. His theme remained essentially the same, and the fresh variations, though frequently vigorous and probing, represented no fundamental new development. In *The Patrician* (1911), in *The Dark Flower* (1913), and in *Beyond* (1917) he pursued his theme of the triangle with great sympathy for the lovers and some excellent illumination of character, but with minimal modifications of the theme and with minimal social implications. In *The Freelands* (1915) social criticism such as we have been discussing is primary. The two strands are woven together in the completion of *The Forsyte Saga* (1920-21), in *A Modern Comedy* (1924-28), and in *The End of the Chapter* (1931-33). Except that as he grew older he grew more tolerant of convention, less sure of the possibility of genuine improvement, I see little change in his basic attitudes, which were formed and had hardened by 1909.

V

In short, Galsworthy's limitations turn out to be limitations of imagination. He learned to ring the changes, for the most part, on one situation, the marriage-triangle in which one partner had some justification for infidelity. The perceptiveness, sympathy, and interpretive power which he learned to bring to his exposition of this situation would appear to be the source of the similar powers with which he analyzed other situations in which individuals found themselves at odds with law or custom, as, for instance, in *Justice* or in *The Freelands*. The defense of the misinterpreted became the very hallmark of his work. He learned principally — not exclusively — to create modifications of three characters — Arthur, the unwanted husband; Ada Cooper, the beautiful and suffering wife; and himself, the gallant lover.

Clearly he burned with a genuine need to communicate the inwardness of his own experiences; equally clearly his imagination did not carry him far from circumstances essentially his. His friend Conrad might be at home with Jim, Lingard, or Nostromo. Galsworthy enjoyed no such freedom. Conrad might analyze the politics of Costaguana or the Bornean tribes. Galsworthy could not. His sentimentality itself — by no means a fatal defect — is an attempt to flog his imagination into interpretations beyond its power.

But within the limited area where he was at home he seems to me to have done well. It should not be forgotten that Soames was so convincing a character that when he finally died a London newspaper headlined his death.[10] Galsworthy never analyzed his characters in genuine depth; but at least the acts and speeches which he chose as symbolic of those aspects of their natures which he did understand and wished to represent do transmit to the reader a sense that these are people, people who have psychic needs and drives, whom we understand the better for Galsworthy's having written about them. The situation into which he put them, though lacking in variety, did in all truth need exploration.

These observations concerning character and situation in Galsworthy's work lead to insights concerning the general nature of his social criticism. Seen against the background of the richly informed and passionately argued social criticism in the novel and the drama of the second quarter of the century, his work is likely to appear so restricted in scope as to lack any substantial critical meaning. Thus Richard M. Kain writes, "The commonplaces of contemporary sociology — power politics, propaganda, demagoguery, the class struggle, and the totalitarian state — in a word, the basic concepts of social psychology, are entirely absent from his program of reform."[11] But to measure Galsworthy's work by such concepts as these is to cast his accomplishment into the shadow of notions totally foreign to the origins and intent of his social criticism. There are two positive aspects of this criticism. In the first place, it analyzes the interaction between personal tempera-

STUDIES IN HONOR OF JOHN WILCOX

ment and the dominant body of social attitudes. These attitudes prevail because they are held temperamentally by the vast majority of people in power; and these people, in turn, are reinforced in their attitudes and restricted in their outlook by the social climate. This is a valid interpretation of some aspects of an essentially conservative society. In the second place, Galsworthy appears habitually as the champion of the individual against the mass. He exposes the crude generalizations with which the law or custom attempts to deal with specific acts, part of whose inalienable nature is their uniqueness. In short, in a century characterized by the destruction of individualism, Galsworthy, ignorant of a developing orthodoxy in the analysis of the social process and unable imaginatively to see far beyond his own experiences, does succeed in expanding his traumatic love of Ada Cooper into a denunciation of the myopia and tyranny of the society.

NOTES

1. The following facts are from H. V. Marrot, *Life and Letters of John Galsworthy* (New York, 1936), pp. 100-104.
2. Ford Madox Ford, "Galsworthy," *American Mercury*, XXXVII (April, 1936), 452-3.
3. *The Island Pharisees* (London, 1925), Chap. 3, p. 26. All references to Galsworthy's works are to editions which should be easily obtainable, but quotations have been checked against first editions except in the case of *The Island Pharisees*. A first edition of this work was not available, and quotations have been read against the edition of 1908.
4. *Ibid.*, Chap. 4, p. 31.
5. *Ibid.*, Chap. 5, p. 42.
6. *The Country House* (New York, 1920), Part I, Chap. 9, p. 91.
7. *Ibid.*, Part II, Chap. 9, pp. 185-6.
8. *Ibid.*, Part II, Chap. 8, p. 180.
9. *Fraternity* (New York, 1920), Chap. 1, p. 8.
10. Edward Wagenknecht, "The Selfish Heroine: Thackeray and Galsworthy," *College English*, IV (February, 1943), 297.
11. "Galsworthy, the Last Victorian Liberal," *Madison Quarterly*, IV (March, 1944), 84.

H. M. Tomlinson, Essayist and Traveller

ALVA A. GAY

I N 1950 the Londoner, H. M. Tomlinson, journalist, novelist, essayist, traveller, published a collection of essays under the title *The Face of the Earth*. One wonders to how many of those who chanced upon it the name of its author evoked nostalgic memories of other of his books not reread in years. To most readers born between the 1914 and 1939 wars the name would probably be no more than just that — a name. But to older readers was there recollection of *The Sea and the Jungle, Old Junk, London River, Tide Marks*? The essays collected in *The Face of the Earth* themselves constitute a backward glance. They are, the author remarks, "remembrances . . . salvaged from books lost in the last war." "It was thought proper," he goes on to say, "to save them; oblivion is inevitable, but it need not come too soon."[1] And he was right; oblivion need not and should not come too soon to his work. There is place for the minor as well as the major, for the quietly persistent tone as well as the shout. One can be delighted and bemused and moved, if in a different way, by Charles Lamb and Thoreau as well as by Herman Melville and Dostoyevsky. Henry Major Tomlinson has been persistent. Although the bulk of his best work was written prior to the outbreak of the second war, at no time since then has he dropped from sight completely. During the war appeared *The Wind Is Rising* (1941), reactions to life in wartime Britain; in 1950, *Malay Waters*, a tribute to the officers, the men, and the little ships of the Straits Steamship Company, "coasting out of Singapore and Penang in peace and war," as the subtitle reads; in 1953, in his eightieth year, *A Mingled Yarn*, a collection much like *The Face of the Earth*, consisting for the most part of earlier essays and sketches; in addition to these, scattered essays that have appeared in a popular travel magazine and elsewhere, and early in 1957 *The Trumpet Shall Sound,* a novel. It is, however, with the Tomlinson of the years prior to the 1940's that I wish to concern myself — not the writer of such novels as *Gallions Reach* (1927) and *All Our Yesterdays* (1930), but the meditative observer, the traveller, the social critic, the author of *The Sea and the Jungle* (1912), *Old Junk* (1918), *London River* (1921), *Tide Marks* (1924), *Gifts of Fortune* (1926), and "Log of a Voyage, 1935," published in *The Turn of the Tide* in 1947.

A frequenter of dockside Thames, as he is seen in *London River,* almost, one hazards, its familiar spirit — he was born in 1873 in one of the shipping parishes — a keenly observant landsman with a love of the sea in its every mood, a love, albeit, somewhat tempered with a knowledgeable fear, and a voyager on most of the oceans of the world, he has an understanding of ships and those who make their living from them and of the sea in its many aspects. The majority of his best books and essays are about the sea and those who live on it. So much has the sea meant to him that often in writing of land matters he uses imagery drawn from it. In "Drought" (*Gifts of Fortune*), describing the encroachment of a city's residential suburb into what had been a peaceful rural village, he notes that the slopes of the adjacent down hang over mason and carpenter like the solidified roller of the sea, a grove of trees riding its back like a raft. And in "A Devon Estuary," in the same volume, the seaside village of Burra becomes a part of a great ship:

> This village, which stands round the base of the hill where the moors decline to the sea and two rivers merge to form a gulf of light, is one I used to think was easily charted. But what do I know of it? The only certainty about it to-day is that it has a window which saves the trouble of searching for a better. Beyond that window the clouds are over the sea. The clouds are on their way. The waters are passing us. So, when I look out from my port-light to learn where we are, I can see for myself there may be something in that legend of a great stone ship on

an endless voyage. I think I may be one of its passengers. For where is Burra? I never know. The world I see beyond the window is always different. We reach every hour a region of the sky where man has never been before, so the astronomers tell us, and my window confirms it. Ours is a celestial voyage, and God knows where.[2]

But what of the voyages across the seas of the world? I cannot here do justice to them. I can hope only that what I give will sharpen curiosity so that the reader will seek to discover for himself Tomlinson's landfalls and horizons. An early voyage, his first he states, is described in "Off-Shore" (*London River*), the account of a voyage by steam trawler, the *Windhover,* to the cod fleet on the Dogger Bank in the days of the Russo-Japanese War. He tells of the almost futile search through several days of stormy, North Sea weather for the trawler fleet, which should have been found directly. Tomlinson was considered a Jonah, but this distinction did nothing to diminish his delight in the prospect of endless ocean upheaved and of leaden sky. The ship herself was for him as sentient a creature as any aboard her, when she pointed her stem to the clouds as she climbed a wave, or lifted her stern to let a mass of hissing gray water pass beneath her keel. Characteristic of the exactness of detail with which he can report what he has seen is the view of the *Susie,* a trawler his skipper hailed in his zig-zag search for the lost fleet: "I shall always see her at the moment when our skipper began to shout through his hands at her. She was poised askew, in that arrested instant, on a glassy slope of water, with its crest foaming above her. Surge blotted her out amidships, and her streaming forefoot jutted clear. She plunged then into the hollow between us, showing us the plan of her deck, for her funnel was pointing at us."[3]

Another voyage, the subject of "The African Coast" (*Old Junk*), took him from Algiers to Tripoli in Barbary on the cargo steamer *Celestine,* with an ebullient Frenchman as master. Again there was a storm — "the barometer, wherever I am, seems to know when I embark. It falls."[4] There had been earlier on his trip from England to Algiers, sun bright glimpses of the land, but off Bougie, "That shining coast which occasionally I had surprised from Oran, which seemed afloat on the sea, was no longer a vision of magic, the unsubstantial work of Iris, an illusionary cloud of coral, amber, and amethyst. It was the bare bones of this old earth, as sombre and foreboding as any ruin of granite under the wrack of the bleak north."[5]

Years later he embarked by cargo ship for the Mediterranean again, this time with a grown son, whose first voyage, when he was a boy, Tomlinson described in "Initiation" (*Old Junk*). The voyage was a leisurely one, with halts at Casablanca, Gibraltar, Malta, Patras, Piraeus (where the ship sailed unexpectedly without them to its next port, while they were on the Acropolis), Istanbul, Ismir, and Alexandria. In his account are the description and reflection that we come to recognize as the hall marks of the man's work: "A mile to port a schooner was dim within the curtain of a cloud, but . . . a beam of [sunlight] found her, and she was radiant in an instant. She became more glorious than a ship ever is. As she heeled she flashed, as if giving out fire. She was signalling eternal renown to us."[6]

The Sea and the Jungle and *Tide Marks* are his two major travel narratives. Concerned with his experiences on his first crossing of the Atlantic, the first covers a voyage from Wales to Brazil and two thousand miles up the Amazon and its tributary, the Madeira, to Port Velho at the San Antonio Falls. The trip was made in the *Capella*, a collier drawing twenty-three feet laden, carrying primarily a cargo of "patent" fuel for a railway construction project. The first part of the book is of the westward crossing — the sea. The ship, almost as soon as the pilot was dropped, was struck by a gale of steadily increasing velocity that, by the time she was out of the Bristol Channel, reached near hurricane force. Few writers that I know of have written so convincingly of the unrelenting fury of the sea as Tomlinson has written here, and I have not forgotten Conrad's power in *Typhoon*. He concentrates his attention not so much on the damage inflicted by wind and weight of water as upon the *Capella's* dogged persistence fighting her way over each monstrous wave hurled against her. She was hurt once and almost overwhelmed when the cover of number three hatch came free. But there was finally relief, and the remainder of the crossing was under a hot sun and warm showers, through slowly surging tropic waters. There follows the second part, the arrival at Para and the long voyage up the rivers, with the *Capella* like a captive creature. Foliage brushed her rigging on occasion, and the fraying of her cable, when she anchored, through the friction of current-borne debris was a constant worry to the first mate. At Port Velho, Tomlinson took a trip further inland to the end of the railway construction and beyond. His breakneck return by mule and handcar to avoid missing the sailing of the ship is a nightmare of speed. To present the book thus summarily is, of course, to miss completely the subtle portraiture, descriptive power, and thoughtfulness that are its marrow.

Tide Marks carries the reader to Singapore and beyond to the island of Ternate in the Dutch East Indies, with stops at Borneo, Java, and Celebes. Returning to Singapore, Tomlinson then made an excursion into the Malayan jungle. This book, satisfying in its own way, lacks the lyric and meditative tone of its predecessor but it has brilliantly realized vignettes of the tropics, both marine and insular. Its high points are the scramble up Ternate's volcanic peak and the sojourn in the jungle with the affliction of ubiquitous and determined leeches.

In the foreword to the first illustrated edition (1930) of *The Sea and the Jungle* Tomlinson chides the original reviewers of the book for their failure to hear the accents of the author who stood in his immediate background, Thoreau. There and elsewhere his indebtedness is evident. Consider the following from "Some Hints for Those about to Travel" (*Gifts of Fortune*):

> It is the chance things in travel that appear to be significant. The light comes unexpectedly and obliquely. Perhaps it amuses the gods to try us. They want to see whether we are asleep. If

we are watchful we may get a bewildering hint, but placed where nobody would have expected to find it. We may spend the rest of the voyage wondering what that meant. A casual coast suddenly fixed by so strange a glow that one looks to the opposite sky fearfully; the careless word which makes you glance at a stranger, and doubt your fixed opinion; an ugly city, which you are glad to leave, transfigured and jubilant as you pass out of its harbour; these are the incidents that give a sense of discovery to a voyage. We are on more than one voyage at a time. We never know where Manoa may be. There are no fixed bearings for the City of Gold.[7]

The attitude toward experience is the same in both men and both are keen observers of the world of nature. Tomlinson, however, takes the waters of the oceans of the world for his province and the great jungles of the New World and of the Malay Archipelago. Thoreau had only the narrowly circumscribed shores of Walden Pond and the New England wood lot and meadow. The movements of one for most of his life were within a ten-mile circle; the other has sailed the seven seas. Tomlinson, in "Log of a Voyage, 1935," writes of his son and himself: "Though we were in the same ship, the two of us must make separate voyages with varying experiences. We should share the same daylight, see the same landfalls at the same time, yet reality for each of us would be anything you like to name. The sea, ancient and changeless, could not reconcile us with its hint of continuity, the same yesterday, today, and for ever."[8] The cabin of a ship at sea serves the same purpose as another man's hut beside Walden Pond.

Like Thoreau, Tomlinson decries the drift of the times. The former deplores the frenetic, and to him inconsequential, quality of the daily press; the latter is distressed that the umbilical cord of radio binds a ship at sea to the news of the world and to the land, so that even the master of a ship "is on a length of string, and an office boy in the owner's office often pulls it, to let him feel the brevity of his liberty."[9] There is virtue in isolation. In

The Sea and the Jungle he writes of his feeling in mid-Atlantic on the fortunately radioless *Capella:* "we confessed, with ease at the heart, and with minds in which nervous vibrations had ceased, that we must have reached the place that was nowhere, and that now time was not for us. We had escaped you all. We were free. There was not anything to engage us. There was nothing to do, and nobody who wanted us. Never before had I felt so still and conscious of myself."[10] To him a ship's radio is but another example of a mechanization of life that can lead only to the merging of the individual difference in the dull gray mass of uniform humanity. This theme he develops in "Log of a Voyage, 1935":

> From Shanghai to Istanbul, people are merging into a uniformity as featureless as the wooly flocks; as if we, too, were mass-produced, like our opinions, our habits, and our flats. . . . There is no excuse for sameness and flatness. It is a crime against the intelligence. Uniformity is the abortion of creation. It is not harmony, but monotony, like the drone of our engines, and numbs thought. It means the death of freedom of the mind, and so the end of the soul's adventure; the hopeful old story of our beginning in a garden will be empty of its purport, for the spirit will be frustrate, good and evil the same, and our eyes blind to the glory of the Lord, should it be revealed.[11]

And again:

> . . . it appears today as if there were but one good we all should respect, whether we want to or not: we must bow to the political use of power directed to full control of the lives of our fellows. The last aim of reason, therefore, is to refuse to human life the use of reason; so down we go to the uniformity of sheep. But will we go down? There is sure to be trouble about that. The individual soul forever, in London, and Pekin, and every Kaffir kraal, against all the assumptions of outside authority![12]

But I would not imply that his is only a derivative importance. There are echoes of Thoreau in his work, yet what he has felt is a reflection of his own individuality, and what he has seen has been viewed from his own angle of vision. And all of it has been set down in a style superbly and exactly molded to his purpose. He is a skilled craftsman of word and phrase.

Tomlinson has not received the serious and extended consideration that his work deserves. Collections of his earlier essays, as has been remarked, have been reprinted in recent years, and one of his pieces — "The Derelict" (*Old Junk*) — has strangely been included in Bennett Cerf and Henry C. Moriarity's *An Anthology of Famous British Stories*, although it is a narrative sketch rather than fiction. Little attention, however, has been paid either to his ideas or to his richly metaphoric prose. In part this neglect is undoubtedly due to the fact that much of what he has said so well as a critic of society has been included in his meticulous rendering of persons and places, of landscapes, seascapes, and personalities — in his travel essays, that is. Creative in quite a different sense from fiction, first rate travel literature nevertheless challenges critical insight.

Without question, it seems to me, he belongs to that noble fraternity of travellers among whom are found the James Boswell of *A Journal of a Tour to the Hebrides*, the Thoreau of *A Week on the Concord and the Merrimack Rivers*, the George Borrow of *The Bible in Spain*, the Charles Doughty of *Arabia Deserta*, the George Gissing of *By the Ionian Sea*, the Henry James of *The American Scene*, the Norman Douglas of *Old Calabria*, the D. H. Lawrence of *Sea and Sardinia*, the E. E. Cummings of *Eimi*. Of such as these Tomlinson may be said to write, and it can be written of him as well: "We borrow the light of an observant and imaginative traveller, and see the foreign land bright with his aura; and we think it is the country which shines."[13]

NOTES

1. (London: Gerald Duckworth & Co., 1950), p. vii. Quoted by special permission of the holders of the American copyright, the Bobbs-Merrill Co., Inc.
2. *Gifts of Fortune* (New York and London: Harper and Brothers, 1926), p. 225. This and a later passage from this volume are quoted by permission of H. M. Tomlinson and the Society of Authors.

3. *London River* (New York: Garden City Publishing Co., Inc., 1921), p. 205. Quoted by permission of Alfred A. Knopf, Inc.
4. *Old Junk* (New York: Alfred A. Knopf, Inc., 1930), p. 22. This and the following passage from this volume are quoted by permission of the publisher.
5. *Ibid.*, p. 27.
6. "Log of a Voyage, 1935," in *The Turn of the Tide* (New York: The Macmillan Co., 1947), p. 8. This and later passages from this volume are quoted by permission of the publisher.
7. P. 22.
8. *The Turn of the Tide*, p. 11.
9. *Ibid.*, p. 14.
10. *The Sea and the Jungle* (New York: The Modern Library, 1928), p. 73. This and a later passage from this volume are quoted by permission of H. M. Tomlinson and the Society of Authors.
11. *The Turn of the Tide*, pp. 56, 57.
12. *Ibid.*, pp. 15-16.
13. *The Sea and the Jungle*, p. 107.

A Preliminary Checklist of the Periodical Publications of Dorothy M. Richardson

15.

JOSEPH PRESCOTT

The following list represents, to my knowledge, the first attempt to register all the contributions of Dorothy M. Richardson to periodicals. I am fortunate enough to have had the assistance of Miss Richardson, and I am very grateful. I am also indebted to Mr. J. Heitner, editor of *The Sphere*.

It has been possible to classify most of the writings, at least approximately, as follows: E — essay; L — letter; N — novel; P — poem(s); R — review; S — sketch; SS — short story. I have made no special effort to list reprints, but give such information, when I have it, for the reader's convenience. Nor have I indicated variations in text between printings.

This list must remain preliminary at least until such time as the unsigned "middles" contributed to the *Saturday Review* from about 1908 on are identified beyond a doubt. In quest of marked editorial files, I have been kindly informed by Sir Gerald Barry, editor of the *Saturday Review* from 1924 to 1930, that "all the files of the *Saturday Review* were destroyed in the bombing of Gray's Inn in 1941 and there is literally nothing left."

I should be grateful for any additions which readers might be kind enough to supply.

"'Days with Walt Whitman,'" *Crank: An Unconventional Magazine,* IV, 8 (August, 1906), 259-263. R

"The Reading of 'The Jungle,'" *ibid.,* IV, 9 (September, 1906), 290-293. R

"'Jesus in Juteopolis,'" *ibid.,* IV, 10 (October, 1906), 331-332. R

"'The Amazing Witness,'" *ibid.,* pp. 332-334. R

"'In the Days of the Comet,'" *ibid.*, IV, 11 (November, 1906), 372-376. R

"The Odd Man's Remarks on Socialism," *Ye Crank*, V, 1 (January, 1907), 30-33. E

"'How We Are Born,'" *ibid.*, pp. 44-47. R

"Socialism and Anarchy: An Open Letter to the 'Odd Man,'" *Ye Crank and The Open Road*, V, 2 (February, 1907), 89-91. L

"'The Future in America,'" *ibid.*, pp. 95-99. R

"Socialism and The Odd Man," *ibid.*, V, 3 (March, 1907), 147-149. L

"A Sheaf of Opinions: Lowes Dickinson's 'A Modern Symposium,'" *ibid.*, pp. 153-157. R

"A Last Word to The Odd Man about Socialism," *ibid.*, V, 4 (April, 1907), 180-182. L

"A French Utopia," *ibid.*, pp. 209-214. R

"Thearchy and Socialism," *ibid.*, V, 5 (May, 1907), 237-239. E

"Down with the Lords," *ibid.*, pp. 257-261. R

"Notes About a Book Purporting to Be About Christianity and Socialism," *ibid.*, V, 6 (June, 1907), 311-315. R

"The Open Road," *Open Road*, New Series, I, 3 (September, 1907), 153-158. E

"Nietzsche," *ibid.*, I, 5 (November, 1907), 243-248. R

"Towards the Light," *ibid.*, I, 6 (December, 1907), 304-308. R

"The Human Touch," *Saturday Review*, no. 2849, CIX (June 4, 1910), 724. L

"Welcome," *ibid.*, no. 2951, CXIII (May 18, 1912), 620-621. S

"Strawberries," *ibid.*, no. 2956, CXIII (June 22, 1912), 778-779. S

"August," *ibid.*, no. 2962, CXIV (August 3, 1912), 142. S

"Sunday," *Art & Letters*, New Series, II, 3 (Summer, 1919), 113-115. SS

Interim, serialized in *Little Review*, as follows:

VI, 2 (June, 1919), 3-25
VI, 3 (July, 1919), 11-24
VI, 4 (August, 1919), 5-28
VI, 5 (September, 1919), 56-61
VI, 6 (October, 1919), 38-54
VI, 7 (November, 1919), 34-38
VI, 8 (December, 1919), 20-28
VI, 9 (January, 1920), 37-48
VI, 10 (March, 1920), 17-26
VI, 11 (April, 1920), 26-34
VII, 1 (May-June, 1920), 53-61   N

"Christmas Eve," *Art & Letters*, III, 1 (Winter, 1920), 32-35. SS

Interview headlined "Future of the Novel," *Pall Mall Gazette*, no. 17,365 (January 20, 1921), p. 7. Reprinted in Meredith Starr, ed., "Dorothy Richardson," *The Future of the Novel: Famous Authors on Their Methods: A Series of Interviews with Renowned Authors* (Boston: Small, Maynard & Company, [1921]), pp. 90-91.

"The Perforated Tank," *Fanfare*, I, 2 (October 15, 1921), 29. R

"Equilibrium," *Little Review*, VIII, 2 (Spring, 1922), 37. Dialogue.

"It Is Finished," *Weekly Westminster Gazette*, no. 60, II (April 7, 1923), 17. P

"Talent and Genius: A Discussion of Whether Genius is not Actually Far More Common than Talent," *Vanity Fair* (New York), XX, 3 (May, 1923), 65. Incomplete. For complete text, see next entry. E

"Talent and Genius: Is Not Genius Actually Far More Common than Talent?" *ibid.*, XXI, 2 (October, 1923), 118, 120. E

"Barbara," *Sphere*, no. 1238, XCV (October 13, 1923), 46; in "Three Poems: Sussex — Discovery — Barbara," *Poetry: A Magazine of Verse*, XXVII, 2 (November, 1925), 67-69. P

"Truth," *Weekly Westminster*, New Series, I, 10 (January 5, 1924), 316. Reprinted as "Freedom" in Louis Untermeyer, ed., *Modern British Poetry: A Critical Anthology*, rev. ed. (New York: Harcourt, Brace and Company, [1925]), p. 312. P

"Death," *Weekly Westminster*, New Series, I, 15 (February 9, 1924), 466. Reprinted in Edward J. O'Brien and John Cournos, eds., *Best British Stories of 1924* (Boston: Small, Maynard & Co., Inc., 1924), pp. 218-220. SS

"Veterans in the Alps," *Sphere*, no. 1262, XCVI (March 29, 1924), 354. E

"About Punctuation," *Adelphi*, I, 11 (April, 1924), 990-996. "De la ponctuation," tr. Sylvia Beach and Adrienne Monnier, *Mesures*, [I] 1 (January 15, 1935), 155-166. E

"Helen," *Golden Hind: A Quarterly Magazine of Art & Literature*, II, 7 (April, 1924), 31. P

"Women and the Future: A Trembling of the Veil Before the Eternal Mystery of 'La Giaconda [sic],'" *Vanity Fair* (New York), XXII, 2 (April, 1924), 39-40. E

"Alpine Spring," *Sphere*, no. 1264, XCVII (April 12, 1924), 44. E

"The Parting of Wordsworth and Coleridge: A Footnote," *Adelphi*, I, 12 (May, 1924), 1107-1109. E

"Waiting," *Poetry: A Magazine of Verse*, XXIV, 3 (June, 1924), 142-144. P

"Buns for Tea," *ibid.*, pp. 144-145. Reprinted in Louis Unter-meyer, ed., *Yesterday and Today: A Comparative Anthology of Poetry* (New York: Harcourt, Brace and Company, [1926]), pp. 152-153, and in Margery Gordon and M. B. King, eds., *Verse of Our Day*, rev. ed. (New York & London: D. Appleton-Century & Co., 1938), p. 284. P

"A Note on George Fox," *Adelphi*, II, 2 (July, 1924), 148-150. E

"Brothers Rabbit and Rat," *ibid.*, II, 3 (August, 1924), 247-249. E

"The Garden," *Transatlantic Review*, II, 2 (August, 1924), 141-143. S

"Discovery," *Sphere*, no. 1280, XCVIII (August 2, 1924), 142; in "Three Poems: Sussex — Discovery — Barbara," *Poetry: A Magazine of Verse*, XXVII, 2 (November, 1925), 67-69. P

"Disaster," *Adelphi*, II, 4 (September, 1924), 277. P

"A Sculptor of Dreams," *ibid.*, II, 5 (October, 1924), 422-427. R

"The Rôle of the Background: English Visitors to the Swiss Resorts During the Winter Sports Season," *Sphere*, no. 1296, XCIX (November 22, 1924), 226. E

"The Man from Nowhere," *Little Review*, X, 1 [*sic* — erratum for 2] (Autumn, 1924-Winter, 1925), 32-35. E

"What's in a Name?" *Adelphi*, II, 7 (December, 1924), 606-609. E

"Spring upon the Threshold," *Sphere*, no. 1314, C (March 28, 1925), 350. P

"Women in the Arts: Some Notes on the Eternally Conflicting Demands of Humanity and Art," *Vanity Fair* (New York), XXIV, 3 (May, 1925), 47, 100. E

"The Status of Illustrative Art," *Adelphi*, III, 1 (June, 1925), 54-57. E

Theobald, R. (pseud. of Dorothy M. Richardson), "Why Words?" *Adelphi*, III, 3 (August, 1925), 206-207. E

"Three Poems: Sussex — Discovery — Barbara," *Poetry: A Magazine of Verse*, XXVII, 2 (November, 1925), 67-69. P

Theobald, R. (pseud. of Dorothy M. Richardson), "Spengler and Goethe: A Footnote," *Adelphi*, IV, 5 (November, 1926), 311-312. E

"Sleigh Ride," *Outlook* (London), no. 1506, LVIII (December 11, 1926), 588. A selection from *Oberland*. N

"Message," *ibid.*, no. 1510, LIX (January 8, 1927), 28; *Poetry: A Magazine of Verse*, XXX, 5 (August, 1927), 256. P

"Continuous Performance," *Close Up*, [I] 1 (July, 1927), 34-37. E

"Continuous Performance: II: Musical Accompaniment," *ibid.*, [I] 2 (August, 1927), 58-62. E

"Continuous Performance: III: Captions," *ibid.*, [I] 3 (September, 1927), 52-56. E

"Continuous Performance: IV: A Thousand Pities," *ibid.*, [I] 4 (October, 1927), 60-64. E

"Continuous Performance: V: There's No Place Like Home," *ibid.*, [I] 5 (November, 1927), 44-47. E

"Continuous Performance: VI: The Increasing Congregation," *ibid.*, [I] 6 (December, 1927), 61-65. E

"Continuous Performance: VII: The Front Rows," *ibid.*, II, 1 (January, 1928), 59-64. E

"A Note on Household Economy," *ibid.*, II, 2 (February, 1928), 58-62. E

"Continuous Performance: VIII," *ibid.*, II, 3 (March, 1928), 51-55. E

"Portrait of an Evangelist," *New Adelphi*, I, 3 (March, 1928), 270-271. R

"Journey to Paradise," *Fortnightly Review*, New Series, CXXIII, 735 (March 1, 1928), 407-414. Personal recollections.

"Continuous Performance: IX: The Thoroughly Popular Film," *Close Up*, II, 4 (April, 1928), 44-50. E

"Continuous Performance: X: The Cinema in the Slums," *ibid.*, II, 5 (May, 1928), 58-62. E

"The Queen of Spring," *Focus: A Periodical to the Point in Matters of Health, Wealth & Life*, V, 5 (May, 1928), 259-262. E

"Anticipation," *ibid.*, V, 6 (June, 1928), 322-325. E

"Continuous Performance: Slow Motion: XI," *Close Up*, II, 6 (June, 1928), 54-58. E

"Das Ewig-Weibliche," *New Adelphi*, I, 4 (June, 1928), 364-366. R

"Gift," *Outlook* (London), no. 1583, LXI (June 2, 1928), 678. P

"Compensations?" *Focus: A Periodical to the Point in Matters of Health, Wealth & Life*, VI, 1 (July, 1928), 3-7. E

"Continuous Performance: XII: The Cinema in Arcady," *Close Up*, III, 1 (July, 1928), 52-57. E

"Films for Children," *ibid.*, III, 2 (August, 1928), 21-27. E

"Madame August," *Focus: A Periodical to the Point in Matters of Health, Wealth & Life*, VI, 2 (August, 1928), 67-71. E

"Decadence," *ibid.*, VI, 3 (September, 1928), 131-134. E

"Puritanism," *ibid.*, VI, 4 (October, 1928), 195-198. E

"Peace," *ibid.*, VI, 5 (November, 1928), 259-262. E

"Post Early," *ibid.*, VI, 6 (December, 1928), 327-331. E

"Mr. Clive Bell's Proust," *New Adelphi*, II, 2 (December, 1928-February, 1929), 160-162. R

"Continuous Performance: Pictures and Films," *Close Up*, IV, 1 (January, 1929), 51-57. E

"Resolution," *Purpose*, I, 1 (January-March, 1929), 7-9. E

Note to eds., *Little Review*, XII, 2 (May, 1929), 31.

Reply to questionnaire — "Confessions" — from eds., *ibid.*, pp. 70-71.

"Continuous Performance: Almost Persuaded," *Close Up*, IV, 6 (June, 1929), 31-37. E

"Leadership in Marriage," *New Adelphi*, II, 4 (June-August, 1929), 345-348. E

Review of Robert Saudek's *Experiments with Handwriting*, *ibid.*, p. 380.

"Talkies, Plays and Books: Thoughts on the Approaching Battle Between the Spoken Pictures, Literature and the Stage," *Vanity Fair* (New York), XXXII, 6 (August, 1929), 56. E

"Continuous Performance: Dialogue in Dixie," *Close Up*, V, 3 (September, 1929), 211-218. E

"The Censorship Petition," *ibid.*, VI, 1 (January, 1930), 7-11. E

"Continuous Performance: A Tear for Lycidas," *ibid.*, VII, 3 (September, 1930), 196-202. E

"Ordeal," *Window: A Quarterly Magazine*, I, 4 (October, 1930), 2-9. Reprinted in Edward J. O'Brien, ed., *Best British Short Stories of 1931* (New York: Dodd, Mead & Co., 1931), pp. 183-189. SS

"The Return of William Wordsworth," *Adelphi*, New Series, I, 3 (December, 1930), Review Supplement, xvi-xix. R

"Man Never Is . . .," *ibid.*, New Series, I, 6 (March, 1931), 521-522. R

"Continuous Performance: Narcissus," *Close Up*, VIII, 3 (September, 1931), 182-185. E

"Continuous Performance: This Spoon-fed Generation?" *ibid.*, VIII, 4 (December, 1931), 304-308. E

Letter to Dilly Tante, in "Dilly Tante Observes," *Wilson Bulletin*, VI (December, 1931), 285.

"Continuous Performance: The Film Gone Male," *Close Up*, IX, 1 (March, 1932), 36-38. E

"Continuous Performance," *ibid.*, X, 2 (June, 1933), 130-132. E

Review of *Documents 33*, April-August, *ibid.*, X, 3 (September, 1933), 295-296.

Contribution to Geoffrey West, ed., "The Artist and the World To-day (A symposium in which various writers define their position in relation to the life and conditions of our time)," *Bookman* (London), no. 512, LXXXVI (May, 1934), 94; reprinted in Geoffrey West, ed., "The Artist and the World Today: A Symposium," *Literary World*, no. 3 (July, 1934), p. 6.

"Nook on Parnassus," *Life and Letters To-day*, no. 2, XIII (December, 1935), 84-88. SS

Two selections from *Clear Horizon, Signatures: Work in Progress*, I, 1 (Spring, 1936), n.p. N

"C. F. Ramuz," *Life and Letters To-day*, no. 4, XIV (Summer, 1936), 46-47. E

"Novels," *ibid.*, no. 6, XV (Winter, 1936), 188-189. R

"Yeats of Bloomsbury," *ibid.*, no. 20, XXI (April, 1939), 60-66. E

Tr., "Prayer," *ibid.*, no. 22, XXI (June, 1939), 7. (Author and original title not given.) P

"Adventure for Readers," *ibid.*, no. 23, XXII (July, 1939). 45-52. R

"A Talk About Talking," *ibid.*, no. 27 [sic — erratum for 28], XXIII (December, 1939), 286-288. E

"Needless Worry," *ibid.*, no. 30, XXIV (February, 1940), 160-163. E

"Nor Dust Nor Moth," *American Mercury*, no. 197, L (May, 1940), 111. P

"Tryst," *English Story: Second Series* (1941), pp. 69-73. SS

"Dark Harmony," *Spectator* (London), no. 5973, CLXIX (December 18, 1942), 573. P

"Haven," *Life and Letters To-day*, no. 84, XLII (August, 1944), 97-105. SS

"Excursion," *English Story: Sixth Series* (1945), pp. 107-112. SS

"Visitor," *Life and Letters*, no. 97, XLVI (September, 1945), 167-172. SS

"Visit," *ibid.*, pp. 173-181. SS

"Work in Progress," *ibid.*, no. 104, XLIX (April, 1946), 20-44; no. 105, XLIX (May, 1946), 99-114; no. 111, LI (November, 1946), 79-88. N

"Novels," *ibid.*, no. 127, LVI (March, 1948), 188-192. E

"A Stranger About," *English Story: Ninth Series* (1949), pp. 90-94. SS

16

Rhythm in Forster's
A Passage to India

RICHARD R. WERRY

In *Aspects of the Novel*, E. M. Forster has given a lecture to the subject of "Pattern and Rhythm" in fiction. He attacks the problem of pattern boldly and with it the novels of Henry James, but he hesitates in approaching rhythm, edging "rather nervously" towards the idea.[1] There are two kinds of rhythm that can be developed in the novel, Forster suggests: an easy rhythm of discernible notation, and a difficult one integral to the whole work but not separable from it.

> . . . Beethoven's Fifth Symphony, for instance, starts with the rhythm 'diddidy dum,' which we can all hear and tap to. But the symphony as a whole has also a rhythm — due mainly to the relation between its movements — which some people can hear but no one can tap to. This second sort of rhythm is difficult, and whether it is substantially the same as the first sort only a musician could tell us. What a literary man wants to say though is that the first kind of rhythm, the diddidy dum, can be found in certain novels and may give them beauty. And the other rhythm, the difficult one — the rhythm of the Fifth Symphony as a whole — I cannot quote you any parallels for that in fiction, yet it may be present.

Forster cites the recurring musical phrase written by Vinteuil in Proust's *A la recherche du temps perdu* as an example of easy rhythm, and suggests, without attempting specific analysis, that one feels the difficult rhythm in *War and Peace*.

In this essay, I should like to make Forster the subject of his own criticism, demonstrating how rhythm, both easy and difficult, pervades *A Passage to India*.

227

I

Throughout *A Passage to India* occur certain obvious restatements of diddidy dum rhythms that any attentive reader must notice and associate. The untracked peregrinations of the ubiquitous wasp, the echo and its echoes, the similarity between the original conversation of Mrs. Moore and Dr. Aziz and that of Ralph Moore and Dr. Aziz are examples. Their obviousness, however, does not reduce them to patterned banality. They are saved from becoming boring because Forster has taken pains to prevent them from "hardening into symbols." We never quite know what to make of the wasp, or of the echo. We can never at any time say, "Here Forster intends the echo to be a symbol of ——"; or, "The wasp clearly signifies ——." The truth is that the echo and the wasp signify nothing effable. Both function in the story, the former binding together Godbole and Mrs. Moore and serving to restrain Adela, the latter connecting Mrs. Moore, even after death, with Godbole and Dr. Aziz.

> Something — not a sight, but a sound — flitted past him [Aziz], and caused him to re-read his letter to Miss Quested. Hadn't he wanted to say something else to her? Taking out his pen, he added: "For my own part, I shall henceforth connect you with the name that is very sacred in my mind, namely, Mrs. Moore."

We remember at once a former incident, when Godbole, thinking of Mrs. Moore, associates her with a wasp. And both, of course, operate as they do because of the scene which closes Chapter III of "The Mosque," the first occurrence, we might say, of this particular diddidy dum.

The novel abounds in examples of easy rhythm. Sometimes the rhythm relies on the repetition of a word or phrase: "Come, come, come, come"; "God is Love," Mrs. Moore thinks early in the novel, and in the "Temple" a draftsman's error results in "God si Love." More often the repetition is imagistic or ideologic. The punkah pusher at the trial, seemingly representing the "Indian body triumphant," is certainly related to the servitor whose "hereditary office" it is "to close the gates of salvation." In the book's beginning, the inhabitants of Chandrapore seem made "of mud moving"; near the end, in the "Temple" ceremony, the servitor "entered the dark waters, pushing the village before him, until the clay dolls slipped off their chairs and began to gutter in the rain," and Professor Godbole "picked up a fragment of mud" and "smeared it on his forehead without much ceremony." The description of the Marabar echo is anticipated by the description of the sunrise which Adela and Mrs. Moore witness on their way to the caves. Compare the two.

> . . . the sky to the left turned angry orange. Colour throbbed and mounted behind a pattern of trees, grew in intensity, was yet brighter, incredibly brighter, strained from without against the globe of the air. They awaited the miracle. But at the supreme moment, when night should have died and day lived, nothing occurred. It was as if virtue had failed in the celestial fount. The hues in the east decayed, the hills seemed dimmer though in fact better lit, and a profound disappointment entered with the morning breeze.

> There are some exquisite echoes in India; there is the whisper round the dome at Bijapur; there are the long solid sentences that voyage through the air at Mandu, and return unbroken to their creator. The echo in a Marabar cave is not like these, it is entirely devoid of distinction. Whatever is said, the same monotonous noise replies, and quivers up and down the walls until it is absorbed into the roof.

Though the melodies are different, the rhythm is the same as both experiences spiral toward a peak of significance which at the very moment of meaningfulness cancels itself into meaninglessness.

It would be a statistician's task to enumerate all of the examples of diddidy dum rhythm in *A Passage to India* which are based on the repetition or association of words, phrases, tapestried descrip-

tions. But this easy rhythm is not limited to such obvious applica-
tions. It has more subtly been woven into action proper. Thus,
it serves to predict what is to come, and the casual reader without
consciously understanding why is prepared to accept what baldly
rendered he would reject as beyond belief. With any kind of
fantasy, the writer's chief problem is always to make the unreal
seem real. There are elements of fantasy in *A Passage to India*.
On the surface a realistic novel concerned with some of the great
social difficulties of our century, it is, underneath, a mystic's approach to the eternal problem of creation. Surface and strata must
be reconciled, the reality of this mechanical age somehow merged
with the great unreality of eternity. But how? Certainly not by
any repetition of symbol or sensation: only by a marked rhythm
of action, which is for the reader direct experience.

In the "Mosque," shortly after Adela and Ronny have agreed
to abandon their engagement but to remain friends, the Nawab
Bahadur invites them to go for a ride with him. He suggests the
trip but leaves it to Ronny to accept or refuse — "The City
Magistrate would decide whether the offer was acceptable." We
suspect that Ronny will refuse, and that the Nawab expects a
refusal. But Adela has chided Ronny for treating Indians without
consideration, and Ronny seizes upon this "opportunity of showing that he could treat Indians with consideration." The Nawab
orders his chauffeur to take the Gangavati Road, but after he
has fallen asleep, the plans are changed. They take the Marabar
Road instead.

Pause now to consider how these events repeat in advance, as
it were, the events leading up to the novel's main incident, that
of the "Caves."

Dr. Aziz comes to Fielding's party with the same "hospitable
intent" with which the Nawab approached Ronny and Adela.
In a moment of enthusiasm, he invites Mrs. Moore, Adela,
Fielding, and Godbole to visit him at home. He expects the invitation to be politely refused (we have been prepared for the
spirit of this invitation not only by the incident of the Nawab

but also by the incident involving Mrs. Bhattacharya) and is obliged to make the best of things, like the Nawab, when Adela and Mrs. Moore accept. However, plans are changed: Dr. Aziz seeks to extricate himself by offering to entertain at the Marabar Caves instead of at home. The manner in which these excursions come into being is not the same, but the rhythm of development is.

Return now to the drive on the Marabar Road. There is an accident. Its nature is not clear to anyone except to Adela in a vague kind of way. She insists it was an animal which ran into them, though exactly what kind she does not know. Goats are suggested, also buffalo, but finally it is decided that the animal was a hyena. In the process of investigating "the external force" that had "impinged," Adela "in her excitement knelt and swept her skirts about, until it was she if anyone who appeared to have attacked the car." Miss Derek in her Mudkul state car appears and rescues the party. The chauffeur, Mr. Harris, feeling very much maltreated, is abandoned at the scene of the accident and does not reappear in the story. The whole occurrence is related to Mrs. Moore. "Mrs. Moore shivered, 'A ghost.'" Adela seems not to hear the scarcely uttered explanation, but later demands an explanation of the word *ghost*. Mrs. Moore does not give it.

At the Marabar Caves there is also an accident — the nature of which is not entirely clear, though from what has already happened to Mrs. Moore in another cave, we may be justified in assuming that the fright which seized Adela, like that which seized Mrs. Moore, resulted from a misinterpretation of a natural phenomenon. But Adela, in great excitement, again so muddies up all traces of fact that it appears before long that she has attacked Dr. Aziz rather than he her. Miss Derek, again in her Mudkul state car, appears in time to justify her name by picking up Adela and rushing her back to Burton-Turton land. The guide is abandoned at the Caves, disgruntled by Dr. Aziz' slap, and does not reappear in the novel. There is much speculation by Fielding and Dr. Aziz and Godbole as to what actually happened, and several alternative explanations to that which the English settle on are considered. Later, after Adela has been much fussed over, she goes to Mrs. Moore for an explanation of the echo.

> "Mrs. Moore, what is this echo?"
> "Don't you know?"
> "No — what is it? Oh, do say! I felt you would be able to explain it. . . . This will comfort me so. . . ."
> "If you don't know, you don't know. I can't tell you."

It is pedagogically pat to say that the one incident functions in the novel to prepare the reader for, to prophesy, the other. This is true, but it is not the whole truth. For the novel is one entire texture of interlinking strands at once prophetic and reflective which constitute a total growth, like life itself. And to some extent, in fact, this quality of adhesion felt in totality gives *A Passage to India* a start toward the difficult kind of rhythm.

II

And now dare we rush in where Forster himself fears to tread.

Easy rhythm Forster defines as "repetition plus variation," and his use of it we have illustrated. Difficult rhythm in music, he says, exists in the relations among the big blocks of the whole musical work, and though he suspects there may be analogies in fiction for this rhythm of the whole which can be heard though it is never actually scored, he prefers not to seek them out except to say that one feels the existence of difficult rhythm in a work like *War and Peace*. In *A Passage to India*, I think we come as near as we ever shall to finding difficult rhythm in a state not altogether defiant of discussion.

Of course, the difficulty in definition is in part responsible for the difficulty in illustrating difficult rhythm. How can one clearly illustrate a reality which must be described by such factitious epithets as *wholeness, expansion, liberation?* Another difficulty in discussing this rhythm of the whole is the fact that it must develop of its own accord; it cannot be plotted into the novel like easy rhythm, for what is calculable is easily demonstrable and ultimately can be reduced to pattern. Pattern is exactly what difficult rhythm is not. Pattern is what Henry James excelled at: rhythm of the whole is what he lacked. Where, then, can a consideration of the nature of difficult rhythm in a work of fiction begin?

I suggest that it must begin with the effect of the entire work. Does it, like Beethoven's *Fifth* or any other great symphony, leave the reader with a summary chordal suspension after the music has ceased? Does the whole reside in the part as well as the part in the whole? Perhaps we can fall back on the terminology of literary scholarship to illustrate this approach, and say that the final perception of the whole work in any fraction of it operates *synecdochically*.

For example, at the mention of echo in any discussion of *A Passage to India*, not one but a dozen separate experiences are likely to leap into the mind of one who has read the book thoroughly (and probably never the same dozen for any two readers): Mrs. Moore in her cave, Adela in hers, Godbole in none yet in all, Dr. Aziz repeating to Ralph what he had said to Mrs. Moore years ago, muddle and mystery — mystery and muddle — on and on the word *echo*, like its image in the book, sets coiling "a snake composed of small snakes, which writhe independently." But nothing in the book is independent, though in the first reading, each experience may seem to be. In a sense, everything is an echo of something that has already happened, and the source of an echo yet to be heard.

Now, if this were true in a cause-and-effect relationship only, we would be saying nothing of the novel except that it is patterned according to a cause-effect concatenation which pursues its course logically forward or backward, whichever way we choose to glance. But though cause and effect certainly is operative in the novel, we cannot say that cause in the sense of the story's action proceeds logically beyond the nature of the characters. In other words, we cannot say, for instance, that the echo is either cause of what happens after its appearance, or effect of what has happened before. Yet it is part of both: it is. The same thing can be said of the Marabar Caves themselves: the book begins with them, proceeds through them, concludes with Dr. Aziz and Fielding still talking of them, and yet nothing about them has been determined; they are, as they have been, as they will be. As with music, one feels in the whole work a certain positive indefiniteness that is, if not absolute, at least stable.

A second approach to difficult rhythm may be made by surveying the structure of the whole work. One can set down classic rules for the form of a symphony, a drama, or a novel, as, indeed, critics have done in some times, and an artist can follow these rules to the letter without achieving or even approaching the quality of difficult rhythm. The kind of structure about which I am speaking has nothing whatever to do with length, balance, thematic development, or other aspects of structural technique. It is developed without design by the novelist; but its development is dictated by that instinct for rightness which distinguishes the true artist from the artistic craftsman. It can lift a work to greatness despite other structural deficiencies.

There is no formula by which such structure can be circumscribed. We can discuss it only in relation to a given work, saying, "This has been done," saying, "The effect of this is so-and-so," definitely *not* saying, "The author, anticipating his need for inspiring this emotion, concocted this arrangement to achieve the desired effect." An author who has succeeded thus amorphously with structure may as clearly as a critic perceive what he has done with total organization when he has done it, but he cannot consciously plan before he creates without committing himself to the crutches of pattern. So as he proceeds, he relies on instinct in molding the material. How has Forster molded his material in *A Passage to India?*

My answer is: Centrifugally.

The "Mosque" sets the structural rhythm for the novel's sections. It opens with an authorial description of an area of India twenty miles distant from the Marabar Caves, Chandrapore, a description colored to reduce human endeavor to its lowest level in relation to the higher absolute of the universe: the inhabitants of Chandrapore seem to be made of "mud moving"; their history for centuries has been one of indiscrete persistence which preserves the "general outline" of the town "swelling here, shrinking there, like some low but indestructible form of life." But "the sky settles everything."

This emotional tone, this process which is movement, this attitude which is theme — in a phrase, this difficult rhythm is maintained in the other two sections of the novel, and in the light of the story intensified. The "Caves" begins with a brief essay, also divinely irrefutable in its authorial prerogatives, again discussing an area of India, the environs of the Caves themselves, again revealing human capabilities on a level of impotency. "The visitor returns to Chandrapore uncertain whether he has had an interesting experience or a dull one or any experience at all." On the other hand, "The caves are readily described," — by Forster in lieu of God, truth, what-you-will. Yet the visitor finds it difficult to discuss the caves; he, like Godbole, is reduced to inarticulateness, or to the expression of his feelings in an ancient and apparently irrelevant song.

> It is as if the surrounding plain or the passing birds have taken upon themselves to exclaim "extraordinary," and the word has taken root in the air, and been inhaled by mankind.

The "Temple" opens with a description of a section of India "some hundreds of miles westward of the Marabar Hills," and, presenting the Hindu ceremony of divine rebirth with an objective whimsicality, achieves an even greater authorial independence than that of either prelude to the preceding sections. Here, not only is the Hindu humility described — it is described so as to be felt sincerely by the reader and yet somehow at the same time made ridiculous, pathetic in its pompous pretense at being what it actually is. The ceremony is in a sense the translation into action of what the other preludes have implied pictorially.

So the novel falls into three movements — the first, "Mosque" — adagio-allegretto; the second, "Caves" — allegro-appassionato; the third, "Temple" — larghetto-sostenuto — and the whole rubato. Each section, without in any sense duplicating the others or falling into schematic patterns, moves with the same relatively leisurely pace into and away from a focal scene in which with pageantry more than with action an effect is produced: the meeting in the mosque producing harmony; the accidents in the caves producing discord, suspicion and isolation; the Temple ceremony producing confusion and resignation — perhaps, too, a hint of wisdom. The Temple ceremony's total ineffectiveness, its indifference to its own state of being, its disruption — all suggest the static flexibility of India and the human race in the chaotic organization of this book's universe. Thus, decidedly, it summarizes a future, which is also a present, and a past we have just experienced. Like a symphony, the novel's sections, though done in different keys and tempos, manage to possess at the conclusion a modal unity which interlinks the sections; superimposes them, we might almost say.

Content has something to do with this unity. So does story, and I am sure so does theme — the Forster theme of conflicting social conventions generating labyrinths of misunderstanding and personal tragedy. Doubtless, without this specific story involving this specific theme, the novel could not have achieved its rhythmic unity. But it is the unplotted, self-generating synthesis of creation which I have tried to illustrate in my description of the sections (a treatment certainly involving repetition and echoing, as with easy rhythm, except that the emotions of creator and reader alike perceive the strokes rather than the intellect) that weaves into the whole work that rhythm which is felt but cannot be tapped to.

Expansion, Forster wrote in *Aspects of the Novel* in 1927 (was he thinking back to the creation of *A Passage to India*?), "is the idea the novelist must cling to. Not completion. Not rounding off but opening out." The extent to which a novel expands, opens out, remains incomplete without seeming deficient to the reader's aesthetic kinesthesia, is perhaps the best method of measuring difficult rhythm. *A Passage to India* expands limitlessly, like the universe itself.

NOTE

1. The quotations in this article, from E. M. Forster's *Aspects of the Novel* (New York, 1927) and *A Passage to India* (New York, 1924), are used by permission of Harcourt, Brace and Company, publishers.

   The interested reader may refer to an earlier treatment of the subject of rhythm in *A Passage to India* in E. K. Brown's *Rhythm in the Novel* (Toronto: University of Toronto Press, 1950), pp. 87-115.

17.
Freud and the Riddle of Mrs. Dalloway

KEITH HOLLINGSWORTH

Mrs. DALLOWAY has always been a baffling novel. It has grown richer as critics have dealt with it, but one of its central features — the one chiefly responsible for the difficulty — has never been adequately treated. Certain critics who admire Virginia Woolf's subtleties of method and style have implied that the book somehow falls short — that it lacks the substance which a sufficiently large theme might give to it.[1] In spite of such obstacles, readers come to it again and again, rightly hoping to find more in it; it is one of those notable books whose suggestive power attracts us even when our understanding remains incomplete.

Mrs. Woolf did not intend to baffle her readers. The references to *Mrs. Dalloway* (once or twice under another title) in the published extracts from her diary, between 1922 and 1925, are of the sort we might expect from such an artist; they show that the book was hard work, that it was intensely personal, that the design interested her "hugely," that her intention was large. They show, too, that she thought she had achieved her aim. In October, 1924, a week after she had written the final words of the novel, she recorded that she felt "rather more fully relieved of [her] meaning than usual."[2] In December she was copying the whole and making minor revisions; she thought *Mrs. Dalloway* the most satisfactory of all her novels so far but had not yet read it "cold-bloodedly."

> The reviewers will say that it is disjointed because of the mad scenes not connecting with the Dalloway scenes. And I suppose there is some superficial glittery writing. But is it "unreal"? Is it mere accomplishment? I think not. And as I think I said before, it seems to leave me plunged in the richest strata of my mind.[3]

239

What she foresaw as the objection of reviewers has remained the difficulty of readers. She did not remove the ground for it — her intention required, obviously, what she had done.

In June, 1928, three years after first publication of the novel, Mrs. Woolf wrote an introduction for a reprinting. She was aware, surely, that reviewers and readers had not seen enough of her design; she quite deliberately gave a clue to it.

> To tell the reader anything that his own imagination and insight have not already discovered would need not a page or two of preface but a volume or two of autobiography. . . . Of *Mrs. Dalloway* then one can only bring to light at the moment a few scraps, of little importance or none perhaps; as that in the first version Septimus, who later is intended to be her double, had no existence; and that Mrs. Dalloway was originally to kill herself or perhaps merely to die at the end of the party.[4]

When we turn from the clue to the novel itself, it is not hard to see that Septimus, the double, is most intricately linked to Clarissa. We notice the merest suggestion of a physical likeness (both have beak noses); we find "Fear no more the heat of the sun" echoing in the minds of both, which serves to link them, though it occurs once, too, in a revery of Peter Walsh. And we notice with heightened attention Clarissa's own sense of identification with the young man who had killed himself. The relationships of form between the two characters, their positions in the successive tableaux, their mental contrasts — all these things which the author wrote into the novel have been examined by critics, and no repetition is needed.[5] But the description of *how* the two are linked is unsatisfactory unless we know *why;* and Mrs. Woolf — offhand but purposeful — seemed to be writing a preface to tell us. The clue, nevertheless, remains a puzzle in itself: when the differences between Septimus and Clarissa bulk larger than the likenesses, how can he be her double?

David Daiches once frankly admitted that the statement shocked him.[6] Others have written about Mrs. Dalloway without mentioning it, and what has been written about it is unconvincing. Mr. Daiches, for example, says in another place:

> Mrs. Dalloway, that is, was originally to lose herself in the flux of experience by dying, while later the same idea was more subtly expressed by making her identify herself with an unknown young man who had already died.[7]

John Graham gives a reading of *Mrs. Dalloway* which makes time the central theme and by it links Septimus and Clarissa:

> Septimus has had the vision of a cosmic unity which Clarissa, rooted as she is in the process of time, can receive only dimly and briefly.[8]

Clarissa, Graham says, triumphs over time; her return to the party, at the end of the book, "symbolizes the transfiguration of time." Of the discarding of Mrs. Woolf's first plan, he remarks:

> An objective correlative is lacking in *Mrs. Dalloway,* where Clarissa, at the end, is herself the symbol of her own vision. That explains, I think, why Mrs. Woolf could not follow her first intention of having Clarissa die: if she had, the meaning of Clarissa's vision would have vanished with Clarissa.[9]

James Hafley has it that both Septimus and Clarissa seek the virtue of surrendering the self to

> what Bergson would call the spirit or supraconsciousness-memory: pure-time existence or duration. . . . Both Septimus and Mrs. Dalloway have therefore to find a way of escaping from the false life to what they believe true reality.[10]

Even when read in their contexts, such explanations seem excessively fine-spun.

Leon Edel, more simply, finds the essential likeness of Septimus and Clarissa in their "failure to feel,"[11] but Clarissa's "failure" is so different in range that one remains dissatisfied. Edel is right, of course, when he says that Septimus and Clarissa "seem to be two facets of the same personality — indeed the projection by Virginia Woolf of two sides of herself." This is significant, but it is not enough; it is akin to the general truth expressed by Flaubert when he said, "I am Emma Bovary."

All these efforts to deal with the author's clue seem inadequate; no one of them justifies the decisive wording of her assertion. They are only partial, moreover, in that they interpret the word "double" as meaning a like figure. If Mrs. Woolf had meant nothing but that, any of several terms such as "counterpart" would have done as well. She chose to call Septimus a double, a *doppelgänger;* and to see one's own double, one's own soul withdrawn from one's body, is a warning of imminent death. The word itself leads us to regard Septimus[12] as a representative of death, separated by the will of the author from Clarissa, whose love of life is the quality presented when first we meet her.

To be specific, Septimus Smith is the incarnation of the death-instincts, Clarissa Dalloway of the instincts of life. The death-instinct was one of Freud's hypotheses; he proposed it in *Jenseits des Lustprinzips* in 1920 and recapitulated his statement of it in *Das Ich und das Es* in 1923. Other and later psychiatrists connected the death-instinct with suicide and self-destructive behavior, as Karl Menninger did in *Man Against Himself* (1938), with a cautionary word that the idea of the death-instinct was still speculative.

I add at once that, like the characters in all good novels, Septimus and Clarissa have a primary existence of their own as created people; the symbolic quality is an aura which clings about them. Such auras are seldom interesting if the characters are not real people first. Clarissa is the will to live, dominant in most of us till we come near our end; and Septimus is the compulsion to die, likewise present in us all, by this theory, and powerful. Life is all eagerness, silly, excited over trivialities, concerned with little things and great ones: a party, the hem of a dress, meeting an old suitor, roses from a husband. But death lurks within: withdrawn, secret, disgusted with human nature, waiting the opportunity to resolve all questions by bringing an end to the meaningless flurry, perhaps on Mrs. Filmer's area railing. It makes this one of us take an overdose of sleeping pills, that one of us drink too much, another drive his car off the road, and still another lie deaf and dishevelled on a couch, with hair unkempt and tears streaming from her eyes. Every reader has felt a painful, a personal intensity in certain parts of *Mrs. Dalloway*; it is with sympathy and admiration that one reads certain words in the author's diary: "Of course the mad part tries me so much, makes my mind squirt so badly that I can hardly face spending the next weeks at it."[13] No one can escape feeling, I think, that Virginia Woolf knew the existence of the will to die — knew it as well when she began to think of *Mrs. Dalloway* in 1922 as when she finally acknowledged it in 1941.

The assertion of Freudian influence must be somewhat speculative, and subject to the judgment of readers. Freud's little book of 1920 was translated into English by C. J. M. Hubback; as *Beyond the Pleasure Principle* it was published by the International Psycho-Analytical Press, London and Vienna, in 1922. It was thus available to English readers when Freud had already come to be much talked of and when Virginia Woolf was only beginning to contemplate her novel, first briefly mentioned in *A Writer's Diary* on June 23, 1922. Somewhat later, with the issuance of the first two volumes of Freud's *Collected Papers* in 1924, Leonard and Virginia Woolf, as the Hogarth Press, became the regular publishers of English translations of Freud's work; but by this time *Mrs. Dalloway* was well advanced. One can only say that, since Freud was talked of in intellectual circles, such a person as Virginia Woolf might easily have heard discussion of the death instinct in 1922.

The question of her knowledge of Freud has been approached elsewhere. Leonard Woolf has said, in a letter to Professor Erwin Steinberg:

> We only began to publish psycho-analytic books in 1924 and I don't think my wife had read any of Freud except perhaps

> the Psycho-Pathology of Everyday Life before she wrote Mrs.
> Dalloway. . . . She never read much of Freud and I don't think
> she ever read the Interpretation of Dreams. . . .[14]

If this removes the reading of Freud, we may still suppose conversation, not so bad a resource as it is sometimes called. In spite
of notions wrongly fathered upon Freud, almost any reader can
recall scraps of reasonably intelligent conversation carried on by
persons who got their information from reviews, magazine articles,
or sources still more distant from Freud's own books. In the
twenties Freud had begun to permeate the atmosphere. Edward
A. Hungerford has pointed out that in book reviews in the *Times
Literary Supplement* in 1920 and 1921 Virginia Woolf showed
herself acquainted with Freudian themes in fiction.[15] We need
not forbid ourselves to find in her work the deliberate application
of a Freudian idea, when it is one which might commend itself
to her experience of life and to her literary purpose.

So much of Freud's theory of instinct as may lead toward *Mrs.
Dalloway* can be reviewed quickly. *Beyond the Pleasure Principle*
springs in part from the long debate about the nature of instinct
which interested biologists as they followed up the consequences
of evolutionary theory. It has the tone of many notable late
nineteenth century documents: the sense of eager inquiry, the
willingness to face the most dispiriting truths about the nature of
man, the exalted naturalistic pessimism. Through reading and
through his clinical observation, especially of compulsive repeti-
tive behavior, Freud had become convinced that instinct was "a
tendency innate in living organic matter impelling it towards the
reinstatement of an earlier condition."[16] The development of
organisms had come as the result of "external, disturbing, and
distracting influences," such as "the evolution of our earth, and
its relation to the sun."

> The conservative organic instincts have absorbed every one of
> these enforced alterations in the source of life and have stored
> them for repetition; they thus present the delusive appearance of

forces striving after change and progress, while they are merely endeavoring to reach an old goal by ways both old and new. This final goal of all organic striving can be stated too. It would be counter to the conservative nature of instinct if the goal of life were a state never hitherto reached. It must rather be an ancient starting point, which the living being left long ago, and to which it harks back again by all the circuitous paths of development. If we may assume as an experience admitting of no exception that everything dies from causes within itself, and returns to the inorganic, we can only say, *'The goal of all life is death,'* and, casting back, *'The inanimate was there before the animate.'* [17]

Such conclusions, Freud remarks, are a strange inversion of common ideas.

The postulate of the self-preservative instincts we ascribe to every living being stands in remarkable contrast to the supposition that the whole life of instinct serves the one end of bringing about death. The theoretic significance of the instincts of self-preservation, power, and self-assertion, shrinks to nothing, seen in this light; they are part-instincts designed to secure the path to death peculiar to the organism and to ward off possibilities of return to the inorganic other than the immanent ones, but the enigmatic struggle of the organism to maintain itself in spite of all the world, a struggle that cannot be brought into connection with anything else, disappears. [18]

Freud then reflects that this cannot be the whole truth: there are the sexual instincts (including of course the maternal). These, he says, are conservative too, though in a wider sense, "since they preserve life itself for a longer time."

They are the actual life-instincts; the fact that they run counter to the trend of the other instincts which lead toward death indicates a contradiction between them and the rest, one which the theory of neuroses has recognized as full of significance. There is, as it were, an oscillating rhythm in the life of organisms; the one group of instincts presses forward to reach the final goal of life as quickly as possible, the other flies back at a certain point on the way only to traverse the same stretch once more from a given spot and thus to prolong the duration of the journey.[19]

These few quotations are not to be taken as a summary of Freud's thought in the book; and one should add that Freud carefully emphasized the speculative nature of his argument. A full summary is unnecessary; there is no point-by-point relation between Freud's work and Mrs. Woolf's novel.[20] She made no use of his one example of the working-out of death-instincts, sadism; and Freud did not, in this book, discuss suicide nor relate it to the death-instinct. Whether at first-hand or not, she was impressed, I think, by the idea of a death-instinct and its opposite, Eros, which Freud called "this exquisitely dualistic conception of the instinctive life."[21] She combined it poetically with what she knew — by intuition, by personal experience — of life and death struggling within a divided self. Then the original central figure of her novel became two persons, whose two sexes, by the way, include the whole of mankind. In arranging for one of them a suicidal outbreak of the instinct to die, she was not following Freud, but she was making the same application of his theory that some psychiatrists were to make after her. On the familiar level of the book, Clarissa is bright busy sanity; Septimus is malign illness. But now they represent more, and we can see the two in a new relationship of unity. She is not the solely normal; he is not truly an aberration. They are inseparable aspects of the innermost, the aboriginal nature of mankind; their being and their actions dramatically represent the exquisite dualism. The apparently tenuous and fragile story of a day has an underlying theme of the greatest magnitude.

Did Mrs. Woolf expect that her readers would know about Freud's theory of a death-instinct? It is not necessary to suppose that she thought they must. I believe Mrs. Woolf expected to draw upon the reader's intuitive understanding that the wish for life and for death dwelt in everyone. The response was not all she had hoped for; she then wrote the explanatory key, which one re-reads now with a new sense of communication.

What does a reading, with the aid of her clue, bring to light in the novel? (Or ought we always to call it the poem?) It reveals, as I have just said, a unifying theme of large dimensions; and in addition a true dramatic element. We need no longer feel frustrated because the principals in the plot never meet, no longer suspect a hidden caprice in the author's putting them into the same book. The symbolic appropriateness of the plot and the unity of the action are evident when the symbolic value of the characters is recognized. The decision to make them two was of course a right one. The embodiment of the life- and the death-instincts in two persons gives us a dramatic separation of the will-to-live and the will-to-die; it isolates both as entities, neither of which, within the story, is subject to the other.

Thus developed, the novel says inescapably that though the two are one — these persons with symbolic auras — in the usual round of life they do not really know each other. Septimus lives withdrawn in the body of vast London; Clarissa is known to somewhat more of London, but not to him. They are near each other; they live within the sound of the same chiming clocks; some sights can meet the eyes of both. Through the measured day, they move in their own orbits, in a kind of mobile balance. When they are so near, how can each fail to feel the other's presence? Will they not meet? When they do, surely they must recognize each other? And what then? But they do not meet, of course. Septimus cannot be bidden to the reception where the easy, happy ones gather, nor can his final assertive act of self-destruction prevent the party. The news of a triumph of death is brought to it almost incidentally, because Sir William Bradshaw is late; and Septimus is made known to Clarissa by the agency of the alienist who has no idea of what he is doing, who does not understand either these two persons or the aspects of being they represent. "Oh! thought Clarissa, in the middle of my party, here's death, she thought." She intuitively knows the young man; identifies herself, contrasts herself with him. She has not actually seen her double, the harbinger of death, but has narrowly missed him. With the news the Bradshaws bring, Clarissa knows what Septimus is and who he is. He is the will to die; he is the other part of herself.

Clarissa's great moments of revelation have now begun. Self-knowledge enlarges her spirit. We have seen her mind as quite ordinary, her human sympathies as warm but incomplete; her endearing quality has been her vivid feeling during every hour she lives. Now she is granted illumination previously impossible for her. The several important themes which have appeared before — the mystery of individual existence, consciousness and time, the instincts of life and death — are combined in an intense lyric expression. In her revery, Clarissa sees the beauty of the world, the distresses of man, and her personal triviality. From the party, the scene of her existence and its emblem, she looks outward to the general life and accepts her proper burden of responsibility. "Somehow it was her disaster — her disgrace. It was her punishment to see sink and disappear here a man, there a woman, in this profound darkness, and she forced to stand here in her evening dress."

When these passages near the end so naturally and so successfully universalize the vision of Mrs. Dalloway, we are certain that her relation to Septimus is neither arbitrary nor capricious. "She felt somehow very like him — the young man who had killed himself. She felt glad that he had done it; thrown it away." (The "glad" that here shocks a first reader cannot trouble us now.) Clarissa has accepted the nature of her other self, his presence in her, the nature of her humanity.

But we are in a novel, not an allegory, and after the important revery scene Mrs. Woolf returns us to the small talk of the party of life, where people are simply people. We wait with Peter Walsh, who is impatient to see Clarissa; at last she comes. The event is slight; the reader who sees it only in its realistic texture finds it inadequate. But when we read with the memory of the symbolic shadows, they hover just behind the focus of our attention and give the ending a tremendous urgency. Clarissa knows death and she lives; we are present at a victory; we feel an elation not quite to be explained by the little incident or by the sense of the words. "What is this terror? what is this ecstasy? he thought to himself. What is it that fills me with extraordinary excitement?

"It is Clarissa, he said.

"For there she was."

NOTES

1. For example: "The dissolution of experience into tenuous insights — this is the real theme of the most important part of Virginia Woolf's work, and it is the real theme of *Mrs. Dalloway.*" — David Daiches, *Virginia Woolf*, Makers of Modern Literature (Norfolk, Conn., 1942), p. 78.
2. Virginia Woolf, *A Writer's Diary: Selections from the Diary of Virginia Woolf*, ed. by Leonard Woolf (New York, 1954), p. 66.
3. *Ibid.*, p. 68; quoted with the permission of Harcourt, Brace and Company, the publishers.
4. Introduction, *Mrs. Dalloway*, Modern Library (New York, 1928), p. vi; used by permission.
5. One account may be seen in Reuben Brower, *The Fields of Light* (New York, 1951), pp. 123-137.
6. *The Novel and the Modern World* (Chicago, 1939), p. 181.
7. *Virginia Woolf*, p. 76.
8. John Graham, "Time in the Novels of Virginia Woolf," *University of Toronto Quarterly*, XVIII (January, 1949), 188.
9. *Ibid.*, p. 191.
10. James Hafley, *The Glass Roof* (Berkeley, 1954), p. 63.
11. Leon Edel, *The Psychological Novel, 1900-1950* (Philadelphia, 1955), p. 197.
12. His name, that of a seventh child, is unusual among the names of Mrs. Woolf's characters. Is it intended to be in keeping with magic or necromancy?
13. *A Writer's Diary*, p. 56; June 19, 1923.
14. Letter quoted in full in Erwin Steinberg, "Note on a Note," in *Literature and Psychology*, the News Letter of the Conference on Literature and Psychology of the Modern Language Association, IV (September, 1954), 64.
15. Edward A. Hungerford, "Mrs. Woolf, Freud, and J. D. Beresford," *Literature and Psychology*, [V] (August, 1955), 49-51.
16. Sigmund Freud, *Beyond the Pleasure Principle*, authorized translation from the second German edition by C. J. M. Hubback (New York, [1922]), p. 44. The three long quotations following from this work are quoted with the permission of Liveright Publishers, New York.
17. *Ibid.*, p. 47.
18. *Ibid.*, p. 48.
19. *Ibid.*, pp. 50-51.

20. If Mrs. Woolf herself read *Beyond the Pleasure Principle,* she must have noticed with interest Freud's few sentences on the Kantian mental category of time and the timelessness of the unconscious processes. (P. 32.)
21. *Ibid.,* p. 62. In following it out, as he says, "we have steered unawares into the haven of Schopenhauer's philosophy." In *Beyond the Pleasure Principle,* Freud most often speaks of life- and death-instincts in the plural, but he also uses the singular.

18

William Ellery Leonard: an Appraisal

CHESTER E. JORGENSON

IT WAS A LATE afternoon in the autumn of 1929 when I first met William Ellery Leonard (1876-1944). I had come to his Murray Street apartment at his invitation. He knew that I (a callow and ambitious student who needed to do a "thesis" to graduate as a major in English) wanted to write on him — as a poet, scholar, and man. He also had heard that my faculty adviser was amiably contemptuous of a thesis on a man not yet interred. And he sensed — better than I — that many of his colleagues were overtly hostile to a scholar who dared to be a poet and a poet who could not help being a scholar. He probably knew that I had been discouraged by my adviser against writing on a man whose private life had been the topic of those who delight in scandalous gossip. I had read Leonard's *Two Lives*, *The Locomotive God*, and the "sensational" newspaper articles on his phobia, his leonine hair, and his purple Windsor tie. I knew that Professor Leonard was more than a poet distrusted by scholars and a scholar whose poetry had been honored by only a discerning few. My interest in the man whom I had seen walking up Bascom Hill to his classes was equalled only by my fear of meeting him — meeting the translator of *De Rerum Natura*, *Beowulf*, the *Fragments of Empedocles*, the author of *Socrates, Master of Life*, *The Poet of Galilee*, *Byron and Byronism in America*, and the poet who had made *The Vaunt of Man* and *Two Lives*.

He let me in, offered a cigarette, and made me feel as if I had a right to his time. His wife joined us and seemed glad that a student wanted to meet her husband as an object of study. And after we had talked I followed him to the attic, where in shadowed corners — beyond bicycles and boxes of journals and books — he found packages of MSS, including elementary school examinations and exercises, unpublished verses, and variants of poems published. I was invited to read and copy out whatever we found. Seldom has an undergraduate been treated more graciously.

This was only the first afternoon. I returned again and again to Murray Street — to ask questions, to return MSS and take out more, to listen to his talk on issues revealed in his poetry and in *The Locomotive God*. And there were intense moments when to clarify a point he would speak out his own verses. One late afternoon he spoke the sonnet from *Two Lives* —

> *"Freut euch des Lebens — Take ye joy of life —*
> *Weil noch das Laempchen glueht — whilst the lamp glows —*
> *Pfluecket die Rose — pluck, O pluck the rose —*
> *Eh' sie verblueht — before it fades"* . . . (my wife!) . . .
> *"Man schafft so gern — we plague from morn to morn —*
> *Sich Sorg' und Mueh' — ourselves with care and strife —*
> *Sucht Dornen auf — we seek too oft the thorn*
> *Und findet sie — and find it"* . . . (O my wife!) . . .
> *"Und laesst das Veilchen — leave the violet fair —*
> *Ach, unbemerkt — unnoticed evermore —*
> *Das dort am Wege blueht — that blossoms there*
> *Along the roadside"* . . . O'er and o'er and o'er
> Ring in my widowed heart the words, the air,
> As if I heard them from the Other Shore.

Never before nor long since have I felt so sharply the passion that a poet brings to his art. It was as if he were making the words for the first time — as if he had only then recreated the poignant and pathetic experience out of the life he had endured. Listening to the poet (even as a casual undergraduate who feels he might find his future in literature) I knew that what he said was not irrelevant to human experience, the depths of which we only occasionally realize.

After nearly three decades, I want less to write a eulogium than to invite readers to consider what William Ellery Leonard phrased in his various works. That he has been ignored by critics may temporarily be less important than that (as he said one day to me) he aimed at the balanced life of Socrates, Dante, Goethe, and Shakespeare. Perhaps an academic vaunt to impress a young man — but I accept his aspiration now, as I had to then.

Before an account of his evolution as poet, I want to recreate his major assumptions of what the creative imagination demands of art — and of life. Early in his adventures as a poet and scholar, he wrote on Socrates and on Jesus: *Socrates, Master of Life* and *The Poet of Galilee*. These monographs reveal that his sense of time was not provincial: "The deepest problems are the same as then, and Socrates was perhaps nearer to their solution than some of us."[1] That is, "a contemporary is not a matter of time, except etymologically. . . ."[2] And from experience and books he was determined to be with those who are dedicated to the "emancipation from all that hobbles or shackles the mind — emancipation from ignorance, uncouthness, stupidity, gloom, fear, and the whole interminable train of devils, among whom sin, though chief, is but one."[3] The artist (whatever his medium) is familiar with the antecedents of his present and is not to be lured "into the pedantry of a narrow intellectualism."[4] Nor is he less "an alert man of affairs" than "a dreamer of dreams."[5]

William Ellery Leonard assumed that the poet's office was austere, that it was more than the devices of "strophe, or metre, or rhyme," more than "mere tumult in the blood." The poet was he who coveted the "realities of the spirit, the sympathetic vision which seems at times almost to penetrate the mysteries of life and of nature — passions and desires of men and women, grass and flowers beneath our too often heedless feet, moon and stars over our unlifted heads. . . . Poetry is vision, exaltation, speech. . . ."[6] It is the "poet's vision of the unseen completeness" that "makes poignant his realization of the imperfection and incompleteness of the world about him."[7]

Leonard as scholar and poet should have become a twentieth century example of Emerson's "American Scholar." He knew the past and he was sensitive to nature as sensuous phenomena and law and he was bold and candid in defending the rights of "men and women, the pitied and bewailed." His was the large desire and will to be a prophet of the nature of things.

Leonard's testament of what man's imagination variously calls beauty or morality is suggested in his "A Little Sermon on Life and Literature,"[8] a critique of Irving Babbitt's *Rousseau and Romanticism*. He maintains "with Aristotle, yes and with Emerson, the sovereignty of ethics for those beings that are human." Man's distinctive nature lies between the "life of the senses," as in Don Juan, and the "life of the intellect," itself amoral, as in Mephistopheles. "To be ethical is to be human," and "the problem of what is human and what is manly might be called at first thought the central problem of civilization; yet humankind, in making its ideal of the type an ethical ideal, and not, for instance, an intellectual, has at the same time been in the great issues — say, loyalty, justice, kindness, gratitude, courage, honesty — so consistent in the specific ethical values, as to compel us to say rather that the making of those values prevail is the central task of civilization. Those values themselves, in their permanence and power (though forever subject to interpretation and readjustment in detail), indicate both what we are and what we aim to be, — what is human and most human." Leonard does not mean that there is an absolute ethic or that the socialization of ethics to the exclusion of individual autonomy is good. That is, although there is a large proximate (but not "absolute") ethical truth, the individual strives to fulfill his organic nature rather than follow the examples of others with mere "mechanical motion" or in the mood of "adoring prostration or complacent pose." As an "ethical positivist," he fears the neo-humanist implication of "universal prescription for obtaining centrality."

Since Leonard, like Babbitt, assumes that the "common-to-all keeps us men and women," one may feel that he disagreed with Babbitt's authoritarian polemics more than with his assumptions and conclusions. Leonard does not deny the primary role of self-discipline in human experience, though he maintains (differing here rhetorically with Babbitt) that "self-discipline means judicious expansion, not suppression." Then, Leonard admits (rather puckishly) that he has written on Socrates "whose daimon seems to be the original inner-check spook" and that "Goethe only came home to me when I was most, most lonely . . . Goethe, to the writer the ideal balance of soul of the modern world." Finally, Leonard himself admits that his recoil from the "inner-check" in favor of "a free, to a daring, a thoroughly experimental attitude to life" is perhaps only "a difference of emphasis" since his qualitative judgments often strangely resemble those of the group he professed to indict! It is casuistry to argue whether the vital energy is somewhat more important than vital control or the vital control more distinctively human than the energy when the two interpretations lead to broadly similar judgments on life and literature.

In the spirit of catholic sympathy Leonard is "particularly unwilling to prescribe with finality what that revelation [that is, of a work of art] may be or should be," but the judicial critic in him hastens to note that "this does not mean for one mortal instant abandoning literature, any more than life, to chaos and caprice; it does not mean for one instant a rejection of standards and tests." That is, "literature is not the report of a psychiatry clinic, or of a hospital, or of a dung-hill, unless to that report are added values that deepen our insight and enlarge our sympathies, touching the mystery and the terror and tragic vileness which is also native to man. Here all is in the earnestness, implications, and dignity of the report." He would judge each life, or each art work, in terms of its solution of "its ethical perplexities in relation to its own temperament and its own environment," but he judicially transcends his wholly relativist theory when he judges the fullness of Goethe or the bestialized eccentricity of Don Juan. Finally qualitative judgment seems to have mastered catholic sympathy (but I doubt that Leonard would view judgment and sympathy as conflict rather than complement).

In 1906 Leonard privately printed *Sonnets and Poems*,[9] a curious fusion of Emersonian idealism and Byronic self-drama and eloquence. With expansive acceptance he would search the "four regions of primordial heaven" to find that which will "feed blood and bone and spirit and desire."[10] In such verses as "For a Decadent," "Rain," "Natura Magna," he idolized primeval nature where husbandmen "wise, shag-browed and large of hand" sought help from the ancient hills.[11] His confidence is that

> The goodman may abide with Mother Earth
> And dream his dreams and have his visions still
> And trust the Infinite to see him through.[12]

The poet's soul searches for "its heritage of light and power,"[13] the "deep self of me written within the Whole" which rebukes "fatal loves and desperate delays."[14] In quest of an ultimate and absolute certainty, Leonard assumed that

> The Good is good — and we shall tend the fire,
> The holy flame that burns behind the veil!
> And each design of ours and each desire
> That would deny the eternal Good shall fail
> And art, that mocks that sunbright temple, must
> Lie soon or late a harlot in the dust.[15]

The master-mood of his early verses is the "ancient law" that the stars "bright, beautiful, unalterable and old" are "beyond earth's nether coasts of gust and flaw."[16] His imagination embraces

> Light, darkness, storms, shapes, demon and divine,
> The inward visions out of Heaven and Hell —
> And choice to make the one or other mine![17]

Owning the "dream of Plato and the hardiness of Kant," he has "all wealth within" him.[18]

But during Leonard's apprentice years, the mood of Byronic suffering and vaunt contended melodramatically with his heroic conviction of self-mastery. While living in Bolton, Massachusetts (where he knew Dr. Thomas T. Stone, "last" of the Emersonian transcendentalists), he "discovered" Byron. In his youth and early manhood Byron's moods became his — "of self-conscious adolescence, of isolation from my kind, of world-pain, of the tragic grandeurs of my fate."[19] Although many of his fevered verses are unpublished (or uncollected), he included more than he should have in *Sonnets and Poems* and *The Vaunt of Man*. His Byronic spleen was directed against a girl (called variously Annie or Marguerite) who had rejected his love-suit (apparently more posed than sincere).[20] With sullen pride he damns her as wanton and vile.

Even in the title poem of *The Vaunt of Man* written to "Agatha" (his wife in *Two Lives*), years after his "Marguerite" passion, the Byronic stance is pathetically evident. With heavy personification and exclamation, he announced:

O when I make my plea before our God,
I shall not boast my sufferance and pain,
The whirlwind snows that blinded on the plain,
The smoke I breathed, the lava fields I trod
With head unhooded and burning feet unshod,
Nor fettered hours in Houses of Disdain
With anarch Ignorance and Custom Vain,
Nor strength achieved by bowing to the rod.[21]

His poetry (before *Two Lives*) reveals that in his art and life there was "a perpetual conflict between passion and reason, between feelings and ideals," that was "abnormally acute."[22]

Leonard's civil war in his consciousness was revealed in his loyalties divided between Socrates and Emerson, Jesus and Byron, Lucretius and Darwin.[23] He was aware of a centripetal morality, and he was equally conscious of centrifugal impulse. He knew the mechanistic world of Empedocles, Lucretius, and Darwin even as he coveted the serenity of New England idealism. By temperament he was humanitarian in his concern for the hag-ridden and dispossessed even as he was austerely contemptuous of ignorance, indolence, and bourgeois mediocrity. His mind was divided in its allegiance to centrality and to flux.

If Leonard had not achieved *Two Lives,* his reputation would be that of scholar and translator. It was his narrative in sonnet form that made him a poet that mature readers of poetry honor. Stephen Vincent Benét once told me that *Two Lives* was the "greatest" poem accomplished by an American in this century.

The story in *Two Lives* can be read in the poem and recreated autobiographically in *The Locomotive God.* Intense, rapid, lyric, and reflective, *Two Lives* is the narrative of courtship, marriage and death, and of a man's endurance after his wife's suicide. Leonard came to the University of Wisconsin in 1906 as an instructor in English. He had come from study at Boston University, Harvard, Bonn, Göttingen, and Columbia, where he received his doctorate — his thesis, *Byron and Byronism in America.* He found a room in the Lake Mendota home of Professor Freeman of the English Department. The professor's daughter Charlotte, the Agatha of *Two Lives,* kept house for her father. Mrs. Freeman had drowned herself in the lake not many years before.

When Leonard wrote *Two Lives* in 1913 (several years after "Agatha," his wife, took her life), he had transcended his egoism and the vindictiveness which he had suffered when Madison's town and gown somehow blamed the husband for his wife's violent death. Had Leonard been what Madison accused him of, he could not have written the epilogue, "Indian Summer," to *Two Lives.* And there is much else he could not have written. Read the sonnet in which "Agatha" sees what her husband has pencilled —

He says, my love's
More than my tact. . . .[24]

Or the sonnet in which her thoughts become "quaintly inco-ordinate."[25] Or our imaginations may be haunted by Agatha's

> . . . olden search for death
> Thrice thwarted by her father, when with breath
> Thrice choked in foamy agony of strife
> Under the summer waters off our pier.[26]

Then, there is the sonnet in which "they led her forth that morning"[27] — and the one in which the poet stands beside his wife's open grave.[28] But the most poignant tells the moment when the wife, feeling she has escaped her threat of madness through love tells her husband

> . . . In France, five years ago
> (When father was ambassador, you know),
> *I lived with a band of ladies wan and wild,* —
> *Myself a shuddering maniac, exiled*
> *With strange physicians, and behind locked door*
> *Mumbling in bed, or tracing on the floor,*
> "The Lord is my shepherd, I. . . ."[29]

How does the scholar mind who translated Empedocles and Lucretius, the poet who is deeply read in the literature of nineteenth century science, interpret the drama he has been through? As if to defend himself, he argued

> I did not doom her: for, if clear am I
> From rhyme to rhyme, this is a story of
> How Time and Circumstance gave birth to love,
> How Time and Circumstance did crucify,
> With manhood's reason standing helpless by,
> Almost to madness.[30]

Retreating to the irresponsibility of determinism, he wants to believe that

> . . . a fate
> Ironic, not alone in scope of plot,
> But in each tragic detail, shaped my lot,
> With cunning masterstroke from date to date.[31]

At this interval, he finds meaning in Thomas Hardy's "studies in the unforeseen accidents and their long results" — studies which he does not regard as "fantastic or unreal."[32]

But Leonard is not free of a sense of purpose, the *élan* of human choice. As he watches university men play baseball and football, youthfully proud of their "exercise of will," he is aware of a "secret soul" that demands a motive beyond the obstacles of time and circumstance. From Goethe, Dante, Shakespeare, yes, and from Socrates, Jesus, and Emerson, Leonard rediscovered the

> . . . challenge to be strong,
> And exercise of valor, for high days
> That lie beyond the mountains of dispraise
> And torture. . . .[33]

As a scholar rooted in ancient lore, he disciplined his mind to say

> I know how ineradicably absurd
> That Man is but a function of the Two,
> Physics and Chemistry — that we can spell
> By atom and motion (or by twitch and cell)
> The ineffable Adventure I've been through. . . .
> I know Love, Pain, and Power are spirit-things,
> My Act a more than Mine or Now or Near:
> One with the Will that suffers, conquers, sings,
> I was the mystic Voice I could not hear.[34]

When many in Madison condemned the poet for the accident of his wife's insanity and suicide, he found inner defenses through his scholarship in the Anglo-Saxon epic-fragment, *Beowulf*. Of all the Anglo-Saxon crimes and sins, disloyalty was chief. Wiglaf over his lord's body rebuked their comrades, "Death itself is better than a life of shame."[35] Whatever the source of his stoic resolution, he was determined to endure and transcend the gossip — the charges made against him. More important than the influence of books and philosophies was his militant sense of the artist's will. This led him to use the sonnet form in *Two Lives*: "The austere form itself, the sonnet (if in any organic creation, whether oak-tree or poem, one can separate 'form itself' from essence, — meaning end) grew inevitably out of the need, an absolute need, of an especially austere control, masterful and unrelenting, over especially intense and fierce emotional experience, while a certain freedom resulted from variations within the norm (rime-arrangement, management of the 'turn,' etc.), and from linking sonnets as stanzas (both in narrative progress and in end-enjambments)."[36] As artist, he creates a rational order which rebukes (if it does not deny) varieties of determinism.[37]

While Professor Leonard still lived, I wrote an article in which I observed that "after *Two Lives* Leonard abandoned the spectacle of man standing alone in his joys, griefs, woes, probing the wisdom of self-mastery, the enigmas of purpose and time, abandoned all these to phrase the 'ominous turmoil' of his age."[38] And he wrote to me,[39] "I suppose the qualities you trace out in their unfoldment are written into the successive years of the verse." He also observed (I suspect, gently warned) that "if all these years I'd been poetically vocal all the time, there'd have been a much harder job for you: you'd have had, e.g., some social poems at 20 and some shameless thrusts of egotism and its woes in the 50's." Having made copies of hundreds of his MSS and unpublished verses and prose I know how right he was. But it is also evident — and this Leonard did not deny — that during any one phase of his adventure a master faith, conviction, resolve, transcended others, transcended but embraced. The Byronism of his "Marguerite" verses is repeated in his more pathetic vituperations in *Two Lives*. And his sonnet in defense of Charles Eliot Norton, who opposed the blatant jingoism of W. R. Hearst's journalism, anticipates his indignation when later he abets Leo Frank, Eugene Debs, Tom Mooney, and the lynched and gelded banjo player in *The Lynching Bee*.

After *Two Lives* Leonard imaged a world brutally irrational and naturalistic, in which Socratic "self-conquest" has little meaning, in which human will is impotent or grotesquely ironic. In our naturalistic century, we may choose to defend Leonard's "growth" from self to society (as some praise Thomas Wolfe who quested beyond *Of Time and the River* to *You Can't Go Home Again*), from Byron, even from Socrates and Emerson, to humanitarian sympathy for those victimized by mad groups and mob fury.

Marked as an outlaw by the society of his town and not a few of his academic colleagues, he found strength in defending those who were merely tolerated or condemned by the "conventional," the "respectable," the "bourgeois."[40] Perhaps it is fairer to say that he recalled the Emersonian temper of his youth as he protested against the *things that ride mankind*. Whatever the *modus operandi* of his social insurgence, his militant indignations, Leonard's poetry reveals the energy of an angry man.

He wrote *Poems 1914-1916*[41] as one who "suffered in spirit, as an American no less than as a believer in Germany, as a humanitarian, and as a philosophic thinker."[42] He challenges those whose interpretations of Germany have become "a cerebral abstraction or a neurotic antipathy. . . ."

In "Confession," Leonard justifies his critique of British imperialism:

> My fathers, sprung from Runnymede,
> Were ancient England's Norman breed;
> Their sons became, beyond the seas,
> Gaunt fellows of our forest trees,
> Among the men of plough and forge
> Who spake that English word to George.
> Myself, New England's scholar, teach
> The master-books of England's speech:
> Yet blood, nor love, nor pride should make
> Man's vision when the world's at stake.[43]

With equal indirection he observes in "My World"

> My world must have, when all is done
> A Lincoln and an Emerson;
> But (if 'tis no offense to you)
> A Goethe and a Fichte too.[44]

Critical of the intentions of the Entente, Leonard believed that "Germany was more honest in her efforts to avoid an European war. . . ."[45] In "The Moral Issue" he announces —

> 'The Issue is a Moral One!' —
> Yes! — Justice! even to the Hun.
> (Justice, the basic moral thought
> That Plato wrote and Lincoln wrought.)[46]

Whatever is history's record of the War of 1914, Leonard distrusted British imperialism more than German militarism. What probably most aroused his indignation was the mobocratic condemnation of all things German from sauerkraut to *gemühtlichkeit*. His attack on indiscriminate hate born of war was not as un-American as organized patriots may want to believe.

Leonard's aversion to a war he had no faith in is an anticipation of his anxieties expressed in *The Lynching Bee and Other Poems*. Inscribed "To those in all Lands who in the Words of Emerson, 'Walk as Prophecies of the Next Age,' " he seeks "to phrase the ominous turmoil of the times." The title poem he regarded as his "best" (beyond *Two Lives*).

> Here at the crossroads is the night so black
> It swallows tree and thicket, barn and stack,
> Even though the sickle of the new moon hang,
> Keen as a knife, bent like a boomerang,
> A witch's bangle in the Zodiac.[47]

The mob assembles "in a monstrous ring." They chain and strip the negro boy. He "stands five fathoms deep in glare agrin."

> His skin-bark on the tree bark-skin.
> Trunk grafted on to trunk.

After he is gelded, the lynched one, his "two great eyeballs, staring white in stone," can no longer see the demon-ghouls

> Screaming round the bonfire's light
> All through the Walpurgis Night.

This is the portrait of no one negro banjo boy, but the voice of "All Ancient Africa" and the pain of all men who suffer martyrdom when people become mobs. Like the negro boy was Leo Frank, who also was hanged "on the gallows-tree" — the mob "hanged God's Justice, hanging him, . . . Leo Frank, the Jew." And there are others in Leonard's parade of men who have endured injustice. Religious pacifists who "would not give their bodies up to war," Tom Mooney who when "free was but a laboring man," Eugene Debs, the Socrates of the proletariat, the "Old Agitator" who "lights on no defense — Except reiteration of his cause," a cause "so wearisomely grim. . . ."

After Versailles, Leonard phrased his disenchantment in "To the Dead Doughboys":

> Be nothing in this book construed
> Against your Hope and Hardihood:
> They mourn you most who're most dismayed
> To see your Golden Stars betrayed.[48]

His prime aversion is for the "Gold-men," the men of power who win unjust victories and the cowardly, ignorant men who lose their rational identity in the herd-mobs of intolerance.[49] After *Two Lives*, Leonard's dominant motifs are of social injustice, of humanitarian outrage against those who would deny the rights of private judgment and action to men morally self-reliant. His major energy as poet is to recreate social issues rather than self-knowledge, the master theme of his art through *Two Lives*.

In answer to a letter in which I asked his permission to use a large mass of MSS of unpublished pieces, he wrote (December 5, 1935), "I'm little concerned with my past — living or writing: the living was too painful and the writing too much the record of that living. And I've been through more since you were here [1930]. There's a record of that too, — but with a more victorious outcome. This, however, can't be published for a long time, perhaps not till after my death. (Maybe then the time won't be so long, either.) I've yet to try to finish what I've wanted to say

in this new long poem; for, even with victory, I'm harassed and
troubled by circumstances. (Savings gone, academic duties, bad
heart, *etc.*)"[50]

The year after he died, *A Man Against Time: an Heroic Dream*
was published. The sensitive readers of his poems may long
debate whether this sonnet sequence was the fulfillment of his
promise of victory or more a dream than an "heroic" confidence.
His Byronic vaunt has become pallid — perhaps even erotic —
with age. And his awareness of what he knew he was in his
youth and middle years is self-consciously revealed in Sonnet LII:

> My fathers shored house-timbers on the rocks
> Timbers of oak with oaken timbers shored,
> Based on New Hampshire's windward mountain-blocks
> With torrents, frosts, and lightnings scarred and scored.
> Large-handed Puritans whom these flabby years
> Disdain with easy jibes, they being dead;
> Stiff-necked come-outers, ruthless pioneers,
> What did they do, on corn and ginger fed? —
> Settling one kingdom east, they built the west
> With ox-carts; built the school-house, voting booth,
> Fought that democracy be more than jest,
> And gnawed the slave's chains with a madman's tooth.
> Come-outers, pioneers! — and I'm their son,
> Though Greek-schooled like Monadnock-Emerson.[51]

In this, the poet and man recalls his life before Aphrodite alone
survives

> . . . in this iron age
> Where temples crumble, sacred fountains freeze,
> And men abandon dance and pilgrimage.[52]

As if to reclaim hope, which he senses he hardly deserves,
Leonard describes his life with his young, new wife in terms of
a swim "from pier to pier across the storm," concluding that
". . . yet for you and me the sun was warm."

Striving for a "brave new sanctity of life and art," he melodramatically associates his love with the essence of passion and beauty as revealed in Sappho, Heloise, Persephone, Diana, Nausicaä, Penelope, and Cleopatra. Yet he knows that "time is king" while he addresses his young wife as "dear child." He reveals himself as "a beaten man and old" who has known and still believes that "the only gods at last are those of Greece." In his determination to live the present, he does not forget that earth did not time "our years aright." But there is pride that in his grey years he has "won such gold." And he is confident that his sonnets

> . . . encompass more
> In brave, fair honesty of love-report
> Than ever artist dared, tried, did before.[53]

A Man Against Time is Leonard's most sustained effort after *Two Lives* and perhaps a victory "after silent years." But only a very young reader will find in Leonard's impassioned amour the depth of heart and mind which the poet brought to the love he shared with Agatha in the white house by the lake.

Who can say what Leonard might have been had he liberated all of his imagination as a poet — or dedicated his mind narrowly to the art and science of translation or sought distinction as a philologian or literary historian? That he chose not to be a specialist argues his sincerity when he dreamed of becoming a poet-scholar in the tradition of Goethe.

Whatever his splendor or failure as a poet, only the sensitive readers of his art can decide. They must determine whether his poetry is fashionable, relevant, prophetic — more or less than whatever poetry should be. Ludwig Lewisohn, his closest friend among the critics who honored his verses, assumed that Leonard's sonnets are "handicapped" by "intellectual severity." A half century later he is ignored by those who favor Pound, Cummings, and Eliot, ignored because he began no school, followed no clever fashion, and failed in "intellectual severity."

I have read enough of his unpublished verses to be confident that he could have been an "Imagist" in the Chicago coterie of 1914 had he chosen to use his skill in phrase to court easy popularity. He knew how to make "a pallid crescent moon in a bleak rose sky," and Coney Island a highway of "rough-up state planking, splintered and worn, in the white glare." He also knew that the Imagists left a gap between sensuous rhetoric and experience. He was not delighted as poet because he could dash off a fragment on "The Telegraph Wires" —

> Harp of the winnowing winds,
> Perch of the sparrow and jay,

a verse that might have been cushioned on a broad page of a magazine dedicated to the "new" poetry. Leonard as poet was dedicated more to the unseen reality than what is too easily seen. Nor did he believe that "modern" poetry need be an image of smoke, skyscrapers, tenements, mechanics, business, and other aspects of the machinery of our age. What he found worth recreating in poems he sensed man had lived with and would continue beyond immediate considerations to have to endure. His learning was too vast to let him accept easy and neat beliefs, and his imagination would not permit him to phrase what was certain to be merely fashionable. What William Ellery Leonard was as a mind, poet, and man can be recreated if one reads *The Locomotive God* and *Two Lives*. For those who read these works, his legacy is a dramatic record of an effort to find a truth to accept, a private life to understand, and a poet's purpose to fulfill.

NOTES

1. *Socrates, Master of Life* (Chicago, 1915), p. 4.
2. *Ibid.*, p. 32.
3. *Ibid.*, pp. 2-3.
4. *The Poet of Galilee* (New York, 1928), p. 51. (First published in 1909).
5. *Ibid.*, p. 104.
6. *Ibid.*, pp. 12-13.
7. *Ibid.*, p. 75.
8. "A Little Sermon on Life and Literature," *University of Wisconsin Studies in Language and Literature*, No. 18.

9. Boston, 1906. Many of these pieces were reprinted in *The Vaunt of Man* (New York, 1912, 1923).
10. "The Windward Slope."
11. See "The Husbandmen," "For Our Fathers' Sons," "The Great Stone Face," and "Mount Washington" in both *Sonnets and Poems* and *The Vaunt of Man*.
12. *The Vaunt of Man*, p. 38 ("With Mother Earth"). This and subsequent quotations from *The Vaunt of Man* are by arrangement with The Viking Press Inc., publishers and copyright holders.
13. *Ibid.*, p. 72 ("Threefold Life").
14. *Ibid.*, p. 80 ("Obscurity").
15. *Ibid.*, p. 82 ("For a School of Artists").
16. *Ibid.*, p. 88 ("For a Drudge").
17. *Ibid.*, p. 91 ("The World and the Soul").
18. *Ibid.*, pp. 110-11 ("Resolve").
19. *The Locomotive God* (New York, 1928), p. 137.
20. *Ibid.*, p. 234 ff.
21. *The Vaunt of Man*, p. 18. *The Locomotive God* describes the Annie-Marguerite experience adequately, although the MS, "A Phobiac. The Case of Professor X — as Recorded by Himself," July 20, 1920, addressed to Dr. Lorenz of the University of Wisconsin, includes a fuller and more intense record. For example: "The hate of the girl was a long wear and tear, and most unlovely. I can say I became obsessed by hatred as I had been by love. I wrote her, in the course of a year or so, several angry letters in the uncontrollable (or at least uncontrolled) desire, first, to relieve my feelings by self-expression (the 'literary,' the 'poet'-motif), and, secondly, to avenge a monstrous wrong that had made me a play thing and ruined my career (I speak from the point of view of my then state of mind only)."

    By 1920 the poet regarded his Byronic mood as "an avenging for the sake of justice, not for the sake of personal satisfaction. It was an intense mood with an intellectually cunning sophistication in self-justification, and an intellectually cunning resourcefulness in the execution in prose and verse." By 1920 he could see that though not unbalanced in reason, he was unbalanced in emotion. When his proposal of marriage was quickly negatived, his "psychic state for six months was most absurd. Rationally, I didn't want to marry her, irrationally, I wanted her 'yes,' but dreaded lest it might come." Thus, the "poor girl became the diabolic instrument of my pain and undoing." Meanwhile, as a graduate student at Columbia, "I walked the streets, worked a little fitfully on my Ph.D. dissertation, drank whiskey, lived on eggnogs and chocolate bars, slept fitfully, wrote verses, and talked about the affair incessantly with any fellow-student who would listen or who wouldn't. This went on for six months. I was more or less discredited with the faculty for years afterwards, which seriously affected my finally getting a university position; while to my fellow students I seemed the half-crazed fool that in very truth I was." Even as a researcher, "I was undergoing a supreme tragedy, I was a marked man, suffering beyond other mortals, and 'the grand passion,' too!"
22. "A Phobiac. The Case of Professor X as Recorded by Himself," p. 54.
23. *On the Origin of Species* was the first book which Leonard as a boy drew from a library.
24. *Two Lives* (New York, 1928), p. 43. The subsequent quotations from *Two Lives* are by arrangement with The Viking Press Inc., publishers and copyright holders.

25. *Ibid.,* p. 41.
26. *Ibid.,* p. 23.
27. *Ibid.,* p. 67.
28. *Ibid.,* p. 68.
29. *Ibid.,* p. 18.
30. *Ibid.,* p. 36.
31. *Ibid.,* p. 48.
32. *The Locomotive God,* p. 260.
33. *Two Lives,* p. 97.
34. *Ibid.,* p. 107.
35. W. E. Leonard, *Beowulf. A New Verse Translation* (New York, 1925), p. 123.
36. *The Locomotive God,* p. 339. Quoted with the permission of Appleton-Century-Crofts, Inc.; copyright, 1927, by The Century Company, copyright, 1942, by D. Appleton-Century Company, Inc.
37. Compare Somerset Maugham's motif in *The Summing Up.*
38. *American Prefaces,* I (January, 1936), 53.
39. December 27, 1935.
40. See *The Locomotive God* for many variations on this theme.
41. Privately printed, "Preface" dated January, 1917.
42. *Ibid.,* "Preliminary Note," dated March 6, 1917.
43. *Poems 1914-1916,* p. 15.
44. *Ibid.,* p. 19.
45. *Ibid.,* p. 4.
46. *Ibid.,* p. 33.
47. *The Lynching Bee and Other Poems* (New York, 1920), p. 11. This and subsequent quotations from *The Lynching Bee* are by arrangement with The Viking Press Inc., publishers and copyright holders.
48. *Ibid.,* p. 84.
49. Compare *Red Bird. A Drama of Wisconsin History in Four Acts* (New York, 1923), and Part III, "Wars" of *Tutankhamen and After* (New York, 1924).
50. Included in his reply was the comment that the MSS I had used were "finally destroyed by me last year."
51. *A Man Against Time: an Heroic Dream* (New York and London, 1945; copyright, 1945, by Clara Leiser), p. 61. This and subsequent quotations are by permission of Appleton-Century-Crofts, Inc., publishers.
52. *Ibid.,* p. 3.
53. *Ibid.,* p. 58.